Praise for GOING FOR BROKE

"These emotionally charged and heart-wrenching narratives are both wide-ranging and powerfully rendered. . . . A penetrating collection that is certain to challenge the readers' views of those living in poverty."
—*Kirkus*

"*Going for Broke* is a gut punch, a collective portrait of precarity, a book of testimony and astonishing courage. This is a book with a pulse. It's angry, as it must be, often beautiful, and always brilliant with the illumination of injustice. These essays and memoirs and poems and pictures—this documentary art—is vital, intimate, and necessary. Please, read this heartbreaking, heart-mending volume."
—JEFF SHARLET, *New York Times*-bestselling author of *The Undertow* and *The Family*

"*Going for Broke* is an illuminating compendium of essays, poetry, photos, and illustrations about the impact of inequality, bias, and poverty on the lives and careers of professional mediamakers. These deeply personal accounts deliver keen critiques of fractured and dehumanizing systems, but they also offer unexpected solutions and reveal the depth of human resilience. *Going for Broke* is ultimately a powerful example of why diversity in media matters—that journalism informed by a variety of lived experiences leads us to a more profound understanding of our disjointed, dynamic world."
—BERNICE YEUNG, author of *In a Day's Work: The Fight to End Sexual Violence Against America's Most Vulnerable Workers* and managing editor of Berkeley Journalism's Investigative Reporting Program

"This moving anthology breaks down the barriers between experience and interpretation. Its contributors explore the underside of American society from many angles. But they do more than document hardship—they show how ordinary people who've been exploited and left behind forge understanding and solidarity out of the experience."
—GABRIEL WINANT, author of *The Next Shift: The Fall of Industry and the Rise of Health Care in Rust Belt America*

GOING FOR BROKE

LIVING ON THE EDGE IN THE WORLD'S RICHEST COUNTRY

An Anthology from the Economic Hardship Reporting Project

Edited by *Alissa Quart* and *David Wallis*

Haymarket Books
Chicago, Illinois

Published in 2023 by
Haymarket Books
P.O. Box 180165
Chicago, IL 60618
773-583-7884
www.haymarketbooks.org
info@haymarketbooks.org

ISBN: 978-1-64259-965-7

Distributed to the trade in the US through Consortium Book Sales
and Distribution (www.cbsd.com) and internationally through In-
gram Publisher Services International (www.ingramcontent.com).

This book was published with the generous support of Lannan Foundation, Wallace Action Fund, and Marguerite Casey Foundation.

Special discounts are available for bulk purchases by organizations
and institutions. Please email info@haymarketbooks.org for more
information.

Cover design by dEEN/Modino Media Design.

Printed in Canada by union labor.

Library of Congress Cataloging-in-Publication data is available.

10 9 8 7 6 5 4 3 2 1

For Barbara Ehrenreich

CONTENTS

SECTION 2: HOME

SECTION 3: FAMILY

SECTION 4: WORK

SECTION 5: CLASS

ABOUT THE ECONOMIC HARDSHIP REPORTING PROJECT

This book was created by the Economic Hardship Reporting Project (EHRP), a nonprofit organization that keeps journalists, essayists, and photographers in the national conversation on economic injustice. We do so by supporting them while they report and publish. Since its founding in 2012, the group has sought to address the classism and lack of opportunity that many reporters face, as well as the ongoing contraction within journalism itself.

EHRP assigns and then places stories in mainstream media outlets in the hope of mobilizing people in the United States to fight for economic justice. Fostering "quality journalism about inequality" continues to be our mantra. It also governs this collection, which focuses specifically on the experiential, first-person work we've commissioned over recent years.

As EHRP's creator, the late, great Barbara Ehrenreich, put it, "As a journalist, I search for the truth. But as a moral person, I am also obliged to do something about it." The anthology that follows does just that.

INTRODUCTION

Alissa Quart

The journalist Bobbi Dempsey was feeling a stark distance between herself and her editors. They tended to assume, for instance, that the town in agrarian Pennsylvania where she lived and worked had high-speed internet. (Back then, in the early 2000s, it did not.) Or they'd tell her to use a certain app, despite the fact that she had only a flip phone; smartphones were too costly. The first few times she had to travel to report, she didn't have a credit card, just a debit card, and couldn't book a hotel or cover a security deposit. Dempsey, now fifty-three, felt that she was fighting a "constant battle" to prove the value of reporting on a "random rural area." Her opponent was a kind of editorial bias, not only financial but also cultural.

Ten years later, the journalist Alex Miller encountered similar barriers as an aspiring writer in New York City. A navy veteran with posttraumatic stress disorder, Miller moved into a shelter when he could no longer afford housing. As he attended college in the city, he continued to contribute to magazines and newspapers, but their slow pace of payments often stymied his ability to pay his bills promptly.

These are just two of the writers whose essays you will find in this anthology, a testament to American life during the lingering pandemic, with its consequent exacerbated inequality, looming economic crisis, and untrammeled reliance on the efforts of those paid the lowest wages. It has been a time when brainwork became gig work and when journalists have been poster children for the increasingly precarious middle class, or what I call the middle precariat. The writers represented here may have lost their jobs, their homes, or even the narrative thread of their lives, but in confronting those hardships they have gained valuable insights into problems facing millions in this country. And lest you think what follows will just make you sad, please rest assured that

1

bold and fresh ideas—about how we can house the unhoused, for instance—arise from these essays, offering hope and ways forward.

We have organized this anthology into five sections—"The Body," "Home," "Family," "Work," and "Class"—all of which contain affecting, honest, and beautiful essays on what it means to be on the edge economically. We decided to start with "The Body" because embodiment is now at the center of both political and psychological concepts of identity. In addition, body politics—for instance, reproductive, queer, and disability rights—fuel some of our most intense political fights. These battles have emerged around who gets to live as themselves and sometimes who gets to live at all, and under what conditions. The urgency of body politics was only underlined by the 2022 United States Supreme Court's *Dobbs* decision, which made abortion inaccessible in much of the nation.

The collection also includes explorations of home, family, how we work, what we earn, and, finally, the structural forces that can hoist us up the economic gradient and take us down as well. This last section, which we have called "Class," is perhaps most reflective of our organization's mindset. Class is not talked about enough in this country, and we have taken it as a mandate—both within the nonprofit and in this collection—to directly address our country's social striation. We can and should give voice to those Americans caught in the legacy of the working poor—growing up without a clear home, for example—and still pinioned by income inequity. The writers in this volume call out the decades of ineffective social policies that have caused this. They are often explicit about the government actions and cruel market forces directly responsible for their or their family's precarity. These range from the absence of affordable housing and gentrification that resulted in one writer's eviction to how psychiatrists' not accepting Medicaid led directly to the untreated mental health problem of another writer. Finally, the high cost of living in an American city caused a third essayist to sell their plasma.

Trying to coax media consumers to pay attention to those who have less is a Sisyphean task. Nevertheless, the work is well worth it, and the results of these attempts can be stunning and politically effective as well. Today, Bobbi Dempsey says she's starting to sense increased sensitivity and responsiveness among her editors to the specifics of her struggles. She admits that she still has to do a lot of code switching to get her reporting out to the world but is bolstered by the narratives she is now able to get published, because people like her can "finally see their stories being portrayed." For Bobbi, it's worth it. As she says, "Readers are amazed and so appreciative: they are glad to know that they are not so alone." We are hoping some of this book's readers will feel the same.

Journalists are used to thinking that they are not the story—that they have no right to be—but all of the writers, photographers, and illustrators whose work we have included here are telling tales that should be shaping policy and inspiring action. In fact, they *are* the story, dedicated to documenting America even as it fractures into a place some of us no longer recognize.

SECTION 1
The Body

INTRODUCTION

Camonghne Felix

In this week's group meeting for bipolar and depressed people, there is a new face. She has never been to a group meeting before but is thrown into our ritual opening of session—say your name, your diagnosis, and a short synopsis of your week. Like a map unfurling, she seems to unrobe as the group progresses and different members speak up about their topics of concern. By the time it's her turn, the robe she'd been clutching had fallen open to reveal her house clothes: it was time to say the thing she'd needed to say all week. "I'm having suicidal ideation. I went looking for help, and every person I met with said they weren't equipped to help me."

I had goosebumps as my own near identical experiences flashed through my mind. How many times had I been in dire straits, deep into a bipolar episode, and someone in an office thirteen floors above ground level would say to me, "You certainly need help, but I'm not sure I'm the one to help you."

She continues, "And when I talk to someone, they say, 'You need to go to IOP,' but I can't afford it, nor do I have time to take off work to go back to IOP; I have a job."

Everyone on screen nods their heads in recognition. Of course we know what she knows, that disabled people, including those with mental health disorders, have been left for dead.

For generations, disabled folks and disability advocates have been the mules of a particular truth, themselves wearing the burden of teacher, of being the ones to teach us all how political the body can be. We seem to understand this during times of war, during times of famine, and during times of catastrophe, because ableism is an equalizer while being disabled remains a category of subjectivity that only the disabled can truly embody. When you understand a mass disabling event (i.e., our government's failure to efficiently respond to a

6

global pandemic), and you understand the ongoing event of disability (when an individual's stated value to our power structure has changed because of "societally constructed ideas of normalcy, productivity, desirability, intelligence, excellence, and fitness"[1]), then it is easy to see how much it costs to have a body in this world. This feels especially true here in the West and more particularly here in the United States, which has failed administration after administration to lead us to universal health care, and which has failed to improve its existing Medicare program—two moves that would easily put our health care on par with health standards of social democratic countries, and even oligarchies like the UK, who themselves remain at odds with the advocates in their countries who believe they can, and should, be doing much better for their citizens.

So how do we, with language, represent these costs? How do we represent the cost of ableism, the cost of a body in existence, the cost of a political system poisoned with the lie of human hierarchies?

In each story in this section, a journalist or writer takes on the task of illustrating the systemic realities that stymie true progress for the working class, and most, if not all, use the stories of their bodies and their blood to tell the particular truth disabled folks have been attempting to tell us about our world. From pregnancy and the fight for bodily autonomy to an individual battle with insurance companies and conglomerates, it's disabled artists and disabled people doing all kinds of critical work who pay the cost for this lack of advancement. As we always have, we pay it in physical labor, an evidence the writers in this section so aptly display.

Camonghne Felix, poet and essayist, is the author of *Build Yourself a Boat* (Haymarket Books, 2019), which was long-listed for the 2019 National Book Award for Poetry, short-listed for the PEN/Open Book Awards, and short-listed for the Lambda Literary Award. Her poetry has appeared in Academy of American Poets, *Harvard Review, Literary Hub*, PEN America, *Poetry Magazine*, and other places. Her essays have been featured in *Vanity Fair, New York Magazine, Teen Vogue*, and elsewhere. Felix's nonfiction work *Dyscalculia* and collection of essays *Let the Poets Govern* are both forthcoming from One World, an imprint of Penguin Random House.

LOVE AND WAR

Karie Fugett

The Washington Post, October 3, 2019

Cleve's prosthetic leg stood in the corner of my living room, its plastic foot still wearing the left shoe of his khaki Converses. It was the third anniversary of his death, and I stared at the socket that once held his nub, remembering its shape. After the amputation, it was rounded, a pink scar cut clean across the top. As the muscle atrophied, his flesh hung like a boneless chicken breast, the scar left amorphous and supple.

On April 1, 2006, men were hiding in bushes on the side of a steaming-hot road in Ramadi, Iraq, when the Humvee driven by my husband, Marine Cpl. Jimmy Cleveland Kinsey II, passed. They waited for the perfect moment, then set off an improvised explosive device, blowing off the door and flipping the four-ton hunk of metal onto its side with Cleve and his buddies inside. "The bomb was double-stacked," he told me. "Twice the power." He held his hands out wide to mimic its bigness. He said the shrapnel flew in all directions like fireworks, ripping flesh from bone. Cleve got the worst of it. Afterward, he was flown to Washington and told that hardly any soft tissue remained on his lower left leg. He was, the doctors said, lucky to be alive.

In fact, his surgeon called my husband a guinea pig. He said they'd never done a leg salvage like the one they did on him. A strap of muscle, the latissimus dorsi, was severed from his back and stitched to his leg. The top layer of skin was removed from his right thigh and placed over the fresh meat of his flesh, a brand-new calf. Frankenfoot, we called it, joking. We joked a lot to cope. Things started going wrong when the tiny veins that had been stitched together didn't cooperate, causing venous congestion. His leg would turn a deep purple and bleed and bleed and ooze. Not long after, bone infection set in, and amputation was the only option. Suddenly, we had nothing left to joke about.

I was twenty-two years old, married only two years, and gingerly rubbing my beloved's stump as we watched *Sopranos* reruns from a box set Rudy Giuliani had given us on one of his visits to Bethesda Naval Hospital, where Cleve was being treated. We'd been living at hospitals on and off in the three months since he had been wounded. I thought about how we'd gotten there. Both of us had come from families who were too busy working to help us with schoolwork and too broke to pay for college. We'd done the best we could with the options given to us, and this was the result: a war hero and his caregiver, two young people who had chosen to serve their country. Or at least that's how the military wanted us to think of ourselves. The reality was much more complicated. Yes, we were proud of his service. But ending up in that hospital, me feeding him cans of Ensure as he lay in his bed after surgeries, felt more like a stumble than a choice. We huddled into each other, and I felt around for bone spurs—fingerlike growths that commonly form at the end of amputated bones. It was soft like dough. "Does it hurt?" I asked, and he told me he'd just taken an OxyContin. "I can't feel anything anymore," he said.

Since the wars began in 2001, more than 52,000 service members have been wounded in action. These men and women are often unable to work and depend on disability benefits to survive. The disability rating system, in my experience, is sketchy. Initially, Cleve was given a low rating—a disability of 35 percent, they said, which meant less money to live on. Thirty-five percent is what you got back then for a single, below-the-knee amputation. I knew he would not be able to work with the severity of his injury, so I spent more than a year collecting his medical paperwork and making phone calls. Finally, someone with some power helped us secure him a higher rating. This kind of experience was common among our friends. A service member with three amputated limbs would have the same disability rating as someone who had no amputations and was willing to work full-time. The rating you got seemed to depend on whom you knew.

At Walter Reed Army Medical Center, where Cleve was transferred after his leg was finally amputated, many patients had missing body parts and, therefore, prosthetics. There were the AKs (above-the-knee amputees) and the BKs (below-the-knee), each further categorized by what limbs were amputated, and how many: single, double, triple, and, God forbid, quadruple. There, the more bionic you were, the cooler you were. The word "disabled" was hardly ever used. It felt like an exclusive club. Humans are so good at reframing terrible circumstances in order to survive them. Cleve ended up thriving in the hospital, mostly. He was comfortable there with friends who looked like him. He felt as if he belonged.

At parties, it was common for the amputees to pop off their prosthetics, all metal and carbon fiber and plastic, fill them with alcohol and pass them around for everyone to drink from. Once, a friend with a prosthetic eye wanted to participate, too, so he popped the glass sphere from his eye socket and passed it around. Everyone took turns licking it. If you participated, you were in the club, even if you didn't have a missing body part. To participate meant you could be trusted. The eye was smooth and cool on my tongue.

So many things we did probably seemed strange to outsiders, but nothing about our lives was normal anymore. If we wanted normal—and we did, even if we didn't want to admit it—we had to create a new version of it, so we did. We made our own rules. We were desperate to take back some control in what felt like complete chaos.

When Cleve medically retired from the military, we moved to Maylene, Alabama, only four hours' drive from Foley, the small town where we'd met in eighth-grade English class eleven years before. We bought a house we could just barely afford next to his best Marine Corps buddy, Matt, and his wife, Shannon. We hoped for the American Dream. Cleve couldn't work, so we lived off what was left of his traumatic-injury insurance payment, monthly disability payments, and eventually the ten dollars an hour I made after finally finding a job. The military by that time called him 90 percent disabled. That meant, in exchange for his leg and mind—he also had posttraumatic stress disorder—he received a one-time check for $100,000 and a little more than $1,700 a month. Neither of us had ever made so much money in our lives. For the price of his body, we were finally somewhat financially stable.

But suddenly, Cleve was the only amputee we knew. So few civilians were willing to drink from his leg. Three years of pain medications—Dilaudid, morphine, Lortab, Percocet, OxyContin, fentanyl—meant he became an addict, which isolated him further. For me, his addiction quickly became scarier than his war wounds. When the military couldn't figure out what to do with him after his first overdose, in the fall of 2008, and then a failed rehab attempt, in the spring of 2009, they retired him: Let Veterans Affairs figure it out. Where the doctors were skilled at treating gnarly wounds, they seemed ill-equipped to treat the addiction that many experienced as a result. Less than a year after his retirement, Cleve died.

Technically, he died of an overdose, but I also think it was isolation and loneliness. It was the summer of 2009, August or maybe July, when he finally retired. It had been two years since the amputation of his leg and a little more than three since the bomb. By January 2010, he'd grown violent. Without the comfort of the hospital and the friends he'd made there, he seemed to have lost his ability to control his temper, a symptom of PTSD that had shown itself in waves since he was wounded. He was pushing me away. In an attempt to save our marriage, he went to what we thought was an inpatient PTSD facility called Project Victory in Houston. There, he was kept in a hotel room across the street from the hospital. In it, he decided to smoke the medicine on his fentanyl patch. I assume he was bored. Maybe he craved the feeling of being high. There was no one there to stop him. He died there, alone.

Cleve's autopsy report took nearly half a year. While I waited for it, my car was repossessed, and our home went into foreclosure. Once the service member is gone, the military isn't as concerned with taking care of the family, not without the correct paperwork. In my case, it was a death certificate and a statement from the coroner that the death was service connected. I was alone, and my grief was so severe, I couldn't work. Before the house was to be taken, I called Matt and asked him to help me sift through Cleve's belongings. We took shots of cheap tequila and rummaged through dusty boxes. We read love letters women before me had sent Cleve on his first deployment, looked at pictures of him as a teen, counted wads of colorful Iraqi money he'd brought home.

Matt and I hadn't had much of a friendship when Cleve was alive, even though they were inseparable. When Cleve and I decided to elope, we had been dating for only three months, and Matt was understandably skeptical. When I asked him years later why he hadn't approved of me, he said it was because I'd missed out on their first deployment by the time I showed up to Camp Lejeune. Cleve and I had known each other since childhood—a rushed relationship didn't feel as odd to us— but Matt thought of me as an outsider, so he picked on me and cracked jokes at my expense. But our unique grief brought us closer. No one else in the world would understand Cleve's death the way we did.

By the time of the foreclosure, I couldn't handle the stress. It all seemed to happen so fast, and I didn't have the energy to fight it, so I let all our belongings go except for what I could fit in my car, including the three boxes of Cleve's things that Matt and I had packed. For months, I lived on a friend's couch reading books like *Eat, Pray, Love*, trying to imagine a new life, until, finally, the autopsy report called Cleve's death "service connected," and the military paid me more money than I could fathom in exchange for his life. *Blood money*, I thought.

After I buried Cleve, I couldn't help but think of his body rotting, the worms, the ants, the heat. I decided the Christian God wasn't real, replacing him with walks in the woods and Buddhist philosophies about life and death. I cried every day. I talked to Cleve in the shower. I slept with his leg, tucking it in next to me as if it were a child. I prayed to Cleve every night, begging him for answers to questions like, "What do I do next?" "How do I go on?" "Are you okay?" I thought I might be going insane. I thought I might want to die. I had been stripped of everything and left to rebuild myself, and I wasn't sure how to do that.

When the insurance money came, things began to change. It gave me space to grieve without having to worry about food or shelter. I had never been in a position where I could choose things I actually wanted rather than choose the only things available to me. Suddenly, I was able to buy a comfortable home and a reliable car without anyone's help. I enrolled in college and no longer identified as a high school dropout. "Student," I repeated to myself. And then "college graduate." And then "MFA graduate." From his ashes, I built myself into something beautiful and new. Could I have done this had my husband not died? No. I don't think I could have.

When Cleve died, I promised him I would live a good enough life for both of us. Grief became a sort of motivator. I was determined to make him proud. For the first time in my life, I had enough money to focus on improving myself, to become the kind of person someone *could* be proud of. Finally, I could find some version of the American dream. When I meditate on the sacrifice it took to get there, guilt and anger burn deep.

I imagine myself as a little girl, born to a young woman and her soldier husband who struggled to make ends meet. Pink cheeks, large blue eyes, and loose brown curls to my shoulders, I wait a year at a time for my father to return home from Korea and watch as my mother struggles to feed and clothe us. I say to my little-girl self: "One day, you will have all the money you ever wanted, but it will come at a price." I am angry for her, at this country for sacrificing us, for sacrificing the working class, to wars and deployments for unclear reasons.

In the nine years since his death, I have come to treasure Cleve's prosthetic leg as if it were a part of his body. I feel lucky to have a piece of him. But I've never known what to do with it. By the third anniversary of his fatal overdose, the leg had collected dust, a thin layer shimmering in the window light, a reminder that enough time had passed for his real body to decay in that hole on a hill in Summerdale, Alabama, where I'd buried him next to his older brother. I was packing to meet Matt to celebrate his life. A week before, Matt demanded that I bring the leg camping, to which I responded, incredulous, "The leg is obviously coming with." I tucked it into my bag along with my deodorant, hair ties, underwear.

Matt and I sat in front of a campfire, filling Cleve's leg with champagne. We passed it back and forth, taking swigs, the bubbles burning the backs of our throats. Trampled by Turtles played "Codeine" in the background, and we sang along and stomped our feet until we were laugh-crying. "That jerk left us here," Matt said. I nodded in agreement. "Total jerk."

I still have the leg in my home, nearly a decade after his death. It is something like decor or a conversation piece. Sometimes it holds fabric flowers or kindling. I wait for visitors to notice it on their own, wondering what their reaction will be. Having his leg around reminds me of where I came from and who I am. It reminds me of what was sacrificed in order to have this home at all.

Karie Fugett is an author and mother living in Alabama. Her debut memoir, *Alive Day*, is forthcoming from the Dial Press in spring 2025.

A STAY AT KINGS COUNTY

Text and photos by Charlie Gross

The New York Review of Books, January 7, 2019

When "the drama of life got too much," Aleeyah tried to hang herself with an extension cord.

I listened to Aleeyah, a new psych patient at Kings County Hospital in Brooklyn, speak, paying rapt attention to her every word and gesture. She was about twenty, dressed in a festive multicolored sweatshirt that spelled "Brooklyn" in arty graphics, and that left some of her wrist and neck tattoos revealed. She pointed out that she designs and does these herself. In spite of her blunted affect, there was a brightness and a glow about her.

She played an original rap track for me on her phone that began, "I love the life I'm living / Pursuing every mission." Then she casually mentioned that she had tried to hang herself the previous month with an extension cord—an act she said had never occurred to her before that moment. The drama of life had gotten too much, she explained, including a bad breakup, two short stays in jail, and a sister with cancer. She would have been dead if her sister hadn't walked into her room at the right time, cut the cord, and brought her to the hospital.

I'm a therapist by profession, though I am not Aleeyah's shrink. I'm also a photographer, and had just met her on the third floor of the Kings County R building, where I have been meeting young people, photographing them, and listening to their stories over the past two years. It's all part of a project I have been working on since 2017, as artist-in-residence. The young adults in the program come from communities all over New York City and suffer from a variety of traumas and disorders.

The psychiatry department of Kings County Hospital in East Flatbush serves one of the poorest, most at-risk, and most diverse populations in a borough that has otherwise become a byword for gentrification. Kings County has a notorious past that culminated in the 2008 death of Esmin Green, a Jamaican woman who died from neglect after being placed on the psych ER's waiting room floor for twenty-four hours. Following a Department of Justice Civil Rights Division investigation of her death that was concluded in 2010, the institution has undergone a remarkable renaissance in the quality of patient care and transparent governance.

Mya discharged from inpatient after another manic episode. She had earned straight As through high school, but her manic episodes kept getting worse and landing her back as an inpatient.

Nathaniel and Anichela, in love for a minute. Nathaniel contributed a poem to a piece I wrote, dedicated to his mother who rejected him in his teens, when he transitioned.

Charlie Gross is a New York–based photographer, artist, and psychotherapist.

I DID MY OWN ABORTION BECAUSE TEXAS USED COVID-19 AS AN EXCUSE TO SHUT DOWN ABORTION CLINICS

Anonymous, as told to and with an introduction by Anna Louie Sussman

Cosmopolitan, August 10, 2020

> One woman reveals the lengths she went to in order to receive an abortion when Texas clinics closed due to the pandemic.

Shortly after "Esmarie" learned she was pregnant in mid-March, the city in South Central Texas where she lives started to shut down in response to the coronavirus.[1] Her college classes went online, and she lost shifts at the two restaurants where she works, leaving her barely able to afford groceries. She knew right away that she did not want to continue the pregnancy but feared abortion clinics would soon be shut down too. It would be another six weeks before she was able to resolve her pregnancy with a self-managed abortion using abortion pills, which, when used as directed, have a success rate of 95 percent and are an increasingly popular option during the pandemic (one study showed a 27 percent rise in requests across the US and a 94 percent increase in demand in Texas). Esmarie, at nineteen years old, told us about her experience obtaining an abortion during the pandemic.

—**Anna Louie Sussman**

The day I found out I was pregnant, I saw all over Facebook that Texas was going to be shutting down the clinics.[2] I thought, "I'm not going to be able to have this abortion." I thought that I didn't have a choice—I was going to have to just live with it. It was very scary because I couldn't tell anybody. I was trying to get as many hours of work as I could.

It was also scary because of everything going on. Everything was closed. I wasn't making enough money. The restaurants were giving me only ten hours a week, so I couldn't make enough to support myself. I was scared I would get COVID-19 because I was pregnant. I didn't have a car, so I had to walk in the heat. No transportation, no work—I couldn't meet my basic needs.

The abortion clinics were closed at that time, but the CPCs, the crisis pregnancy centers, those were open.[3] When I was making phone calls, trying to see which clinics were open for abortion, they were the only ones who answered. They said, "We don't do abortions, but you can get an ultrasound and we can talk to you about your choices." But they really only give you two choices—adoption or parenting. I was definitely not going to do adoption, because I was adopted and it just didn't go well. But I knew I couldn't raise my child at this time.

They try to tell you, "We're going to help you do this, we're going to help you do that." I've had friends say they told them that too. But once the baby was there, there was no help. So I was just scared, just thinking, "I'm really going to have to give birth." I just felt stuck. They just kept saying, "When you *do* have the baby." I was wondering, "Who am I going to tell? How am I going to get money? How am I going to get to my prenatal appointments?" I was barely even able to make the two-hour bus ride to that CPC.

I started reaching out to anyone who could try to get me to a different state. A few years ago, I had an abortion in a clinic. I took the first pill in the clinic, then the second one at home. I reached out to someone who was out of state who had helped me the first time. I thought they weren't going to be able to do anything. But they said they could fly me out to a different Texas city or to a different state if clinics in Texas close too.

Like I said, I've had an abortion before, so I know how it is. If I had to go out of state, who knows what state it was going to be? I only have family in Texas. I wouldn't have had anywhere to stay. I didn't have money for a hotel. I could barely even get food for myself. They found me an appointment at a clinic, but then they asked, "Do you want to go to that clinic or do you want to do it at home?" I said I would do it at home.

It took two weeks for the pills to arrive. I'm pretty sure the mail was backed up because of COVID-19, so after a week, I asked them to send another package. While I was waiting for it, I was just thinking, "I'm only getting further and further along." It was so stressful. The people who sent them buy them outside of the US and send them to women who need them.

The first time I had an abortion, I was eight weeks along. Eight weeks and ten weeks is actually a very big difference. The first time, it was not that bad—I was able to handle the pain, I guess. But the second time, it was so bad. I couldn't move, I had chills, and my stomach was hurting. It was so bad I brought my blanket into the restroom just so I could be next to the tub, be next to the toilet. I feel like this wouldn't have happened if I would have just gotten the help earlier.

I was staying with a friend, and I didn't tell him anything about the pill. I remember my hair was all wet like I had been in the bathtub. It was around three in the morning. I was crying and I was bleeding; I bled through three maxi pads. You're not supposed to bleed through more than two during a medical abortion. I was trying to take as much pain as I could, and I actually dealt with the pain for a good two hours. But then I just couldn't do it anymore. I couldn't lie down. I couldn't sit down. I couldn't do anything, so that's when I decided to go to the emergency room even though there were COVID-19 patients there. My friend took me. The hospital was not that far off, maybe five minutes, but it felt like the longest drive ever. My phone was dead so I couldn't tell anybody I was there. I was just on my own during that time.

I had forgotten my mask—that was not on my mind at all. I was nervous. I didn't want to touch anything. I think I was having a panic attack, because I couldn't tell them I was having a miscarriage. They were asking me what was wrong and what I needed, but I couldn't breathe, because I was in shock. I just remember holding my stomach because it was hurting, and I was crying because I was scared. I told them, "I'm bleeding and I was pregnant."

Then I lost so much iron from bleeding that I passed out on the floor. I'm four feet eleven, and I weigh about ninety-eight pounds. I remember a receptionist told me to go put hand sanitizer on. I walked to go get hand sanitizer and I woke up on the floor. They put me in a wheelchair. It was kind of embarrassing—I was bleeding all over the wheelchair, all over the floor and the restroom.

They gave me morphine for pain through an IV. I was on anesthesia, because I guess they had to finish taking out whatever was left, so I was asleep. When I woke up, I used the hospital phone. I was trying to get ahold of my mom or my brothers or sisters. I wasn't going to tell them what happened, but I did want to tell them I was in the hospital and I needed a change of clothes. I had bled through my pants and didn't have extra clothes. I got ahold of my brother at six thirty in the morning. He came to give me some clothes and stuff but I couldn't have visitors, so he gave it to the front-desk person and they brought it to me.

The baby's father gave me a ride home from the hospital, but I didn't tell him why I was there. No one knew about the abortion, which I was sad about, but still, everyone was calling me, asking, "Are you okay?" My mom told other family members that I was in the hospital, so they started blowing up my phone: my sisters and my *tías*, my *tíos*. They started asking questions, so I told them, I don't know, I was asleep, they had me on all kinds of medicines. I didn't want to tell them anything, because they're going to judge me. They wouldn't be supportive. I haven't told my friends either.

To the politicians who closed down the clinics, abortion is a basic human right. Young ladies have the right to this. If they know what they want, they shouldn't have to wait longer, because it can just make things worse.

CODA

Less than two years after Esmarie's story was published, in June 2022, the Supreme Court of the United States overturned the constitutional right to abortion in *Dobbs v. Jackson Women's Health Organization*.[4] In the months that followed, seventeen states passed abortion bans or restrictions,[5] dozens of clinics stopped offering abortion care,[6] and many more clinics have closed.[7] According to one analysis, roughly thirty-four million American women of reproductive age[8] live in states where abortion is banned, restricted, or likely to be in the near future.

Stories of patients denied abortion care for pregnancy complications, forced to travel longer distances and often across state lines,[9] or to seek clandestine abortions, as Esmarie did, are now common. Renee Bracey Sherman, the executive director of the abortion storytelling organization We Testify noted that the additional legal and logistic barriers are already having a disproportionate impact on people of color. She is also concerned that people of color and those living in poverty, who are already overrepresented among people criminalized for self-managing their abortion,[10] will face heightened scrutiny post-*Dobbs*.[11]

At the same time, a massive resistance has emerged of activists around the country seeking to fill the void created by clinic closures and legal restrictions. Abortion funds are ramping up their work, serving more patients than ever. Clinic-based telemedicine, as well as informal networks that help women self-manage abortion and provide them with the means to do so have grown in scale. Many of the activists involved in this work take their inspiration and practical models from similar networks that have long served communities in countries where abortion is illegal or highly restricted, such as across Latin America, in Poland, and in numerous African countries. As of 2020, medication abortion already accounted for over half of all abortions performed in the US.[12] Although abortion opponents have sued[13] the Food and Drug Administration to overturn the agency's approval of the abortion pill, it is likely its use will only increase in the post-*Dobbs* era, and activists will figure out new and creative ways to support those in need of an abortion.

Anna Louie Sussman is a New York–based journalist covering gender, economics, and reproduction. She was a 2022 Russell Sage Foundation Visiting Journalist and a Class of 2022 New America Fellow. She has written for the *New York Times*, the *New Yorker*, the *Atlantic*, the *New York Review of Books*, and other publications, and she was previously a staff reporter at the *Wall Street Journal* and Reuters.

"WOMEN AFRAID OF DYING WHILE THEY ARE TRYING TO FIND THEIR LIFE"

Alissa Quart, with an introduction by Katha Pollitt

Literary Hub, May 6, 2022

The leak of the Supreme Court vote to strike down *Roe v. Wade* caused waves of outrage across the land: The 1973 decision provided federal constitutional protections of abortion rights. Now it appeared women would be shorn of a guaranteed protection they had had for forty-nine years.

For Alissa Quart, the leaked decision reminded her of the women she had interviewed in abortion clinic waiting or procedure rooms or by phone from their homes, across three different states. Most of them were poor; even without an unwanted pregnancy they'd be living on the edge of crisis.

It's not surprising that that reporting found its way into the documentary poem "Clinic" that follows. There are the women with mothers "full of God," the one with the boyfriend who dropped her over the abortion, the one whose boss will fire her if she's pregnant. One woman has a boyfriend to hold her hand, but for most there doesn't seem to be much empathy or help beyond the clinic walls.

In the waiting room, the terrifying mingles with the mundane: the specter of an antiabortion killer—"a man / with a Santa beard and a long gun / enters a clinic in Indiana"—coexists with a woman talking about how she "got a cold from / her two year old." The experiences of wealthier women aren't so great either, at least as far as decor goes—"a paneled private / room, Reagan-era / red, with fake curtains, / a bad stage set." But there's a reward: "the surprise / guiltlessness." Women expect to be miserable; the surprise is when they're not.

In this complex, moving poem, Quart captures both the determined resistance and the fatalism of women trying to get some control over their lives in a milieu that doesn't particularly want them to have any. For far too many women, this is just the way it is: "Women afraid of dying while / they are trying to find their life."

—Katha Pollitt

_____ _____

Clinic

1.
When we type "abortion"
autofill writes, *I am pregnant.*
I am pregnant in
Spanish. I am having
a baby and have no
insurance. I'm scared of having
a baby. What trimester am I
What trimester is abortion illegal?
Google says: *I need your love.*
I need an abortion.
I am pregnant can I eat shrimp?
Am I having a miscarriage?
I need help paying for abortion.
Abortion clinic violence.
Not ready to have this baby.

2.
God will punish, old ones
say in unison. They sing,
"Genocide." A man
with a Santa beard and a long gun
enters a clinic in Indiana.
In Mississippi, it's day-glo
signs, floppy hats, tiny
peachy fetus dolls.
Their lawn chairs
too near Women's Health,

their flesh sunscreen white.
Metal-detectors-
as-framing-devices.
Surveillance cameras as
glass birds.

In a place like this, in America, a long gun.

Women afraid of dying while
they are trying to find their life.

3.
On a normal day, women aged
23, 19, 41, 35.
Work at Kmart, Home Depot,
at daycares, at the hospitals
at night. Today, they learn
a new vocabulary.
Ultrasound, waiting period,
Trailways, TRAP law,
witnesses. They learn
the way euphemisms mostly tell
the truth. That the polite
word is always "discomfort."

The door clicks when it locks.
Hungry to talk, no words.

4.
She's got a cold from
her two-year-old.
The doctor talks through
the procedure. The someone
holding her hand, not
her husband.

From a Baptist town, her mother
full of God. So she lied,
got on the bus here. Drove
for three hours, borrowed
money for the hooker
motel, then the overnight
waiting period. Wondered whether
God cared or was it the care
her mother managed.
One girl was a sturdy teenager,
tall enough to play center.
Signed the parental notification
with a broken ballpoint.
Another, redheaded, the hottest
number at the Bingo Hall in
Shreveport. Grandma drank.
"What about your boyfriend?"
She answers, "He stopped
talking to me. All he wanted
was the baby."
With her own body, hurtling.

One boss wouldn't let
the woman sell car parts
if she was pregnant.
One minister called
the clinic "baby parts."
One was doing this *for*
the other baby.
The soldier said she was
doing this so *I can fight*
for this country.

5.
The ATM spits $500.
She slid inside the office

building, paid money to
a counter lady, was led into
a paneled private
room, Reagan-era
red, with fake curtains,
a bad stage set.
Silk fishtail fern,
mustard satin bedspread.
She was put to sleep
woke up to Saltines,
other posh sleepy women
in gowns, a cultic circle.
Her friend called it
"The Anaconda."
Always the code
words and then the surprise
guiltlessness.

6.
Bed rest with the mysteries. Old blood.
A mandala of succor and suffering.
Dark blood could mean anything.

It gets sloppy when you are trying to find love.

A glass of water, a small
pill. Hard candy, Saltines
afterwards. Silk
flower in your hair.

7.
Poems about abortion,
poems about abortion and feelings
of sorrow. Google says: *shame or guilt;*
Remorse is Forever: Abortion Poem.
Post Abortion Stress Syndrome

Support. Poems about abortion from
a baby's point of view.

8.
Say: No shame.
We can say: The
birth spectrum.

Choices are always field work,
freedom song, elegy,
captivity narrative.
This feeling won't forget them;
won't forget you.

Alissa Quart is the author of *Bootstrapped: Liberating Ourselves from the American Dream* and executive director of the Economic Hardship Reporting Project. She has written for many publications, including the *New York Times*, the *Washington Post,* and *Time*. Her honors include an Emmy Award, the SPJ Award, and a Nieman Fellowship. She is the author of four previous books of nonfiction, including *Squeezed: Why Our Families Can't Afford America* and *Branded: The Buying and Selling of Teenagers,* and two books of poetry, most recently *Thoughts and Prayers*. She lives with her family in Brooklyn.

Katha Pollitt's Subject to Debate column, which debuted in 1995 and which the *Washington Post* called "the best place to go for original thinking on the left," appears regularly in the *Nation*. Subject to Debate won the National Magazine Award for Columns and Commentary in 2003. Her most recent book is *Pro: Reclaiming Abortion Rights,* which the *New York Times* listed as a Notable Book of 2014.

MEDICAID HAS BEEN GOOD TO MY BODY, BUT IT HAS ABANDONED MY BRAIN

Katie Prout

Chicago Reader, September 29, 2021

Early in April 2020, my boyfriend Carter asked, not unkindly, if I've ever been diagnosed with anything besides my generalized anxiety disorder.

"What do you mean?" I asked innocently, my pockets full of rocks. He warily eyed the front of my pink raincoat, which bulged like the pouches of bullfrogs. "Can we keep the rocks down to maybe five a day?" he said. We shared the apartment with four other people and two dogs; in our tiny bedroom, the rocks I'd been collecting from the nearby Lake Michigan beach lined the base of our lamps, pooled on the warped surface of the plastic bedside table, and balanced on the radiator. "Oookay," I lied.

It wasn't just our new rock roommates, he said now. It was the way I cleaned for hours when my body and brain felt bad, or the way I went immobile whenever a bad call or text came in from home. My anxiety got so intense that I fractured a molar from grinding my teeth and my jaw once popped out of its socket; my dentist thought I had been in a car accident. Then, there was my terrible sleep, with its 3:00 a.m. wakings, muffled screams during night terrors, sleep paralysis, and, on limber nights, the convulsive jerks that torqued my whole body, startling Carter awake.

I didn't feel pathologized by his question; I was relieved that somebody had finally asked about my mental health. Carter knew about my family's intergenerational history of addiction and mental illness, and how often my siblings or dad have nearly died. In childhood, I coped with hyperreligiosity, then moved on to checking the breaths of my family when they were sleeping, to see if they were still alive, and collecting rocks that I thought were lonely. As an adult, there was bulimia and compulsive exercise, some reckless decisions

29

with my life, and then—thankfully, when I had private insurance—various medications, therapies, and care. But still, I struggle.

All spring and summer 2020, I kept kicking the ball of my fritzing brain down the field to some imaginary goal of (gestures vaguely) "things" getting, if not better, at least more stable. But as I stared down the November 2020 election and a bleak pandemic winter, I knew I needed more tools to survive. And so, like many across the country, in September 2020, I went back to therapy. Or tried to. I'm on Medicaid, and while the insurance I receive through the program—Blue Cross Community Health Plan—is accepted by many dentists and primary care physicians, finding a therapist who takes it has been, in my experience, impossible.

I'm not alone. Americans, particularly if they're low-income, elderly, young, or a minority, are both seeking and struggling to find mental health care in record numbers. In Illinois, funding cuts and the pandemic have left 38 percent, or 4.9 million people, in "designated mental health shortage areas." Even though Governor J. B. Pritzker recently signed into law a bill intended to fund more Medicaid mental health and substance abuse disorder treatments, it comes with a call for a more "comprehensive behavioral health strategy" from the Department of Healthcare and Family Services to be delivered to his office . . . by July 2022.

Meanwhile, lives hang in the balance as the number of practices accepting Medicaid have declined. That's due, in part, to the dearth of available psychiatrists; in 2018, NPR reported that 77 percent of US counties faced a severe shortage of psychiatrists. Additionally, despite increased Medicaid funding, many psychiatrists don't want it. "Medicaid pays low fees, has delays in reimbursement, and comes with extra administrative burdens," the internist and Johns Hopkins School of Public Health professor Dr. Albert Wu told Reuters in 2019. The rising demand for psychiatric services among Medicaid patients and the dwindling Medicaid-accepting providers has left those providers overstretched and Medicaid patients underserved, enduring wait times that can extend for months. For people like me, with every passing week without care, our conditions can grow more disruptive and life-threatening.

When I tried to start therapy in September 2020, I used *Psychology To-day*'s search tool and found fewer than four therapists in the Chicago area who said they accepted Medicaid. Only one returned my email. During our intake call, she asked me a number of detailed, personal questions, including whether or not I was experiencing suicidal ideation, to which my answer was a firm "yes." She determined that yes, she thought she could help me and that we would work well together. But I never heard from her again.

I haven't been ghosted since my twenties, and certainly never by a mental health professional. So I gave up on my search for a bit. It wasn't until late November when I finally found someone who would see me. The downtown clinic didn't accept Medicaid, but for twenty-five dollars a session, I could pay out of pocket to be treated by their clinical intern who was finishing up his last year of school. "Z" was five years my junior and a man, both firsts for me, but with America's motto "beggars can't be choosers" singsonging in the back of my brain, I decided to give him a try.

I'm glad I did. Z was patient, enthusiastic, compassionate, and attentive. After a few weeks, Z asked me to consider the possibility that my anxiety was a symptom, rather than the correct diagnosis itself. He read back to me some of my own words, collected in his notebook since our first session. Then, he read through some of the criteria for stress disorders, like secondary traumatic stress and its more famous cousin, posttraumatic stress. So many of the words were the same.

Suddenly, a swirling number of experiences I've never thought to connect were organized like constellations. A correct diagnosis could not only bring greater clarity, it could help me heal. That's why I needed a psychiatrist, as Z suggested, trained to give me a psychological evaluation. It had been fourteen years since my first, and only, psych eval, when an unsmiling man asked me ten minutes' worth of questions, diagnosed me with generalized anxiety disorder, and prescribed me my first SSRI (selective serotonin reuptake inhibitors, a commonly prescribed type of antidepressant). When I came back and told him the medication was making sex difficult for me, he was unmoved. "You still enjoy sex sometimes, right?" he asked. I was nineteen, terrified to tell a grown man that I was sexually active, let alone try and advocate for my right to sex that was pleasurable more often than "sometimes." I'd stay on that medication for another four years, but I never went back to him.

Brains change, Z reminded me, like every part of our bodies. I would never, if I could help it, take fourteen years between dentist appointments or gynecological exams. Shouldn't my brain also get a regular checkup as part of my general preventive health care?

Z emailed me a list of psychiatrists to contact in December 2020. Of the five he recommended, four didn't accept insurance. One, however, was listed as accepting Medicaid. When I called this psychiatrist a few days later, he apologetically told me he did not, in fact, take my insurance, but knew someone else who did. That person, when I emailed them after the new year, told me this was also incorrect, but they'd be happy to take me on as a patient if I was willing to pay out of pocket. If I could pay a couple hundred dollars out of pocket per session, I wanted to write back, I wouldn't be on Medicaid.

In the next eight months, attempting to get myself care—preventive care to tend to my brain before she got any worse—cost me time, mental health, and money. I asked for help from my in-network primary care physician, who can refill the meds I currently take but who is mysteriously unable to evaluate whether or not they're appropriate for me. Two messages and one month later, she wrote to say that (despite treating Medicaid patients) she knew no psychiatrists who accepted Medicaid to refer me to, ending the message with a well-intentioned but unhelpful ";-(." After combing the internet, I found five other Chicago-based psychiatrists who had "Medicaid" listed on their profiles. They never returned my emails or my calls.

In February, I got close. For a week, I emailed a representative from 7 Hills Healthcare, a medical group with three locations in the Chicago area. I confirmed twice, in writing, that they take my insurance, that they provide psychological evaluations, and that there is no copay. A week later at the beginning of my telehealth appointment, the person doing my intake apologized for the confusion. They don't provide psychological evaluations. She reminded me that I can always call the back of my Medicaid insurance card for help getting in-network services, something Z has also said. I thanked her, cried, and got high.

Studies show that being poor is correlated to higher rates of mental illness. What is perhaps less widely understood is that poverty causes mental illness too. As anyone who has tried to get "help"—financial, physical, mental—knows, the process dispatches whole days to the dump. I'm a freelance journalist. When I don't have time to work, I can't earn income to live. This is time I could've spent filing a story. It's time I could've used to call my mom, clean my fridge, apply for a job, run around the block—literally anything. I remind myself that in some ways, I'm lucky: I don't have kids, I'm housed, I have a partner who loves and supports me and with whom I'm safe.

For weeks, I put "Medicaid psych" on my list of things to do, then don't. Finally, in May 2021, I call the DHS helpline (800-843-6154) listed on the back of my Medicaid card and speak to a woman named Denise. I tell her exactly what I'm looking for—a psychiatrist who can give me a psych evaluation, prescribe meds, and monitor if they work. She asks for my zip code, and provides me with four names: Advocate Chicago, Asian Human Services, Community Counseling Center, and Heartland Alliance.

When I call Advocate Chicago, I get put on hold, and then the call ends. I try again. The person I eventually reach says they're at capacity and can't accept new patients: the newest people on their docket are waiting at least three and a half months for initial psychiatric appointments. A counselor at Asian Human Services apologizes as he tells me they don't provide psychiatric care, only therapy. Community Counseling Center says they do offer "medication management" together with therapy, but that means I'd have to leave Z, the therapist I like and already have a working relationship with. At Heartland Alliance, a representative tells me that they only provide psychiatric services *after* you're established with one of their own primary care physicians, meaning I'd have to leave my current PCP. It's unclear to me what is to be gained by disrupting the stable care I already have established in exchange for the uncertain promise of eventual help.

I interviewed Theresa Eagleson, the director of the Department of Healthcare and Family Services in Illinois, hoping to make sense of this system. She was sorry to hear about my experience and noted that the state is trying to address this issue. When I asked why psychiatrists and therapists regularly don't accept Medicaid as insurance, Eagleson said she hasn't seen this statistic. According to Illinois Healthcare and Family Services, 2,126 psychiatrists are actively enrolled in Medicaid. (I was told by Kristine Herman, bureau chief of behavioral health at the Illinois Department of Healthcare and Family Services, that in recent years the state has added thirty-three additional behavioral services offering counseling to address capacity issues, although those services don't include psychiatrists.)

But the number of enrolled psychiatrists doesn't account for the phenomenon of "phantom networks," which is when "errors" in provider directories include wrong numbers or list physicians who aren't actually accepting new clients—and, in some cases, list providers that do not accept that insurance. In the approximately two years I've been on Medicaid, this has been true in my experience, and not only in my search for a psychiatrist: when looking for a general practitioner, it took me several weeks and over a dozen emails or phone calls before I found a provider on the Blue Cross Community Health Plans list who (1) actually took that insurance and (2) was accepting new clients.

"There's a lot of capacity in Medicaid," Eagleson reassured me. "Medicaid provides more for behavioral health than most private insurance." But research tells a different story.

"Ultimately, the literature is clear that psychiatrists (especially child and adolescent psychiatrists) are more likely to accept private insurance than Medicaid, if they accept any insurance at all," wrote researcher Dani Adams in an email to me. Adams, a PhD candidate at the Crown Family School of Social Work, Policy, and Practice at the University of Chicago, researches the "availability, accessibility, and quality of mental health services in under-resourced neighborhoods." She pointed me to a number of studies that show the inequities those on Medicaid face, including a 2011 study done in partnership with the Illinois Department of Healthcare and Family Services itself. Callers posing as parents looking for psychiatric care for their children had an 82.9 percent chance of being denied an appointment if their insurance was public (Medicaid-Children's Health Insurance Program) versus a 48.8 percent chance of denial if their insurance was private (in the case of this study, Blue Cross Blue Shield). Neither number is great, but it's evident that a psychiatrist is more likely to accept private insurance over Medicaid, if they accept insurance at all.

Some days, I still can't believe that, more than a year into a pandemic which saw massive layoffs, record unemployment, hundreds of thousands of deaths, and untold numbers of long-haul COVID survivors, as well as an increase in mental illness, this country still ties "good" insurance to your employer. Medicaid has been good to my body—I got a dermatologist, a primary care physician, a gynecologist, and a gastroenterologist with relative ease—but it has abandoned my brain. I want timely, accessible, affordable care. And I want choice, not a fistful of deeply unhelpful options wrestled, after months, from the banal, cruel system we currently make poor people navigate to access health care.

We deserve so much more. We deserve access to experimental medication when appropriate, stable access to therapy, and processes that don't consume whole days. We want to live. We want more than mere survival. For me, I want to be present in my existence, in the ordinary bickering and loving with my partner, rather than getting lost in the endless twilight plains of my mind.

Z and I ended our sessions in June but not for a bad reason. He graduated and got a job at a new place where, of course, Medicaid isn't accepted. In August, I started looking again for psychiatrists. During our last session, Z said I have a lot of emotional "heartiness," something that fortifies me even in the worst of times. I'm glad someone else can see that, but I wish I didn't have to be hearty. It's a finite resource, one best replenished with the right medication, therapeutic support, and a plain and simple break. I wish I didn't have to rely only on my heart and my rocks to make it through.

Katie Prout is a staff writer for the *Chicago Reader* and a freelance writer for a number of outlets, including *Belt*, *Literary Hub*, and *Longreads*. Previously, she was a creative writing instructor at the University of Iowa, a nonprofit program coordinator in Kalamazoo, and a farmer in Ireland.

MY DISABILITY IS MY SUPERPOWER— IF ONLY EMPLOYERS COULD SEE IT THAT WAY

Andrea Dobynes Wagner as told to Deborah Jian Lee

Elle, June 24, 2021

Twenty-seven years ago, Andrea Dobynes Wagner didn't pass her preschool vision test. She was later diagnosed with retinitis pigmentosa, a group of genetic eye disorders that lead to peripheral vision loss and difficulty seeing at night. Growing up legally blind, doctors warned Andrea that she'd never lead a normal life. They recommended she work a clerical job after high school and live with her parents.

Andrea rejected that destiny. She learned to navigate the world with her limited vision and enjoyed a childhood full of academic achievement, sports, dating, and friends. In college, she lived independently and by age twenty-four she bought a house. Today, at thirty-two, Andrea holds multiple advanced degrees and lives with her husband in Tuscaloosa, Alabama.

Despite everything Andrea has overcome, one challenge persists: navigating the job market with an invisible disability. Even with laws prohibiting discrimination, people with disabilities face many obstacles to employment. In this piece, Andrea shines a light on the cracks in the system and why she's devoting her career to advocating for those pushed to the margins.

—Deborah Jian Lee

In March 2019, I was giving a presentation for a job in tutoring services at a university in Alabama. What the five-person hiring committee saw: a petite Black woman dressed sharply in a crisp shift dress and tweed power blazer, standing at the front of the room. What I saw: mostly darkness.

Through my eyes' narrow aperture—imagine peering down a skinny paper towel roll—I could make out the small conference room and the multiracial panel of men and women smiling brightly at me. They did not know about my retinitis pigmentosa, a genetic disorder that gives me permanent tunnel vision.

As a Black woman with an invisible disability, I was used to this. I stand at a fraught intersection of identities often discounted by society. In some instances, I face outright employment discrimination. Other times, hiring practices unintentionally exclude me. Even with those earnestly recruiting people with disabilities—from social services to companies intent on hiring us—I'm often cut out of the process because I'm not disabled in a way that's obvious or because my young age and advanced degrees disqualify me from public benefits. In the eyes of employers and public service providers, I'm disabled, but not disabled enough.

Even if it was more visible, the unemployment rate of disabled people generally with advanced degrees is almost twice the unemployment rate of nondisabled people with advanced degrees, according to the Bureau of Labor Statistics. Only 25 percent of disabled people with advanced degrees are employed, compared to 72 percent of people without disabilities with the same educational attainment.

That's why even though the hiring committee said nice things about me to my face, when weeks passed and they never called, I wasn't surprised. After the interview for that job, I reached out to one committee member, hoping for intel. She told me that I had aced my interview, but one panelist dinged me for my lack of eye contact—that was the deal breaker.

I was crushed by her remarks. I am legally blind; eye contact will never be my strong suit. For most of my life, I've viewed my disability as a superpower—it's made me adaptive, innovative, and empathetic. But on the job market it has complicated my path to success. Even with my advanced degrees and experience, I can only go so far in a system that fails to understand and accommodate people with disabilities. In the US, sixty-one million adults live with a disability, according to the Centers for Disease Control, and many of them show no outward sign of disability. They may have hearing or vision impairment, epilepsy, autism, a chronic illness, or a mental health ailment, among other conditions. The majority of disability job discrimination claims filed with the US Equal Employment Opportunity Commission (EEOC) between 2005 and 2010 were associated with invisible disabilities, according to research by Cornell University's Employment and Disability Institute.

Technically, the EEOC protects us from job discrimination, but I've seen enough to know better. When I taught a high school journalism class, an administrator regularly commented on my disability, calling it my "crutch." Whenever she observed my teaching style, she'd pull me aside and level critiques that always began with, "I know you have vision problems but..." She criticized me for not walking around the room while I lectured, for not catching every student who peeked at their cell phone, or for turning off the lights while screening a documentary, all circumstances that stemmed from my retinitis pigmentosa. Even after students voted me Educator of the Year, my boss continued to fixate on my disability. Eventually, her bullying became untenable, and I quit.

Ever since I couldn't spot the Christmas tree in a routine preschool vision test, my family worked hard to ensure I wouldn't be left behind. My parents drove me hundreds of miles across the southeastern United States for appointments with eye doctors and retina specialists. My grandparents—all four of them retired educators—routinely showed up at our doorstep bearing stacks of books and learning games.

Born the same year as the Americans with Disabilities Act of 1990, I grew up navigating disability benefits with my family. After attending a free summer camp for the deaf and the blind, where other parents happily shared resources with my mom and dad, my world opened up. Soon our home filled up with free talking books, text-enlarging machines, and other assistive technologies. I leaned into my love of learning, quickly outpacing my peers by two grade levels.

Doctors had practically damned me to a life of solitude, dependence, and unemployment. But my childhood was full; in high school I ran track, did cheerleading, dated boys, and enjoyed my close circle of friends. In college, I learned to live independently and by age twenty-four, I had bought my own house in Tuscaloosa, Alabama, after just a few years of teaching.

Despite my success, disclosing my disability to employers remains dicey; it could cost me the job or invite harassment. Unless I'm positive disclosure will help, I typically wait for a job offer before divulging.

It doesn't help that most applications have migrated online and require details such as a driver's license number. I'm legally blind. I have no peripheral vision, let alone a driver's license, so I'm booted from the process before it's even begun. I've tried accessing ride services for people with disabilities, but I can't qualify for these services without a job, and I can't apply for these jobs without the ride service set up. When I applied to virtually teach English to kids in China, I couldn't take the role, because the script I'd need to read was in their software, which didn't have text-enhancing capabilities. This international company was not bound by EEOC mandates to accommodate me.

Company programs that specifically recruit people with disabilities do so for lower-wage jobs with fewer benefits. I regularly see postings from big-box stores hiring cashiers and store greeters. These jobs won't help me climb out of graduate school debt or advance in my chosen field, advocating for diversity, equity, and inclusion in education. Meanwhile, I no longer qualify for public programs that would help me through leaner times; my advanced degrees and previous higher earnings made me ineligible for social security, food assistance, and housing assistance.

These barriers have taken a toll on my career and economic security, but still, I know I'm one of the lucky ones. I grew up with a supportive family. Today, I'm surrounded by friends who love me, give me rides to doctor appointments, and, when I shatter a dish, rush over to safely clean it up for me since I can't see the shards. I've also been lucky in love. Like many modern relationships, my marriage sprouted from flirty DMs on Instagram. On our first date, Justin assumed I was just tipsy when I grabbed his arm and wobbled in my heels up the steps of a darkened jazz club. By our second date, I knew he was the real deal, so I told him about my retinitis pigmentosa, about the chance of passing it along to my children, about the possibility of losing what little sight I had left. My stomach was in knots as the words tumbled out, but he just looked at me tenderly and said, "Why would you think that'd change anything?"

There are always optimistic signs. Recently, over Zoom, I interviewed for a position as curriculum coordinator for a middle school social justice summer academy. When asked, "What does diversity, equity, and inclusion look like to you?" I took a deep breath and decided to take a risk.

"It looks like me," I replied. "I'm Black, female, and legally blind. I cannot drive, but I do have drive to do this work."

I saw the three panelists smile back at me from my screen. This time, I didn't have to wait weeks for an answer. I was offered the job.

Deborah Jian Lee is an award-winning journalist, radio producer, and author of *Rescuing Jesus: How People of Color, Women, and Queer Christians Are Reclaiming Evangelicalism.*

A TRIP TO THE NAIL SALON WITH MISSING FINGERS

Kim Kelly

Allure, July 31, 2020

Last summer, I attended Coney Island's sideshow school. After encountering a culture in which having eight fingers was seen as a bona fide asset, I left the experience with a deeper appreciation of my status as a human oddity, and a feeling of familial camaraderie with the long line of disabled performers whose ranks I was lucky enough to join.

To put it simply, I have eight fingers. The clinical term for my condition is ectroldactyly, which is a congenital deformity that occurs in approximately one out of every 90,000 births and manifests differently depending on the person. My case is fairly mild in that only one of my limbs, my left hand, is affected; my right hand and all ten toes are standard-issue. All that is to say: it's really not that big a deal.

Most people don't clock this about me, though. My disability is relatively minor, and I've developed effective behaviors at hiding it. As I've gotten older and more comfortable in my own skin, my hands have ceased to bother me. They are now more akin to mild inconveniences, like when they prevent me from opening jars (my lifelong obsession with pickles is just one cruel irony). Painting my own nails is another.

Before the coronavirus pandemic hit, I got my nails professionally done every four to five months. As a freelance writer, gel and designs were above my pay grade, so I always went for basic manicures, gravitating toward muted shades in icy or pastel tones to counterbalance my all-black wardrobe. My last manicure was lavender. None of this is particularly unique—surely, many of you get your nails done, whether sporadically or with religious regularity. (How else would the nail salon industry have become an $8 billion industry in the US alone?) The only thing that makes me stand out within this context is the *number* of nails I bring to the salon—and the significance of being treated so well by the workers who handle them.

Nail salon technicians are the only group of people with whom I have public, personal interactions who get an up-close look at my gnarled hands. Getting your talons done should be a soothing, pleasant experience—and it often is, but for me, it also comes with a bolt of initial dread. How will the technician react to my hands? How will they handle my left hand, with its three stunted fingers and scars? I'm always a little afraid, but nearly every time, that fear has been proven unwarranted.

While some (often privileged) strangers react to my limbs with naked curiosity or cruelty, these technicians seem almost uniformly unperturbed, at least to my face (and I can't blame someone for commenting on an unusual thing they saw at work that day once they're off the clock). While they are often underpaid and mistreated by their employers, I have found them to be uniformly kind when unexpectedly confronted with my digits. This wordless acceptance is such a rarity in a country that so often castigates, isolates, or otherwise oppresses those with physical differences. None have ever called me a freak or sneered in disgust when presented with my fingers—which isn't something I can say for everyone I've encountered in my thirty-two years.

In some cases, manicurists are extra gentle, handling my fingers like butterfly wings, which is a show of kindness, but nevertheless makes me feel weird in the pit of my stomach. I always worry that I'm making an already demanding, underpaid, and hazardous job more difficult by needing them to adapt to the unexpected shapes of my atypical fingers, or that I've made them feel they need to mask their surprise. Dwelling on this additional emotional labor takes away from the small luxury that is getting one's nails done, and even though I go out of my way to be grateful and polite (and directly tip the technician at least 30 percent in cash), it can be hard not to feel like a burden.

It's not the same as other salon experiences: I get the occasional facial treatment when I can, but everyone has skin, so these vulnerabilities and anxieties aren't present. Lobster claws feel like another matter entirely.

Now that nail salons are beginning to open back up—regardless of whether or not it's actually safe for some states to do so—many of the workers who lost their livelihoods as a result of the initial closures are heading back to work. The future of the industry remains a question mark, but it does seem inevitable that customers will start going back.

I might, eventually, though I can't imagine returning before the danger passes for everyone—not just those who have the option of choosing to stay home. My disability doesn't place me at an increased risk from the coronavirus, but that's certainly not the case for many other people in the disability community or the workers themselves. And there is always a power dynamic from the moment you step into a nail salon as a customer, so it's your responsibility to ensure you're doing so as ethically as possible—especially now, when wearing a face mask and following safety protocols can be a matter of life or death.

And when that point does come, for me, going to the nail salon will remain the only time I can go into a public place and feel truly, utterly unremarkable—almost *boringly* human. The last time I got my nails done in New York City, I summoned up the courage to apologize for making things harder, and asked the technician who was absorbed in applying my topcoat whether she'd ever seen anyone like me before. She looked up with a warm, reassuring smile, shook her head, and said, "Honey, I've seen a *lot*." The comment was a kindness she didn't need to offer me, but I am still so grateful for it. The absence of surprise (or horror) at my hands felt like a gift.

Like many other groups who are marginalized by American society—including immigrant workers of color—people with visible disabilities are rarely afforded the luxury of banality. Moving through the world while being noticeably "different" can be exhausting, and in the age of Zoom calls and FaceTime, those of us who would normally be out and about haven't gotten much of a break from that feeling. As much as I struggle with even identifying as disabled, those visits to the salon really help to reinforce the comforting idea that no individual body is really all that interesting, but everybody deserves to feel cared for—and to have cute nails if they want to.

Kim Kelly is an independent journalist, author, and organizer based in Philadelphia whose writing on labor, politics, class, and culture has appeared in *Teen Vogue*, *Rolling Stone*, the *Nation*, the *New York Times*, the *Washington Post*, the *Columbia Journalism Review*, among others. Her first book, *Fight Like Hell: The Untold History of American Labor*, is out via One Signal / Simon & Schuster.

TRAUMATIC PREGNANCIES ARE AWFUL—<u>DOBBS</u> WILL MAKE THEM SO MUCH WORSE

Alissa Quart

The Washington Post, June 24, 2022

Some pregnancies and births are difficult enough to give mothers PTSD. When a pregnancy is unwanted, the physical and psychological strains will be even more severe.

When Justice Samuel Alito's draft opinion in *Dobbs v. Jackson Women's Health Organization* leaked, signaling that *Roe* was about to fall, I felt sick, both figuratively and literally. First, I thought of the faces and the stories of the women I had interviewed in abortion clinics in three states, for various articles and documentaries. I felt shaky, thinking about what would happen to women like them now, women who often had other children to support.

But I also felt actual nausea as I flashed back to my own difficult pregnancy. I suffered from hyperemesis gravidarum—a detached-sounding clinical term that describes vomiting constantly while pregnant. It's like morning sickness but all day and for all three trimesters (waning only, in my case, in the very last month). I couldn't swallow prenatal vitamins; cucumbers were one of the few foods I could keep down. My throat ached from stomach acid, and I was weak. Sometimes I was bedridden and almost never was I able to get work done (except to write occasional poems about, yes, pregnancy and nausea). Eventually, I wound up on Zofran, a drug sometimes prescribed to patients undergoing chemotherapy. (It didn't really work.) Mercifully, my husband and I had some savings, so I could sink into an entropic duvet existence till I gave birth and was no longer imprisoned in my own ill body.

As many as a third of women experience some form of trauma during pregnancy or birth—caused not only by illnesses like mine but also by such things as complications during delivery and inadequate support during labor. And a significant fraction who experience this suffering also end up with posttraumatic stress disorder (PTSD). After I gave birth, I had some of the classic signs of posttraumatic stress disorder: I constantly replayed the worst moments of my pregnancy; I suffered from anxiety spikes; and I avoided anything that reminded me of pregnancy. In fact, I tossed my maternity clothes as soon as I could. The latter was part of my effort to dissociate from that time.

That disassociation may explain why it took *Roe*'s demise to grasp that what I suffered from was psychologically diagnosable: yes, that was indeed PTSD. Estimates of the proportion of women with pregnancy- and birth-related PTSD range widely (from 4 percent to 19 percent, depending on the study), but it is known to disproportionately affect women who have had previous trauma or who are financially stressed—as well as women of color.

Of course, the statistics about prevalence come from a world in which most pregnancies are wanted. In the world the Supreme Court has just created, women will be forced to carry unwanted pregnancies to term, which will only increase the physical and psychological stress on mothers.

For decades, the antiabortion camp has inundated the public with claims about the ostensible suffering of groups of fetal cells (in propaganda like "The Silent Scream"); those who worked to reverse abortion rights point to the electrical impulses in these cells and call them, misleadingly, "heartbeats." Meanwhile, the very real bodily and mental suffering of many pregnant women gets short shrift. Until I myself developed hyperemesis gravidarum, I had no idea that 0.5 percent to 2 percent of pregnant women confront it, or that, among those, more than half end up with at least one PTSD symptom, according to one study, and fully 20 percent experience "full criteria" PTSD.

Counting on the Supreme Court to uphold key rights was always a mistake. And hyperemesis gravidarum is far from the worst physical ailments that pregnant women can face. Other afflictions include life-threatening diseases such as preeclampsia, which affects an estimated 5 to 7 percent of pregnant women, or pulmonary embolisms.

People who give birth willingly can, with difficulty, reconcile themselves to pregnancy-related trauma because they want to have a child. But if I had not desired my daughter with all my heart, the physical pain I experienced, which also caused psychological scarring, would have been akin to torture.

Antiabortion activists like to throw around pseudodiagnoses like the "trauma of a past abortion" and "postabortion syndrome," glossing over, or flatly ignoring, the afflictions that pregnancy can cause. Yet pregnancy-related trauma needs to be part of the discussion about the implications of forcing women to carry fetuses to term.

We need to tell stories like the one Courtney Lund O'Neil related in *Parents* magazine, in which she described twenty-eight hours of labor that nearly killed her. When she was finally put on oxygen, "A sea of people stood around me, screaming for me to breathe." The experience, worsened by what she describes as subpar care, led to PTSD: "I suffered from insomnia, nights spent staring at the ceiling as the past rewound in my mind."

We should tell stories like that one for political reasons but also, more basically, because the silence around pregnancy-related trauma comes from stigma. It took the shock of the *Dobbs* decision for me to recognize the pregnancy-related suffering I endured. *Dobbs* also reminded me what I already knew: that these mental and physical maladies should be part of the debate over abortion—and, like abortion itself, they should be spoken of without shame.

Alissa Quart is the author of *Bootstrapped: Liberating Ourselves from the American Dream* and executive director of the Economic Hardship Reporting Project. She has written for many publications, including the *New York Times*, the *Washington Post,* and *Time.* Her honors include an Emmy Award, the SPJ Award, and a Nieman Fellowship. She is the author of four previous books of nonfiction, including *Squeezed: Why Our Families Can't Afford America* and *Branded: The Buying and Selling of Teenagers*, and two books of poetry, most recently *Thoughts and Prayers.* She lives with her family in Brooklyn.

THE TWISTED BUSINESS OF DONATING PLASMA

Darryl Lorenzo Wellington

The Atlantic, May 28, 2014

Since 2008, plasma pharmaceuticals have leaped from $4 billion to a more than $11 billion annual market. Donors desperate for the cash incentive from high-frequency "plassing" may be putting their health, and the public's, at risk.

I needed the cash.

That was how I found myself lying in a plasma "donation" room filled with about forty couches, each equipped with a blood pressure cuff and a centrifuge. A white-coated attendant (workers aren't required to have medical or nursing degrees) pricked my arm. He separated my plasma from my whole blood into a large bottle, and returned my protein-depleted blood, which flowed back into my arm to rebuild my nutrient supply.

"My house is so noisy with four kids so I come here for my relaxation," said a middle-aged, haggard-looking woman on the next couch, the plasmapheresis machine at her side whirring. A clinician instructed us both to pump and relax our fists, like cows milking our own udders.

Before leaving I received a calendar that mapped out my pay, *if* I maintained a twice-weekly schedule for subsequent donations. Even a ten dollar bonus on my next visit!

How did I get here? My rent was due. I had insufficient funds in the bank. I was forty-eight years old, a journalist running short on cash from writing assignments and odd jobs. That was when I saw an ad offering fifty dollars per plasma donation: blood money, or more specifically, payment for my time and any small pain involved in the process of having protein-rich plasma extracted from the blood. Regulars call it "plassing."

The ad I'd seen featuring smiling attendants suggested an experience similar to one at a sedate hospital. The facility I entered buzzed like a school lunchroom. There were first-timers waiting to complete the initial medical exam, and regulars hurrying to check in at automatic computer terminals. Easily fifty to sixty "plassers" were present at any given moment, the crowd continually ebbing and flowing. All were like me—hopeful, needy, and impatient to get paid.

I received an oral examination. I was not surprised by the many questions about my sexual behavior, but I was taken aback by repeated questions regarding tattoos. Three times I was asked if I had lied and "really" had tattoos. After the clinicians tested a blood sample for protein levels, I underwent a bare-bones medical checkup. But I questioned its efficiency given that my examiner ran through scores of questions so fast I had to ask him to repeat himself. I spotted a sign: "no payment unless donation is completed."

Plassers receive payments on a special debit card that extracts a surcharge whenever they use it. Curiously, while my examiner hurried me through the screening, he *did* patiently lay out the payment scheme. Did he know how desperate I was? His "don't worry, you'll pass" attitude may have expressed condescension, unprofessionalism, or benevolence.

My extraction went smoothly. I left with a ray of hope that I could "plass" next month's rent money. The literature provided at US centers ubiquitously states that "donating plasma is safe." Its side effects are limited to "mild faintness and bruising." (My brochure also added, "Other possible side effects will be explained by our medical staff," though I can't say any such explanation stayed with me.) But the following day my body received an impromptu schooling in the price tag of the world I had entered.

It happened at about five o'clock the next day. Unexpectedly, with no apparent cause or logical relationship to physical exertion, I felt my legs go rubbery. I was Silly Putty. This was something more than "mild faintness" and particularly disturbing because of the aspect of a random attack. I suddenly felt so weirdly fatigued that I couldn't stand on my feet. I barely reached the couch before I passed out for five hours straight. Luckily, I was safely ensconced at home. But because I substitute teach as well as freelance write, I woke up wondering: What would I do if that happened at my day job?

What had happened? I had received my welcome to the subtle physical changes, possibly exacerbated by work and poverty, which may be the upshot of plassing. And my research began.

Biotest, CSL Plasma, Yale Plasma. These are some of the funny corporate names that dot my state, New Mexico, and maybe yours. Or Octapharma. Or Biolife. Plasma reaped from paid US donors makes up about 70 percent of worldwide collections.[1] The United States is conversationally known in the industry as "the OPEC of plasma collections."

But why plasma?

Proteins in the plasma collected at places like Biotest are necessary for the manufacture of a wide range of pharmaceuticals produced by for-profit corporations. The industry burgeoned in the 1950s thanks to a boom in new drugs for hemophiliacs. Plasma centers have historically worn the scarlet letter in the blood-collection universe.

Prior to the AIDS crisis, plasma-collection practices were often under the table, but the medical community still operated under a general assumption that those standards for plasma were good enough. The assumption proved disastrously wrong. Industry practices eventually cost the hemophiliac community dearly.

Throughout the 1960s and '70s, plasma companies minimized their own overhead costs by relying on chancy prison populations paid a pittance: five to ten dollars per plassing donation. Roughly 50 percent of American hemophiliacs contracted HIV from bad plasma-based pharmaceuticals (a much higher infection rate than that suffered by gay men at the time), making worldwide plasma medication HIV outbreaks the industry's most publicized scandal.

People with hemophilia filed class-action suits. These included substantial evidence that a major plasma company continued to distribute "old supplies" of bad medications after becoming aware of the AIDS infection. The public was dismayed to discover that the industry operated under the protection of federal and state blood shield laws, limiting its liability.

By the 1990s, the industry's public reputation reached a low point, with American collections dwindling, US federal regulators clamping down, and revelations coming to light that spoke poorly of industry oversight and humanitarianism. Even before the AIDS crisis devastated US plasma collections, other controversies, such as incidents of hepatitis C infection in plasma pharmaceuticals, led corporations to keep overhead low and avoid regulation by transporting the payment-incentives collections system to penniless countries abroad.

In the 1990s, China attempted to develop a plasma market to compete with Western companies by touting money for plasmapheresis in China's most impoverished province, Henan. Villagers who were too poor to afford condoms soon realized they could earn more money by selling plasma than by farming the land, but the facilities offered substandard sterilization techniques, needles, and blood bags. By 1995, Henan Province had become a blood farm built on a criminalized plasma economy. Thousands of Chinese donors became infected with AIDS and hepatitis C.

Today, many plasma products for hemophiliacs have been outdated by medical advances, but the industry thrives on producing albumin for burns and intravenous immunoglobin used to treat immune disorders and neurological conditions. The industry has returned to the United States in a big way with the help of brighter, user-friendly advertisements that include appeals to public service and reminders of the economy's downfall to encourage donors. The number of centers in the United States ballooned during the Great Recession, with a hundred new centers opening and total donations leaping from 12.5 million in 2006 to more than 23 million in 2011.

Monopolization has transformed the industry, which now consists of five international corporations operating in the United States under FDA regulation: Baxter International of Deerfield, Illinois; CSL of Australia; Talecris of Research Triangle Park, North Carolina; Grifols of Spain; and Octapharma of Switzerland. A possible sixth big player is Biotest AG, the for-profit arm of a Dutch nonprofit corporation, Sanquin. Since 2008, plasma pharmaceuticals have leaped from an approximate $4 billion to a more than $11 billion annual market.

Santa Fe, New Mexico, where I live, has a crowded but reasonably clean Biotech Plasma center. But the state's largest city, Albuquerque, population 552,804, has three plasma centers that would have challenged my willingness to plass no matter how needy I was. Yale Plasma, located on a strip where panhandlers convene, resembles a pawn shop. The exterior window sports a motto for in-house lotto games; the interior is remarkably cramped. Another Albuquerque center, CSL Plasma, is larger but has no chairs. Donors crouch on the floor or stand in long lines until they plass. Asking a young man if he minded squatting, I was told CSL removed complimentary seating to "keep the bums out of here."

Plasma is "pooled" or collected in containers to prepare it for a process called "fractionation," which will render it usable. The bigger the plasma pools, the cheaper they will be to process—which Dr. Lucy Reynolds, a research fellow at the London School of Hygiene and Tropical Medicine, cites as an example of the industry cutting corners.

Large pools maximize profits. Furthermore, although large pools are subject to advanced safety analyses (twenty-first-century viral testing has made hepatitis C and AIDS contamination rare), health officials have raised the concern that as market plasma spreads globally the harm that could result if another AIDS-like pathogen infiltrated the system would be exponentially greater.

"Certain governments are people and people's-rights centered," says Reynolds, who recently published a paper castigating the plasma trade.[2] "In those places they make the plasma corporations play by the rules; sometimes they just choose to have as little as possible to do with them. But the United States is a corporate country" that maintains the Western world's least restrictive plasma regulations.

US centers also have a policy assured to reel in those with an ongoing, immediate need for small sums of cash: fifty dollars for the first five donations, then sixty dollars a week if you willingly go under the needle twice a week.

"I call it a grubby business because they knowingly endanger the health of donors in the US by harvesting them twice a week, while in every other place in the world you're only allowed to donate fortnightly," Reynolds says.

I interviewed plassers in Albuquerque but, given that my questions included asking if they lied to pass medical examinations, the people I spoke with often asked me not to use their last names.

"Going into the center makes me feel like a lab rat," says Ron, a thirty-three-year-old single father and unemployed schoolteacher who began regularly plassing six years ago to make ends meet for his new son. He was disqualified at a local center because he had many visible tattoos but accepted at another center "that was less picky." Ron reports no particular bad side effects but still worries. "They tell me there are no long-term effects but the answers they give at these places are so robotic."

A haggard man with bloodshot eyes standing outside the CSL center identified himself as "Bubba" and said he was homeless and an alcoholic. He had suffered a serious head injury in youth and had been plassing for nearly fifteen years with no ill effects other than "sometimes my arm hurts really bad." He also continually falls asleep on the couches. In fact, Bubba once collapsed in the standing lines at CSL, but he appreciated the extra cash. He says he was unhappy when he had been drinking too much to pass the protein-level test, but claimed he later discovered, "If I swallow ketchup before going in I can pass any test they throw at me."

Bubba was cognizant that donors who were homeless, were alcoholic, or had suffered head injuries like his own were, in theory, barred. "Everybody lies," he said. "Nobody is honest on all those questions."

I left the conversation wondering whether Bubba was an example of why other nations don't want to expose their citizens to the commercial plasma trade, and many make (increasingly unsuccessful) efforts to limit imports of commercial plasma from the United States.[3] Should a homeless alcoholic be banned from plassing for his safety and ours?

Gabriella, a fifty-one-year-old mother of three, began plassing eight years ago after she was laid off in a cut-back of state-government employees. She admits to having lied to pass the screening after realizing that she had become too thin to pass the weight test, and "put on extra clothes, just to squeak past the weight minimum" of 110 pounds. Gabriella knows other regular plassers, many homeless, who use ankle weights.

Kevin Taylor, a twenty-seven-year-old student at the University of New Mexico, plassed to meet expenses but found that over two years of plassing he lost fifteen pounds.

"I definitely wasn't eating regular meals, and I think the pressure of keeping up my two donations a week was making me sick," he says.

Kevin Crosby, forty-eight, began plassing ten years ago to provide for his six-year-old daughter.

"Every time I've had this weird hollowed-out feeling. And a lot of times the next day I will have serious fatigue," he told me. "Then, about five years ago when I was working night shift at a security job, I had that weird fatigue. I don't know what hit me but I woke up on the floor. They accused me of falling asleep; I know I blacked out."

Crosby has had several blackouts, including one that hit when he was driving.

"I had to pull over," he said. "I had to sit there several minutes in a daze. It really freaked me."

The fact that other Western nations adopt a "better-safe-than-sorry" attitude (when they sanction commercial collection centers at all) by insisting on two-week intervals between donations should raise eyebrows about US practices. Many people I interviewed left me questioning whether, when poverty is the primary motivation, the advisability of twice-weekly plassing should be reconsidered. Not to mention the other likely health complications donors may suffer from, including stress, poor nutrition, and inadequately treated or untreated medical conditions.

All told, I interviewed almost three dozen regulars at CSL and Yale Plasma. More than half of them confessed to frequent, bizarre tingling sensations; pains; rubbery legs; and severe dehydration, as well as to having been homeless, having lied to pass medical exams, and having used "tricks" that allowed them to pass protein-level tests. They lived in circumstances that made plassing a hardship, but said, "I can't eat if I don't plass."

I described the experiences above to the medical historian Harriet A. Washington, also the author of *Deadly Monopolies* and *Medical Apartheid: The Dark History of Medical Experimentation on Black Americans*. Washington told me, "Our blood supply is now very safe, although not perfectly so." Hepatitis C and HIV infection are as rare as one in every one million blood recipients.[4]

Washington is not opposed to payment centers that observe safety standards and adhere to regulations. Neediness and economic hardship don't necessarily make a donor unsafe, which is a historical prejudice. The crux, Washington said, "is how we screen donors."

"If these companies are winking at donors' deception, then they're putting us all in serious danger. In an ideal world, I'd want more government oversight to closely monitor these collection sites."

Why do donors, including myself, suffer fatigue akin to blackouts? During plasmapheresis, centers often use a chemical, sodium citrate, to keep blood from clotting, Washington explained.

"Sodium citrate and other citric-acid derivatives bond with the calcium in your blood, and afterwards the calcium is no longer available to your body. We know that some people respond badly to sodium citrate. The worst case is rare: extreme hypocalcaemia, which can be fatal. But more often, people will suffer fainting, tingling and numbness, muscle contractions, or even seizures. Walking around with depleted calcium can be extremely dangerous. It can lead to serious health-care issues."

These issues include heart arrhythmias, seizures, osteoporosis, eye strain, breathing problems, brittle bones, and chronic kidney conditions.

A summary of a 2005 report by Jeffrey L. Winters published in the *Journal of Clinical Apheresis* states that "the most common aphaeresis-specific reaction is hypocalcemia due to citrate anticoagulation, which, while usually mild, has the potential for severely injuring the donor."[5] In fact, Winters writes, compared to whole-blood donations, "the risk of reactions requiring hospitalization is substantially greater." Plasma centers that don't inform donors of these risks are abrogating patients' medical rights—yet none of the people I interviewed who experienced "funny fits" or weird tingling sensations were knowledgeable of the possibility of hypocalcemia.

Several reported that they had inquired about such symptoms at centers but were given absolute guarantees of safety. And it seems preposterous to expect them to diagnose themselves when centers prominently display statements like the following one from a Baxter Inc. press kit: "Donating plasma is a low risk procedure with minimal or no side effects."

I sat in a pizza parlor with Kevin Crosby near the Yale Plasma center. He rolled up his sleeves and showed me a huge sore where ten years of needles had gone into his arm.

"I never in my life thought I would have to do this to survive," he said. "A lot of the staff aren't competent with the needles. People get jittery talking about that stuff, but a lot talk about how much money they make off us. I say, if they're going to exploit us they could at least pay us. I say they could pay us a hundred dollars for twice a week."

Crosby has also always been pestered by doubts: Why does he have blackouts, and how safe is this plasma? Looking at the suspect patrons, "you can tell something is wrong with them," he says.

I tell Kevin about the industry's history of negligence: the tragedies in South America, the American prison collections, and the AIDS outbreak among hemophiliacs who received medications tainted because the industry put market share above safety controls. I explain that today the monopolized industry harvests in the US because only the FDA will allow it to reap enough plasma to support an international market. Nowhere else in the West believes twice-a-week donations are advisable, and the international community isn't as sanguine regarding detrimental health effects. Kevin's blackouts are probably a bad reaction to an anticoagulant, sodium citrate.

"I have read every word of every paper I've signed at CSL and Yale," Kevin said. "I haven't seen a mention about this."

Critics today still question the wisdom of cutting costs by maintaining massive plasma pools. Safer systems operate on a not-for-profit basis, and require only sufficient amounts of plasma to meet domestic needs. A 2005 report published by writers at Ghent University in Belgium says that in Belgium, "approximately 5,000 donations are mixed into such pools. In Germany, pools containing up to 60,000 donations are considered." In the United States, "some donor pool sizes are in excess of several hundred thousand [donations]." The authors recommend alternative pooling strategies because the "risk of contamination of these pools increases rapidly with the pool size."[6] Zealous precaution today could spare us untold misery tomorrow.

"Hearing all this," Crosby said, "I never want to walk into those places again."

CODA

I never received as much attention for a story as I did after I published "The Twisted Business of Donating Plasma" in 2014. Years later, I still receive commentary—sometimes irate, sometimes appreciative, and sometimes instigative.

The appreciative correspondents have been troubled souls who have always felt queasy about the impact the practice has on their bodies. They may have spent weeks, months, or years debating "plassing," but they quit after reading my piece.

Journalists, nonprofits, and think tanks have contacted me, asking for my insights into the plasma industry. The attention is gratifying.

I am aware there have been changes in the plasma industry since 2014. During the pandemic, plasma companies began producing drugs that eased the symptoms of COVID-19. Plasma donors have been slightly better compensated. Business Insider reports that "Centers that usually offer between $35 to $50 per visit have paid an average of $65 per donation." Donors with COVID-19 immunity have become prized cash cows.

But sixty-five dollars a pop still foremost of all incentivizes the poor, the desperate, and the hungry. Other writers who have explored the subject have asked the same questions that I did: Why is the US the only country that allows donors to sell their plasma twice a week? Why is the US one of the few countries that legalizes cash incentives? Why hasn't a major oversight body sponsored a thorough study of the health effects of selling plasma? Shouldn't this industry be regulated? Given the paucity of a US social safety net, isn't the country effectively abandoning the health of its poor to mysterious international corporations?

I note with chagrin that none of the articles I have read feature a single response to these questions from representatives of the international plasma industry, or an indication the industry intends to respond to public concerns. The poor supply the plasma, while the bosses remain shrouded in secrecy.

Darryl Lorenzo Wellington is a poet and journalist based in Santa Fe, New Mexico. His work has also appeared in the *Nation* and *Dissent*.

TO HELP THE HOMELESS, OFFER SHELTER THAT ALLOWS DEEP SLEEP

Lori Teresa Yearwood

San Francisco Chronicle, December 28, 2018

I barely slept for the full two years I was homeless. One night, I searched for places to sleep in all the wrong places, including the top of a plastic slide in a playground. At about 3:00 a.m., I curled up on a portion of soft, thick grass. But an hour later, automatic sprinklers came on, drenching my feet. I sloshed to the edges of a wilderness park, where I finally found a generous-size wooden bench. I changed my socks and fell in and out of sleep for the next two hours, waking up to my own violent shivering.

Sleep deprivation haunts unhoused people, worsening the trauma that sometimes caused their unsheltered situations in the first place, as well as any mental and physical illnesses they have. Bobby Watts, chief executive officer of the National Health Care for the Homeless Council, says that "sleeplessness in homelessness is a public health crisis."

There are more than 554,000 homeless people in this country, estimates the US Department of Housing and Urban Development. Of those, 7,499 people are homeless in San Francisco, according to the 2017 San Francisco Homeless Point-in-Time Count. Shelters aren't providing the needed respite—70 percent of homeless individuals who had experienced shelter stays reported that they sometimes felt so tired that they could not function normally during the day, according to a 2011 study conducted by the House the Homeless in Austin, Texas.[1]

Yet the simplest way for people to drastically improve the quality of their lives, Watts notes, is: "Get more sleep."

This simplicity, however, begs a few questions:

What if homeless people were provided with more comfortable sleeping environments, where they could get the rest required to function better? Would homelessness then be reduced? I definitely think so. After all, without the clarity that a decent night's sleep provides, how can someone climb the herculean mountain of self-sufficiency that housing oneself demands?

The first issue that homeless people inevitably face is a loss of control, Watts points out. This loss becomes acute when it comes to regulating sleep, as the majority of shelters place people in barrack-type rooms where residents can't control the noise, the temperature, the lighting, or even what time they must go to bed or wake up.

This was my experience. That night, in 2016, I curled up on that bench outside a Salt Lake City apartment complex. I had already walked more than three miles from the homeless shelter, which didn't have any remaining beds that night—only thin rubber mats on tiled floors in fluorescent-lit rooms filled with sad, angry, and often loud women.

After a half hour on the bench, someone opened an apartment door and walked across one of the upstairs corridors. Since I no longer slept deeply—homelessness had trained me to remain constantly vigilant—I instantly opened my eyes. I feared being accused of trespassing. I grabbed my backpack and garbage bag with my possessions and set back onto the streets.

Situations like mine have finally reached the attention of builders and architects. Now, along with shelter staff and case managers, they are turning their attention to therapeutic, "trauma-informed" shelter care, meaning that there is an attempt to reduce the experiences of powerlessness for those caught in homelessness.

New York architect Ira Mitchneck designed a new shelter for homeless residents ages fifty and older, dubbed Valley Lodge. Until a few months ago, the shelter resembled college dorms, and relied on windows for ventilation. The new Valley Lodge offers a ventilation system and electric power for each resident, along with acoustically rated windows and air conditioning. A range of spaces in the building accommodates different sleep schedules, and the lighting is designed to work with most people's circadian rhythms—the approximately twenty-four-hour cycle in the physiological processes of all living beings.

While clearly many steps beyond what has been expected of homeless shelters, Mitchneck believes this new therapeutic model can—and should—be emulated.

There are more modest solutions to combat sleeplessness, which, according to the Centers for Disease Control and Prevention, makes the human body unable "to function well, resulting in fatigue, confusion, depression, concentration problems, hallucinations, illness and injury."

In Lane County, Oregon, at the ShelterCare organization, short-term housing units come with locked doors, allowing clients to manage their sleeping environments. This helps her clients, says Melissa McCloskey, a case manager. Before being able to avail themselves of these options, her clients often exhibited such deep states of exhaustion that it is difficult to differentiate between the symptoms of sleep deprivation, mental illness, and self-medicating addictions, McCloskey said.

Journey of Hope, a Salt Lake City nonprofit that helps harmed women, regularly provides the privacy of its conference room so homeless clients can catch up on sleep during office hours. Shannon Miller Cox, the executive director, said: "Often, they fall asleep sitting upright in our chairs, and snore and sleep for hours at a time. We feed them coffee and snacks and cover them with blankets. They are exhausted."

And even these extended naps can do a world of good. One of Miller Cox's clients, a woman who had been living in her van, got enough sleep to reach an epiphany, Miller Cox recalled.

"After getting enough rest, she gained the clarity that she wanted to change her life. She got sober, got a job as a dishwasher, and now has her own apartment."

My own homelessness ended when a pastor at a homeless outreach center recognized my need for housing, and brought me to Journey of Hope. There, Miller Cox gave me a job as a house mom in a transitional residence for recently homeless women.

But on that seemingly unending spring night months earlier, I never did find real rest.

I got up from that last bench and walked to a food pantry as the sun rose. There, I drank a free cup of black coffee, something I hoped would keep me awake enough to search for the next place to rest my head.

Lori Teresa Yearwood is a national housing crisis reporter for the Economic Hardship Reporting Project. Her work has appeared in the *New York Times*, the *Washington Post*, the *Guardian*, *Mother Jones*, *Slate*, and many other publications. Lori is currently working on her memoir.

INEQUITY IN MATERNAL HEALTH CARE LEFT ME WITH UNDIAGNOSED POSTPARTUM PTSD

Courtney Lund O'Neil

Parents, March 23, 2022

After twenty-eight hours of labor with my first child, I struggled to breathe. In the hospital, a nurse strapped an oxygen mask to my face. A sea of people stood around me, screaming for me to breathe. Breathing, something we're born knowing how to do, escaped me.

I had no idea this moment would later bring about weeks of enervating postpartum posttraumatic stress disorder (PTSD) symptoms. Researchers estimate postpartum PTSD, often triggered by birth trauma, impacts anywhere from 10 percent to 17 percent of birthing people—but I didn't even know it existed.[1] Limited literature has curbed awareness and symptoms are often misinterpreted as depression or anxiety. PTSD, well-known and well-researched among veterans, has common symptoms including flashbacks or nightmares, intrusive reimagining of past events, panic attacks, or a sense of detachment. Many patients go undiagnosed. Myself included.

My lower-income status didn't help. My husband was in graduate school and we had just moved to a new city. I was juggling three low-paying jobs with no benefits, which placed me on Medi-Cal, California's Medicaid health-care program, through a clinic east of Los Angeles. The payout for Medi-Cal patients is lower, so doctors who take it slot these appointments back-to-back to compensate.[2] The first OB-GYN I saw said, "You shouldn't care how you're treated. You don't work. You aren't paying." I told her I had been paying government taxes since I started working at sixteen years old, and still was. I walked out of her office and never looked back.

It's no wonder my symptoms went undiagnosed. Poverty is a leading factor in maternal vulnerability in the US, according to 2021

61

data released by Surgo Ventures.[3] Beyond the physical impact of health-care disparity for birthing people, maternal depression rates are an estimated 40 to 60 percent higher for low-income people, according to the Georgetown University Health Policy Institute.[4] As a white woman who did not grow up in poverty, I have much more privilege than some. There is staggering racial disparity in maternal health care: Black, American Indian, and Alaska Native women are two to three times more likely to die from pregnancy-related causes than white women, according to the Centers for Disease Control and Prevention.[5] When birthing people of color live in low-income communities, the inequities increase even more.

The OB-GYN whom I ultimately stayed with never got to know me. He sped through each appointment; I barely got a question in. When he told me he wouldn't be in the delivery room, I shouldn't have been caught off guard, but I still was.

MY TRAUMATIC BIRTH CAME BY SURPRISE

In the hospital delivery room, my body had entered a panic. I arrived the day before on an instinct of fear—I couldn't feel the baby kick. Over the next twenty-eight hours I was pumped with Pitocin, Demerol (or possibly Fentanyl), antibiotics, and a failed epidural. My water was broken without my consent. I could not move my body, but I could feel substantial pain. I forgot how to breathe.

In the final moments before my baby's birth, I yearned for comfort from a familiar face at the other end of the hospital bed. Instead, the on-call doctor, whom I'd never seen before, took out a knife and sliced me without warning—a violent, bloody episiotomy. He pulled out my baby and the NICU team swooped my son away for examination. My body shook in shock as I cried. After the APGAR score confirmed that the baby was healthy, he was passed to my husband for skin-to-skin. I was told I could not hold my child until I stopped shaking. I clenched my teeth, but I continued to scream and shake for what felt like hours. The stranger called "doctor" sat at the foot of my bed as I watched the thread pull up and down, yanking nearly fifty stitches through my raw skin. I yearned to hold my baby.

STRUGGLING WITH POSTPARTUM PTSD

That loss of autonomy is one of many kinds of mistreatment in child-birth. Researchers found that in the US one in six people reported experiencing mistreatment during labor or delivery. Based on the Giving Voice to Mothers survey, I was one of the 18 percent of low-income white patients in the US who report a mismanaged birth. The rates among low-income patients of color are starkly higher, at about 27 percent.[6]

In the weeks that followed, I felt stuck, voiceless, and unsure of how to make peace with what happened. Once home, I was unable to exclusively breastfeed.[7] I bled for months. I couldn't sleep. My physical pain was enormous, as were the hauntings. I would dip further back in time to when I cared for my only brother, an infant in hospice care. He would wail from a rare disease electrifying him, damaging his brain. These traumas would replay in my mind, and I'd feel my whole body shudder.

I suffered from insomnia, nights spent staring at the ceiling as the past rewound in my mind. At my six-week checkup, I filled out a form—the obsolete Edinburgh Postnatal Depression Scale—that could possibly diagnose me with postpartum depression or anxiety.[8] I did not feel like myself, but I didn't feel like I had either of those completely. I hoped the nurse would see something I could not vocalize.

During my visit, I was pushed through a system not meant to support me. I tried to explain to the nurse that I was experiencing feelings of reliving my birthing experience that would keep me up at night.

"You may have a slight case of depression—you can see someone or not. Up to you," she said, hand already on the doorknob. No one checked on my postpartum health again. I was never formally diagnosed. It wouldn't be until three years later, during my PhD program, when I would learn from a psychology professor doing research in the field that postpartum PTSD even existed.

THE COST OF A FAILING SYSTEM

Many people who experience traumatic childbirth and postpartum PTSD feel isolated without appropriate care and affirmation from their medical team. After an undiagnosed seventeen-day fever and severe postpartum bleeding left her unable to walk without intense pain in her pelvis, groin, and back, Stephanie Bernard, thirty-six years old, from Atlanta, did not even get to see her OB-GYN at the typical six-week checkup.

"My husband lost his job shortly after I gave birth, which meant that we no longer had medical insurance," says Bernard, who is African American. Her doctor's office did not accept Medicaid, and it wasn't until a full year later that she learned she was suffering from diastasis recti. "Had I received the care I needed, my recovery process would have been much smoother," she says. "I had no idea about the dangers of postpartum hemorrhaging, fevers, infections, pulmonary embolisms, and heart-related issues that are common." She says she was heartbroken during those first two years when she couldn't even pick up her child and feels lucky to even be alive to share her story now.

Bernard was uninsured at the time of her postpartum appointment and did not have access to the medical care she needed. Her experience also highlights the medical bias and racism Black women experience during pregnancy, childbirth, and postpartum. "I was alarmed to learn the rate at which maternal mortality affects Black women due to not being listened to by medical professionals, staff, medical bias, and medical racism."[9] She calls for increased education for health-care professionals, especially non-Black health-care professionals, on institutional racism, racial biases, especially how to identify and address both within patient care.

The national cost of perinatal mood and anxiety disorders (PMADs), such as postpartum PTSD, from pregnancy through five years postpartum registers at $14.2 billion, or an average of $32,000, for those affected but not treated.[10] These costs break down to health consequences for mothers and children, maternal productivity loss, and increased costs for social services. For parents like me who could barely afford groceries, because we lacked paid parental leave, finding, navigating, and affording such treatment felt impossible.

Research into postpartum PTSD began around 2006 and awareness has expanded since then, but the lack of patient education persists. Doctors still tend to misdiagnose PTSD symptoms as depression or anxiety.[11]

Lyra Matin, thirty-seven years old, who is of Filipina descent and lives in Los Angeles, experienced a traumatic birth, which included a blood transfusion and episiotomy that developed an infection. When she tried to discuss her trauma with her OB-GYN, he misdiagnosed her. "He tried to normalize it as baby blues because of 'hormones fluctuating.' He referred me to a therapist for postpartum issues, but the therapist did not take my insurance," says Matin. She had government-funded health insurance.

The experience motivated Matin to become a psychotherapist specializing in healing trauma.[12] After seeing the obstacles so many people face—from misdiagnoses to insurance hurdles and steep costs—she believes the entire system needs to be overhauled. "Trauma-informed care needs to be institutionalized and become required education for all medical professionals, not just mental health ones," she says.

There are regional trauma-informed care programs trying to address this, like the California-based Beba: A Center for Family Healing, which offers families early intervention and care.[13] But national programs like these must have a larger presence during the perinatal and postnatal periods. Some families may be able to afford out-of-pocket therapy, night nurses, and postpartum doulas, but many are not in the economic position to do so. We need a system that doesn't shut out low-income patients or Black patients and patients of color. We need humans treating humans in every appointment, in every room. Those with fewer economic resources bear the brunt of our maternal health crisis; it's costing birthing people their physical health, their mental health, and their lives.

We also need improved education for our doctors and health-care professionals. Just this year, the American Psychiatric Association published the first comprehensive educational textbook for understanding, diagnosing, and supporting reproductive and maternal mental health for use in medical education.[14] At least that's a start.

THE JOURNEY TOWARD HEALING

Almost four years later, I was pregnant again. This time, as a PhD student, my OB-GYN visits were covered by my insurance. I also qualified for secondary coverage under my husband. During this pregnancy I became vocal in my prenatal doctor appointments. I was physically and mentally able to self-advocate, but the responsibility should not be on the birthing person. We are negotiating with a systemic problem.

Six weeks after I delivered my second child, I went to my postpartum appointment. When the Edinburgh Postnatal Depression Scale form was handed to me, I asked how diagnosis happens. The nurse told me that they only intervene if the patient is in crisis during the time of visit, but this designation is left to a clinician's own judgments. It's clear that there is no universal care directive to assist postpartum birthing parents in a tangible way.

"There has yet to be a measure created that does [appropriately test for PMADs], unfortunately," says Stephanie Freiburg, a licensed therapist certified in perinatal mental health. "Better assessment of postpartum PTSD starts with awareness and training within our health-care system. This would mean OB-GYNs, perinatologists, lactation consultants, and nurse practitioners would all need to take part in a training on perinatal mood and anxiety disorders."

WHERE TO GO FROM HERE

I'm optimistic we will see change in this country, but the change is slow: The Build Back Better Act aimed to improve pregnancy outcomes and lower postpartum complications and death by allocating $3 billion for maternal health.[15] After the plan being on hold due to Senate negotiations, the Senate reconciled and passed the Inflation Reduction Act of 2022. The bill intends to lower the cost of health care for American families but fails to adequately support the whole-body health of birthing parents as originally outlined in the Build Back Better Act. For example, the Senate reconciliation omitted the provisions of the Black Maternal Health Momnibus Act included in Build Back Better, which would address maternal mortality rates in our country. Second, Build Back Better also included funding to expand the perinatal workforce and would require states to offer continuous Medicaid coverage for a year after childbirth, closing a serious gap in care for lower-income Americans, which was not included in the Inflation Reduction Act.

Because the provisions to support maternal health of the original Build Back Better Act were not passed, it's the time to fight for the rights of birthing people. We need to voice our concerns in health-care offices. We need to call our congressperson, to speak up about better support in the postpartum period. We need to advocate for ourselves and the generations to come. If you're a patient experiencing mistreatment, find a new doctor who makes you feel heard—there are organizations that can help you advocate for your care.[16] If you are angry about birthing people being left behind at the federal level, take action. It's not just people who are pregnant that must do this work, but collectively, we must engage in actively pursuing better care for parents after birth.

Courtney Lund O'Neil is an educator at the University of California, San Diego. She completed her PhD in English at Oklahoma State University and earned her MFA in creative nonfiction from the University of California, Riverside. Her writing has appeared in the *New York Times*, the *Guardian*, the *Washington Post*, *Harper's Bazaar*, the *Normal School*, the *Chicago Tribune*, and elsewhere. She is currently completing a narrative nonfiction book, *Postmortem*, about what survives the John Wayne Gacy murders.

ANYTHING OF VALUE

Lorelei Lee

The Believer, September 1, 2020

"We believed that trading sex meant never asking for help."

I worried that the gravel outside the train station would scuff the shine on my too-small, thrifted platform heels. It was such a find—thrift store shoes not yet scuffed. The man had told me on the phone that his name was John. He would pick me up and we would drive to a hotel. I would stay with him overnight and the next day he would drive me back to the train station.

A month earlier, I'd had a job at a big chain coffee shop. The coffee shop was in a historic neighborhood where the street signs had been transformed by graphic designers into replicas of their former selves and the Victorian houses had washer-dryers and a sandwich cost an hour's wage. Most of us who worked at the shop lived a forty-five-minute train ride away. We had a three-minute grace period to punch in at the start of our shift. Any later and we'd get a write-up. Three write-ups meant probation. Four and you were fired.

Later, I would learn that all the men wanted to call themselves John. Did they think they were funny? Was it the only name they could think of? Later, I would be curious about these things, but in 2002, I was not. I was not curious about the men at all. My feet hurt. My rent was due. I had not asked this John what his car looked like or how I'd recognize him. I just stood on the curb in my slip-dress and hefted my heavy purse and waited for someone to call my made-up name.

"Lulu?" he said.

His car was gray. He was a thin white man with black hair and a suntan. I got in.

All of us who worked at the coffee shop had a lot of emergencies. Our electricity got shut off, our apartments caught fire, our friends got stabbed or OD'd, we had miscarriages or fevers we'd let go too long and we had to spend the night in the public hospital waiting room where you could heal yourself faster than you could get in to see a doctor. The coffee shop gave benefits if you worked over thirty-two hours, so no one was ever given more than thirty except Jimmy, who had cancer. The rest of us left the ER at five a.m. for our six a.m. shift, scheduled the community college course we were trying to take around the thirty hours we were allowed to work, hung up on our parents if we had parents, skipped class, showed up late to our other jobs, were late to everything except the coffee shop.

John drove us north on the highway. He said he was a musician, that he used to play backup keys for the Grateful Dead. He pointed in a general direction out the car window.

"Over there, we dropped acid. We played baseball against Jefferson Airplane until we started peaking and couldn't find the bases anymore."

He had promised me two hundred dollars. At the coffee shop that would have been nearly a week's pay. I had not yet done the math that I would be working the same number of hours for it. It was the end of the month. Two days was faster than five days.

The third time I missed the three-minute grace period, Jefferey, the day manager, followed me into the break room. I rushed to punch my time card, to drop my bags, to tie my apron on, to get my ass out onto the floor with him in my ear saying, "You're on probation," as if I didn't know. As if I hadn't spent two years building my whole life around those three minutes.

That morning, on my break, I went out and grabbed the free weekly papers from the sidewalk boxes. I sat at the count-out station and called the numbers listed in tiny ads with no copy except "women ages 18–28, make $$$ fast, no experience necessary."

"My dog died last year," John said on the drive. "He was a damn good dog. Why do they make dogs' lives so fucking short?" His voice was uneven, and it occurred to me that he might cry. I watched the trees pass. They seemed to go faster or slower depending on how I turned my head. We'd been driving for half an hour, and it was all trees for miles.

John swerved into a pullout and stopped the car.

Today, I have guides. I have pamphlets on how to screen clients. Always trust your gut. I have pamphlets on how to plan in case of your own arrest. Have a support person, memorize their number. I have pamphlets on what to expect from a lawyer, on how to talk to cops. Act calm. Say, "Am I free to leave?" I have guides on what to do when you get kicked off yet another online platform, where to apply for food stamps, how to deal with Child Protective Services. Act calm. I have guides on how to lobby your congressperson and how to talk to the media. Trust your gut. I have guides on avoiding burnout, on the necessity of building a network of sex worker friends. Have a safe call. Have community. Today, I help write these guides. I help disseminate them. There are so many ways we can have each other's backs.

I looked up and down the road. Sun filtered through the redwoods and eucalyptus. A car passed, then it was gone. John got out and ran to the trunk. He grabbed something and came around to the passenger door.

"Let's go! Let's go! Let's go!"

I could have stayed in the car, but then what.

"Quick," he said. "Let's go! Get going!"

I got out.

Years of minimum-wage work had taught me that getting my money meant doing what I was told. Doing what I was told by managers and customers, over and over again, hour after hour, day after day. The difference between me and rich people, it seemed, was that they could do what they wanted, they could—like Barbara Ehrenreich, whose book we'd passed around the coffee shop—wear our lives like clothes and then go on the radio and talk about it. My gut, if I had considered trusting it, would have said rent is due. I did not get full names. I did not have a safe call. I did not circle the car before getting in. I did not get the money up front.

It must have been fall because the leaves were brown and covered the ground. Wear shoes that you can run in. I shifted my long purse strap. Avoid shoulder bags that can be pulled or tightened around your throat. He led me into the trees.

"Let's go!"

We walked, crunching leaves, until I could no longer see the road. I did not have a network of sex worker friends. I had friends who

traded sex and who knew as little as I did. No one had told us: Negotiate from a distance. Don't wear big earrings that can get pulled out.
Wear mentholated chapstick in your nose to cover other smells. Instead they'd told us: Never get in cars with strangers. Sex means disease. Whores get killed. We believed we had to choose. We believed
that trading sex meant never asking for help.

Deep in the woods, John stopped. He began to unbutton his shirt.
His hands shook, and he looked back toward the road, checking if
we'd been followed. He kicked out of his shoes and took his pants off.
He handed me the camera he'd taken from his car trunk.

"Take my picture," he said.

He ran, weaving through the trees, barefoot and wildly off kilter,
his hands between his legs to protect the weakest part of his body. I
framed him in the lens and shot.

Lorelei Lee's fiction, nonfiction, and poetry have appeared or are forth-
coming in *Salon*, the *Rumpus*, *WIRED*, *Denver Quarterly*, the *Establishment*,
Buzzfeed, *The Feminist Porn Book*, *Coming Out Like a Porn Star*, *Hustling
Verse*, *n+1*, and elsewhere. They owe their life to other sex workers.

SECTION 2

Home

INTRODUCTION

The Organized Abandonment of Shelter

Keeanga-Yamahtta Taylor

The summer before seventh grade, my mother and I began a nomadic journey across the Metroplex, the geography-laden name for the city of Dallas and its surrounding suburbs. My mom had filed for bankruptcy in 1982 and could never catch up. We moved from our house in the lush Oak Cliff neighborhood, where the waxy green leaves of magnolia trees and sturdy pecan trees were fed by Five Mile Creek, to a condominium complex several miles away that sat on the edge of a freeway. The next year we moved again, this time into my uncle's three-bedroom ranch house in a completely different part of Dallas. Brown carpet and endless wood panel, but with a cold, white-tiled bathroom and a bedroom a quarter of the size of my previous one. We lied about our address so that I could stay at my junior high school. After eighth grade, we moved again. We were in a new neighborhood, blocks away from the movie theater on Jefferson Avenue where Lee Harvey Oswald huddled after he assassinated President John F. Kennedy. This time, we shoved our steadily dwindling belongings into the shell of a house that my mother imagined could be remade into a windfall.

By that point, my mother had taken up part-time work as a home appraiser, feeding a delusion that investment into real estate could transform debt into prosperity. She hired a contractor who was mostly skilled at draining her bank account. We were left with a hulking structure that had no hot water, no heat, and a kitchen infested with nutria, rodents that look like gigantic rats that made their home on the exposed pipes where the kitchen walls should have been. We ceded the kitchen to the nutria and plugged in a hot plate in another room that was used for heating up water for baths.

This during my first year of high school, when anxiety and anticipation were already cranked high. Texas winters were mild, but without heat or hot water, my morning routine—heating up small pots of water to dump into a bathtub—became interminable. After a year of living in a house that barely constituted shelter, my grandmother moved from Nashville, Tennessee, to live with us. Her income, combined with my mother's, was enough for us to rent a house in the suburbs of Dallas. We were on the move again.

There are a handful of necessities that define what it means to be human, binding our vastly disparate experiences into one. We need some combination of food, water, air, and shelter. Of course, there are other things that may constitute a better or worse life, but these four are a baseline for human survival. And yet, in the United States, whose leaders like to imagine this nation as the absolute pinnacle of human achievement, none of these are readily available to all who need them.

I share my own story to communicate the universality of housing instability, housing insecurity, and housing precarity in the United States. The stories, poems, and photographs in this section illustrate the fragility of housing security and the breadth of its reach. This can be measured in the more than three million people formally designated as homeless or living in shelters,[1] while millions more languish in what social scientists describe as "housing insecurity,"[2] which is measured by unpredictable housing costs and threats to habitability, quality, and continued access. This crisis of shelter in the United States has been a feature of our society for the duration of the twentieth century and now in the twenty-first. If crisis indicates a periodic rupture in the otherwise routine occurrence of daily events, then what we are actually experiencing, in the words of Ruth Wilson Gilmore, is the "organized abandonment" of the human and social obligation to shelter our species. This abandonment is abetted by gender and racial discrimination that has left Black women, in particular, facing eviction, homelessness, and the attendant social catastrophes that come when your housing is fleeting. Alex Miller's piece illustrates the "organized abandonment" of homelessness with the absurd contradiction of homeless veterans in the most powerful nation in the world.

The deep roots to our housing disaster lie in the market economy that has historically regarded housing as a commodity and not a right. This process has worked to drive the price of rent well beyond the rate of wages and salaries earned by ordinary workers. From 2021 to 2022, rents across the United States for both one-bedroom and two-bedroom apartments increased by 24 percent.[3] It has been long established that the paltry national minimum wage of $7.25 is not enough to cover the rent for a two-bedroom apartment in any state in this country. This has translated into an astonishing 51 percent of American households being "rent burdened" or spending more than 30 percent of their income on rent.[4] That's the experience Joseph Williams describes in his piece "Evictionland."

The enduring character of the organized abandonment of housing means that it's very easy for housing insecurity to look normal. But the pandemic brought this instability to the surface. Individuals and families on the brink of eviction or foreclosure were able to see each other as mutual victims of corporate, landlord greed. Their collective endeavor might one day cohere around a different kind of consciousness of resistance.

Many stories of housing insecurity center or describe the fear and personal insecurity that gestate when it's unclear where or what home is. This does not have to be the case. Housing should be treated as the human right it is, along with the other things like food and water which actually constitute the building blocks of human life.

Keeanga-Yamahtta Taylor is a professor in the Department of African American Studies at Northwestern University. She is the author *Race for Profit: How Banks and the Real Estate Industry Undermined Black Homeownership,* long-listed for the National Book Award and a finalist for the Pulitzer Prize in History, and *From #BlackLivesMatter to Black Liberation,* winner of the Lannan Cultural Freedom Award; and she is the editor of *How We Get Free: Black Feminism and the Combahee River Collective,* winner of the Lambda Literary Award for LGBQT nonfiction. A 2021 MacArthur Foundation Fellow, Taylor is a contributing writer at the *New Yorker* and a former contributing opinion writer for the *New York Times.*

HOMELESS IN A PANDEMIC

The Housing Poetry of Jennifer Fitzgerald

Poems and images by Jen Fitzgerald,
with an introduction by Alissa Quart

Literary Hub, July 28, 2020

STRUGGLING TO NAVIGATE A BROKEN SYSTEM

For the poet and photographer Jen Fitzgerald, "'a series of unfortunate events' began unfolding. And in New York City, we don't have cushion to handle one unfortunate event, let alone twelve.'" She is now one of nearly one million New Yorkers who may be unable to pay their rent and are thus at risk of eviction during the pandemic.

It started even before COVID-19 landed in March. But it worsened then, when the Airbnb Fitzgerald stayed at was swiftly no longer a housing option. She was unable to afford another month upfront, Fitzgerald says.

She grew desperate. A single mother, Fitzgerald was also unable to return to work for the foreseeable future due to the coronavirus, as she teaches poetry and writing in New York City's jails, including Rikers Island, places that have been epicenters for infection. Fitzgerald's other profession is writing poetry—she was previously the author of a 2016 poetry book, *The Art of Work*, about the members of New York City's Butcher's Union, UFCW Local 342, including her own family—but poems do not pay by the word. Eventually, Fitzgerald created an open call on social media to her friends asking for support.

But Fitzgerald was able to put this experience to some use in the fact-based poems and personal images that follow. "My difficulties did not start with the coronavirus but the virus is showing me that there is actually a level of struggle that is simply not possible to contend with," as Fitzgerald puts it.

Fitzgerald was born and raised on New York's Staten Island. Thanks to her social media outreach Fitzgerald was introduced via a friend to friends of hers who had left their lower Manhattan apartment vacant during the quarantine. "The open minds and open hearts of this couple astound me," she says. She and her daughter are currently living rent-free in the donated vacant apartment. They will have to leave soon, however.

For other cost of living expenses, Fitzgerald has, as she puts it, been battling "the Unemployment Ins. gods since April 6th." She waited for the money to arrive with "millions of other New Yorkers: calling, calling, waiting, calling." Fitzgerald's unemployment money came through toward the end of May.

In addition, protests against police violence as well as the effect of COVID-19 on communities of color have roiled American public spaces in recent weeks. These protests, and the experience of housing instability during a health crisis, have edged into the poems and images that follow. They stand as testaments to the wearying nature of eviction and homelessness. They are also records of what it is like to be alive in an extreme time and place, accompanied by Fitzgerald's photos. Fitzgerald says they are examples of her "feeling out this new reality."

In German, the word "uncanny," *umheimlich*, a favorite word of Freud's, also means "unhomey." These poems show how synonymous the uncanny—or the disturbing—and the loss of our homes, really are. For Fitzgerald and so many others in American cities, no longer having or being pushed out of their homes during a national crisis is strange indeed.

"The city is opening back up and my continued presence will quickly morph from 'crisis help' to 'free-loading,'" says Fitzgerald. "I am keenly aware of that and am too grateful for this help to ever cross that threshold."

"I do not know where I am going, but I know I am going to start heading there in a couple of weeks," says Fitzgerald of her and her daughter's future.

American Landscape: Inheritance

This is not a poem
about losing an apartment
nor is it a poem about losing
three apartments in three months,
which I could write for you
with deftness; this is not a song
for my job long gone, I'm afraid
this is an answer.
I'll not be so bold as to insert myself
into 200 years of the dream—
of who still dreams it
and who still comes,
of who was born in it
and what's been done
but geography is fate
and I've been here
far too long for gratitude
in the immigrant city,
of the immigrant nation—
after five generations,
the best I could do
was a single room
and some money for food
If I am an answer
then is failure my question?
My images, like my lineage: too grand—
but I am the song my ancestors sang
on their ocean voyage West;
raised on the Statue of Liberty
and the Irish starving in the streets;
raised the impossibility of survival.
I can't make allegory of an entire life;
at some point I will have to start living.
But I remain at the impossible nexus:

five generations in and ousted
cannot be dressed up in eloquent language, poet.
Disinherited, at last!
from the monolith
I am afraid, but in that fear,
liberation, I tell myself—
because even my homelessness
must have glory written in the margins.

North Bronx: Morning light from the couch of my dear friend's apartment. From
Thanksgiving through New Years, I stayed there through the darkest time in my
life, whenever my daughter visited her father.

When My Daughter Writes the Poem of This Day

I will be distant—in black and mourning; I will be leaning
into the open window as I drive us up and over; hauling
only what we could carry, through three boroughs; I tell
myself she will remember nothing I want her to forget
as though I could shield her from failures I call attempts;
these formative failures I swore to never—forgive me;
not all scenes can be painted in favorable light; she sees
the view from back seat, clenched jaw, my rising tide;
forgive me; for some of us, grief is unshakable anger—
it takes up residence within us; for we well-practiced few,
anger throws us into the dust of the new; forgive me;
I have dragged my child into my childhood where I was
more wildflower than girl, cast to soil by wind; rootless
yet never free; incapable; me, again—me again, here now—
somehow not just me; forgive me; I burned through all
the saints and call on any deity that will have me, let her
painlessly unsee all but my hair catching wind as a bright
but tenable flame, let her remember me only as the woman
who carried water up the hill for everyone to finally drink.

First night in the Lower Manhattan miracle apartment, wearing the shirt purchased in Times Square on the last evening that stores were allowed to be open.

The Heart Divided Has Many Rooms

1.
Of the normally four walls that comprise a room,
Of the plaster, lathe, gypsum, gas lines veining the lamp-lit walls,
Of the layers
the layers of paint, paper, poster,
we decorate vacancy

Of the pine floors,
the stripped, peeled, stained, patched—
Of the necessary steps we take
to not be too many steps away—

but that's how they get us—
the absurdity of structure

and our inherent tenancy;
Of walk up, of split level, of detached, semi-attached two family
Of costs that defy reason—

that's how they gut us.
And we let them,

all to prove,
I will do whatever it takes
to stay with you

2.
what language
have we made
for each other?

I am afraid I don't know what to say
I am afraid I shouldn't say
and afraid not to say
the heart divided has many rooms

3.
my claim to this city
has nothing to do with birth
but that I have loved
and laid my head
in every borough.

I am native;
you cannot evict me
from the people
who sustain this heart divided

4.
words obfuscate meaning, so I will do my best:
This vision is no city without you

no country
no heart;

a vacant lot,
absent your voice

I may not know what we look like
after all this burning but
I will sit with you in the rooms of this heart;
we'll eat from a charred table,
view our scorched street
through singed curtains, eat of whatever is left—
hear me: anything, anywhere, but only with you

Staten Island: I was proud to preserve the original hardware, doors, and transoms from the Boarding House and Brothel that inhabited this apartment in the past. I was proud to put my labor into this lineage.

Jen Fitzgerald is a poet, essayist, photographer, and a native New Yorker who received her MFA in poetry at Lesley University and her BA in writing at the College of Staten Island (CUNY). Her essays, poetry, and photography have been featured widely, over the past decade, in venues such as *PBS NewsHour*, Tin House, *Boston Review*, and *Colorado Review*, among other publications.

MEET TOMEKA LANGFORD

Anne Elizabeth Moore

The Guardian and *Bridge Detroit*, October 18, 2022

Miraculously, Tomeka Langford is willing to talk to me.

The forty-seven-year-old Black woman is a long-standing Detroiter. A career pharm tech with four kids and six grandkids, her family has lived in the city ever since her grandparents came up from the South.

I am white, single, and childless. In 2016, I was given a house by Write a House, a short-lived Detroit-based organization founded in 2011 to award homes to low-income scribes. The gift was meant to support writers with some of the city's plentiful housing stock—and thus change the stories that get told about Detroit.

It was, on paper, a great idea. But the house I was given already belonged to someone: Tomeka Langford.

I didn't know it at the time. Neither did Tomeka.

I settled into the adorable house, which sits in a cheerful neighborhood dubbed BanglaTown after the area's majority-Bangladeshi community. But the organization started to crumble once I moved in, and soon the roof of the house did, too—needing immediate replacement.

After the roof was replaced, I realized I was now living in a surprisingly expensive free house, trying to fulfill the mission of an organization that no longer existed. It was frustrating and unsustainable.

When I was offered a job in another state, I took it, and put the house on the market. This is when I realized I'd never been listed on the house's title. Legally, the house did not belong to me.

Shortly after that is when Tomeka first came across my name. It was on the documents she received when I sued her for ownership of a house I'd been told was mine, a house that had, confusingly, already been taken from her years beforehand.

This isn't a story about gentrification—at least, not how we usually think about it. It's a story of a Black woman losing her home to municipal greed, and a white woman benefiting from her loss. It's a story about the racial wealth gap, and how the median white American household accrues almost eight times the wealth of most Black American households.

But it's also a story about what we do next: how we calculate damage, and what we might do to repair it.

—**Anne Elizabeth Moore**

Tomeka bought the house in 2010 for only $700, knowing there would be back taxes to pay off. She had always been a renter, and wanted to trade in monthly rent for home equity. People were selling houses in Detroit for dirt cheap then—$5,000, $2,000, $500, $1—but they needed a ton of work and came with hefty property tax bills.

Tomeka's husband introduced her to a guy who was offloading a house in BanglaTown. It was a fixer-upper, but Tomeka's husband is a contractor. Steady employment meant she could cover the cost of the house, purchase supplies for repairs, bring in family to do the labor, and start paying down back taxes.

She says the seller, William C. Murray II, was straightforward about both repairs and back taxes. They would amount to at least $10,000.

Documents show that Murray had purchased the house in 2009 for $1,000 from Deutsche Bank National Trust, the German multinational bank and financial services company that had acquired the house when the previous owner, a man with a Bangladeshi name, defaulted on his bank mortgage and abandoned it at the peak of the financial collapse.

This unusual chain of ownership explains how a house in the tightly knit and long-standing immigrant community ever fell out of Bangladeshi ownership—and eventually into my lap.

In 2015, five years after Tomeka bought it, the house was sold for $5,000 to Write a House. A year later, it was given to me under the condition that I upkeep the property, pay taxes, be a good neighbor, and write. The city even gave me a Spirit of Detroit Award for moving into it.

After she bought it in 2010, however, the house technically remained in Tomeka's name. But that didn't stop Wayne County from selling it out from under her without telling her why.

When I moved into it, I was told the house had been abandoned, and that it sat unoccupied for eight years. In 2016, it made sense: a lot of people had abandoned houses during the financial crisis.

Write a House had built a fast reputation on the claim that it wasn't capitalizing on the city's foreclosure crisis. I was wary—property tax foreclosures were still happening at alarming rates—but the organization had done due diligence, and I was in love with my neighborhood.

After a two-year period, the house was supposed to go in my name. The deed did—the document that gives me the right to own the property. But this is different from a title, as mortgage companies will describe it, because a deed is a document while a title is a legal framework, a set of conditions that confer uncontestable ownership of a property. The title didn't change hands.

I discovered this when I put the house on the market, two and a half years after I had moved into it. That was when my title agency informed me that the title to the house was still in Tomeka Langford's name.

I found fifty-two Tomeka Langfords on Facebook, and soon gave up any attempt to make direct contact. After all, I was told the legal process from here was straightforward—it even has a name. My title agency suggested a law firm, Quiet Title, that specializes in quieting titles.[1] For a set price ($1,200 back in 2018) and in lightning speed (90 to 180 days), clients are guaranteed a squeaky-clean title and uncontestable ownership of a property.

Detroit property ownership is a strange experience. The land was only ceded by Indigenous inhabitants in 1807, over a century after the city had already been founded. Selling a house as a white person in a brown community is even more distressing, as pricing, the language used in the listing, and how word of sale spreads are coded to maximize sellers' profits, not maintain community integrity.

Yet the quiet title process is inherently violent. Lawyers for reputed homeowners take swift legal action against all contenders to a property's title. Few opportunities exist for distressed homeowners to have legitimate claims heard, and in places where disputes may be common—like Detroit—the process itself may fuel displacement.

I found the quiet title process perplexing and sad, but that was before I met Tomeka. That was before I heard, firsthand, how a process made relatively easy for me was in fact traumatic for her.

We tend to think of foreclosure as a logical consequence of too many skipped bank mortgage payments—indeed, the vast majority are bank-driven.

In the US, one in every 854 properties faces foreclosure, numbers that are rising again after a pandemic downturn.[2] But most foreclosures in Wayne County, where Detroit is, are over unpaid property taxes. Few other municipalities treat their bases so aggressively.

There are *a lot* of property tax foreclosures. Between 2002 and 2016, 143,958 Detroit houses were foreclosed and listed in the county's tax foreclosure auction, the vast majority after the economic crisis of 2008.[3] The number totals an astonishing 37 percent of the city's 384,840 properties.

That's over a third of the city sold at auction, often for less than $5,000.

The press ate it up, churning out story after story about white artists moving to the city, installing new windows and paying off back taxes—but such articles overlooked who, exactly, bought those foreclosed homes.

A staggering 90 percent of all properties purchased at auction between 2005 and 2015 were by "investors buying in bulk," a 2019 report from the University of Michigan shows.[4] These were often abandoned or turned into rental properties. The report shows that 60 percent of the properties purchased by bulk buyers underwent evictions two or more times.

And evictions target Black women. According to Princeton's Eviction Lab, nearly twice as many Black renters as white were evicted in 2020.[5] The same study showed that 7.7 percent more white women than white men were evicted that year, whereas a full 36.3 percent more Black women than Black men were evicted.

When Tomeka bought her first house, she hoped she had escaped the precarity of the rental market. It was a starter home, barely big enough for her family of six, the youngest members of which was just starting school. "It was never a forever home, but maybe we could have given it to the kids," she says.

This is no small thing. The primary means by which Americans pass along generational wealth is through home ownership. A 2020 report from the Brookings Institute finds that 30 percent of white households received an inheritance in the year before the pandemic, averaging just under $200,000.[6] In comparison, just 10 percent of Black households did, for an average of $100,000.

The pandemic-fueled housing crisis has only deepened the racial wealth gap.[7] Like foreclosure rates, eviction rates are returning to prepandemic numbers as the price of renting has skyrocketed.[8]

Housing insecurity doesn't merely strip the emotional safety of a place to live from neighbors; it forces entire families to give up their investment in future generations.

One lost house can disable a whole bloodline.

———————

Throughout 2010 and 2011, Tomeka and her family stayed in their rental and made visits to the new house for repairs.

"We had to do all new wiring," she tells me. "We had to put in an electrical box. Lighting. Hot water tank. Furnace. We had to put a few windows in, and then we had to put in some doors and some storm doors. We sanded the floors."

The rehab was expensive. "I would probably say $6,000 or $7,000," Tomeka estimates, adding that it would have been more expensive if they'd had to pay for labor. "We were gonna do that attic, finish it off." She's getting excited, and I get a glimpse of her from over a decade back, sharing with me a dream made reality through hard work and substantial investment.

Then she straightens, fades, and withdraws into herself a bit. "But we never made it up there," she says sadly.

At the end of 2011 or the early days of 2012, the whole family got the flu and it disrupted their schedule, she says. They couldn't visit the house for weeks.

"When we did get back there, somebody had broken in and stolen all our furniture. Literally cleaned the place out. I was like, 'What the hell! They done clinked us out!'"

"They stole the storm door!" She's nearly fuming with rage. "We had furniture there. We had, like, a whole house!"

The clothes, toys, and furniture there were all used, but Tomeka estimates they'd spent about $2,000 furnishing the house. "We had put all this money in it," she says, catching herself getting worked up again. "It made me angry," she admits. "It was a lot of hard work, a lot of money. The fact that somebody would do that—I found that very, very upsetting."

After that, they didn't spend much time at the house for a few months.

Then in spring 2012, Tomeka was at a birthday party, poking around the county's property tax auction website with a friend. "I was helping somebody else look for houses," she says. She was seen as an expert among her peers in making the dream of home ownership come true.

Then she saw a listing—for her own house.

The white two-and-a-half bedroom BanglaTown bungalow was listed on the Wayne County tax foreclosure auction website.

She had only owned the house for two years and knew—everyone in Detroit did then—that it was supposed to take three years before the county can foreclose on a property. She says she was on a payment plan, and making regular payments on her back taxes. She admits she'd been having trouble receiving all her mail at the new house, but wouldn't the Treasurer's Office have alerted her to the pending foreclosure when she dropped off another property tax payment?

———————————————

On paper, the Wayne County tax foreclosures auction works like this: property taxes are issued twice a year by the city. If a property owner doesn't pay taxes after that first year, the debt is transferred to the county.

Two and a half years later, after multiple reminders, late fees, and the addition of an 18 percent annual interest rate, if a homeowner fails to pay those taxes to the county, the house is foreclosed. Then the county puts the property up for auction.

According to documents from Wayne County, my own court case, and separate FOIA requests, Tomeka made only one payment of $689 on an outstanding tax bill of over $5,000.

Her house went into foreclosure.

County records indicate that Tomeka was notified of foreclosure proceedings via an in-person visit and a note left on the door. There's a document testifying to the former signed by a process server with Rancilio & Associates, and a photograph of the latter. But these documents also show that two postal mailings to Tomeka are still marked "Delivery Information Pending."

Tomeka says she never received foreclosure warnings or notices. Since she knew she owed back taxes at purchase, she says she dutifully entered a payment plan with the treasurer's office. She admits she may not have always made her payments on time, but she says her payments were regular.

Records show she still owed around $4,449 in taxes when the house was foreclosed, but she remembers paying down her debt to $1,500 or $2,000. "I would make multiple payments, like when I'd get my tax [refund], I'd go drop off a lump sum," Tomeka says. "Then in between I only had to pay off a hundred dollars, or a hundred and something dollars per month."

Queries to Wayne County about missing payments and lack of receipt of notification have gone unanswered, but the city explained via email that the foreclosure was over unpaid property taxes from 2009.

Sent by Stephanie Davis, communications manager in the office of the chief financial officer, the email reads: "When the 2009 taxes went unpaid for a third year, the 'Judgment of Foreclosure' was issued by the Wayne County Treasurer for this property. This happens often when someone purchases a home without checking first to see if the prior owner had unpaid taxes, which the new owner becomes responsible for."

The city's email continues: "It would not have mattered if she had paid the 2011 property taxes to Detroit, she owed Wayne County for 2009 and 2010."

But seemingly missing payments and lack of notification are not unheard of among those who've lost homes to Wayne County. Nearly twenty families facing foreclosure had sued the county in federal court by 2016, alleging the foreclosures were illegal because owners "didn't receive notices and believed they had more time to pay taxes and save their properties," according to the *Detroit News.*

Two companies are mentioned in the lawsuit—Wolverine Services of Detroit and Rancilio & Associates, the very same process server contracted to deliver Tomeka's notifications. Each company was paid more than $9 million over four years to deliver foreclosure notices for the county.

The families behind the lawsuits share familiar stories: payments on back taxes owed, false or no information from county officials regarding foreclosure status, and foreclosure notices that never showed up, whether submitted by mail or taped to front doors with flimsy painter's tape and blown away in the wind.

Unlike those families, Tomeka didn't sue Wayne County. She didn't have enough information.

———————————

How much Tomeka paid in property taxes may be less important than how much she was being charged.

Documents list her 2010 tax bill as over $1,800, and the back-tax bill from 2009 as over $2,500. This is more than double what she paid for the house in property taxes, every year.

When Tomeka and I speak, I show her a packet from a nonprofit that pulls information from the Detroit Assessor's Office. "The year you bought the house for $700," I point out, "it carried an assessed value of $17,720."

That's high, but Tomeka is not impressed.

"The year before, when William C. Murray II bought it for a thousand dollars, it was assessed at $20,136," I read.

Tomeka remains unfazed.

"Inflated property tax assessments are a violation of the Michigan State Constitution," I say. No property can be assessed at more than 50 percent of its market value, I explain.

The year she bought it, Tomeka's house was assessed at 2,500 percent of what she paid for it.

At the time, over-assessments were common. Detroit overtaxed

between 55 percent and 85 percent of properties above that 50 percent threshold from 2009 to 2015, researchers found. Between 2011
and 2015, close to 100,000 families lost their homes.

A good quarter of the foreclosures that resulted from unconstitutional property tax assessments, a 2018 report from the University of
Chicago says, were of homes priced at $9,000 or less.

That she was among thousands of Detroiters being charged illegally high property taxes for low-value houses finally raises Tomeka's
eyebrows.

At an assessment rate of 50 percent of the purchase price of her
house—or half of $700—property taxes for 2010 would have been
less than thirty dollars. A constitutional assessment would have meant
slightly higher taxes for the year prior, but Tomeka's $689 on-record
back-tax payment would easily have covered the total.

There's no doubt that property taxes generated income for the
city that was much needed at the time—Detroit would declare bankruptcy the year after Tomeka's house was foreclosed.

In fact, in a June 2017 article, *Bridge Michigan* found that Wayne
County made $421 million from interest rates and fees from residents
repaying back taxes since the beginning of the financial meltdown. In
2013, the year Detroit declared bankruptcy, Wayne County's surplus
from fees and interest on back taxes alone was $64 million.

But while the heavy reliance on property taxes for income might
explain why the county was so quick to foreclose, the sky-high assessments are more complicated.

"We believe this home was not over-assessed," Davis, a City of Detroit spokesperson, writes in response to my follow-up queries. Based
on a mortgage appraisal conducted in 2007, the city holds that the
2010 $17,720 assessment—representing a cash value of $35,440—
was fair.

"Before Mayor Duggan took office in 2014, there was widespread
over-assessment of properties, however in this particular case, because of the mortgage, the assessment was fair and in line with market
condition," Davis writes via email.

Marie Sheehan, the director of the Coalition for Property Tax
Justice and a certified assessor in the City of Detroit, sees things

differently. Her job is to help homeowners repeal their assessments; over and over, she's seen the city downplay the problem of over-assessments.

"Of course that makes no sense," she tells me on a video call. "In 2008 values plummet and what [the property] was worth in 2007 is undoubtedly not what it was worth in 2010."

Founded in 2017, Sheehan's group aims to stop illegally high property tax assessments, compensate Detroit residents who've lost their homes over unconstitutional property tax assessments, and suspend foreclosures on owner-occupied homes until their assessments are deemed legally viable.

"From our perspective," Sheehan tells me, "for the tax foreclosure crisis and over-assessments to be happening in predominantly African American municipalities in Wayne County, but not in predominantly white municipalities in Wayne County . . . this is a violation of equal protection." She says that houses of lower value are assessed at much higher rates on average than houses of higher value, which points to a systemic problem.

Sheehan sends me video of a city council meeting in which Alvin Horhn, city assessor, refutes the findings of the Coalition for Property Tax Justice. "There is no systemic problem of assessments in Detroit," Horhn says on video.

Even years later, Tomeka is still in shock over the quick loss of her house.

When I ask what it was like to find it on the auction website, her eyes widen. "I was like, 'Wow. This is really for sale! They done clinked it out!'"

We both stay silent for a moment, marking the unfathomability of the experience. Slowly, something clouds Tomeka's sunny disposition. Not anger, but whatever anger becomes after a decade without outlet.

The anger she exhibited earlier in our conversation when detailing the gutting of her home by unknown thieves is gone. Yet the taking of the home *itself*, by a government agency that she says she steadily paid income, sales, *and* property taxes to, sparks little reaction.

A couple of thieves will anger her. But officials elected to provide her protection that instead do her harm? What can she do with the heartbreak and the fury, but let it go?

"You can't harbor stuff," she says when I ask if she's angry they took her house. "You can't believe it, but when you're the little person, what can you really do? You don't have anything to fight with."

She says she spent most of 2012 trying to find out why a municipal entity was auctioning off her house. She called the Wayne County Treasurer's Office, the deed people, and the city, "but nobody could never give me any information." She told anyone who would listen that she couldn't be that behind on her taxes, that she'd only owned the house for two years, less than the three-year deadline imposed by the county. No one had any explanation.

Eventually she got tired of asking and gave up. When the house went to auction, it failed to sell. Twice. It was eventually offered to the city's Land Bank, who sold it to Write a House the following year.

I moved in a year later.

When I brought my lawsuit forward in 2019 to claim the house's title, Tomeka fought it with everything she had.

"We went to housing court twice, because the first time, I told the judge I wanted to look over the documents. He was like, 'Do you want to sign?' and I was like, 'No, I wanna take time.' I made another court date. That's when I tried to do some more research," she says.

"I even asked the lawyer, 'If you want me to sign off, I should be getting some type of monetary settlement or something,'" Tomeka continues. "And the lawyers—they never said nothin'. They said, 'Get your own lawyer.'"

Annoyance has finally crept into her voice.

"So then I was like, 'Look. If somebody wants the house that bad . . .' I just can't keep going back and forth, around and around."

That was when, she says, she signed the papers they gave her. Papers that conferred the title of a house that had been awarded to me.

My lawyers had never informed me of any of this, and I'm ashamed to have put her through it. I'd been given the impression, throughout my lawsuit, that Tomeka was not locatable. Instead, she had contested my claims of property ownership right up until she finally agreed to sign.

I pull out the collection of legal documents I've amassed over the years that had suggested she could not be tracked down. Maybe I missed something?

I didn't. The documents state that Tomeka Langford's "whereabouts are unknown."

"I was told no one could find you," I tell her, feebly.

"Oh, they found me just fine," she says, referring to my lawyers, in 2019. Then she scoffs, annoyed that I would put any credence in a system that attempted to erase her.

It would be easy, I imagine, for Tomeka to feel unseen in this process, simply for trying to be a homeowner. But political action is already being taken to address some of what Tomeka's gone through.

Early this year, the Detroit city council president, Mary Sheffield, and the Coalition for Property Tax Justice outlined a new plan for compensating over-assessed homeowners.

The proposal states in clear language that the city and county stole family homes, reduced or destroyed intergenerational wealth, broke community bonds, and dehumanized and/or infantilized residents, resulting in a theft of dignity. "Dignity takings require more than reparations," the plan reads. "They require dignity restoration, which puts dispossessed individuals and communities in the driver's seat, allowing them to determine how they are made whole."

The preliminary plan suggests that those who lost homes to foreclosure between 2009 and 2020 be offered: employment and small business support; a one-dollar side lot; and either a Land Bank–rehabbed property, a Land Bank property and home repair grant, or a rental voucher.

It's a small, local effort at restitutive housing, but such programs have been gaining ground across the country, even if they help only a fraction of those who qualify. In Santa Monica, California, residents, children, or grandchildren displaced by a freeway construction project in the '50s and '60s are given priority in the city's affordable housing rental program, and in Evanston, Illinois, qualifying Black residents are offered funds for home purchase or repair in deliberate attempts to redress generations of housing discrimination.

It's a far cry from federal reparations, but city-based programs are a step in that direction.

It's a new day, and the house we both owned has been returned to Bangladeshi ownership.

Sitting with Tomeka on the front porch steps of our former neighbors' home and chatting about an upcoming birthday party on the block feels profound. Maybe even healing.

But I have been dreading this meeting. Writers can be complicit in structures that benefit them while silencing the voices of their subjects. I got a house out of the deal, and then a Spirit of Detroit Award for moving into a home taken from a Black woman and second-generation Detroiter.

How to account for that, face to face?

"What appears to have happened," I summarize, "was that the county had decided it wanted your house by the time you bought it, and then took it."

"Pretty much," Tomeka agrees.

"And even though that was years before I became involved, I did end up benefiting from that. And I am so sorry." I'm trying not to cry. I don't want Tomeka to feel like she has to make me feel better about how I came to be living in her house.

She does anyway. "Well, it's not your fault, Anne. You had no idea."

I gesture toward the house and ask what might undo some of the damage it brought her way. "Have you thought at all about what it would take to make you feel whole?"

Tomeka thinks for a moment. "You have put a lot of answers to some of my questions, as far as finding out what happened. That makes me feel better about the whole situation," she says.

"I used to think, 'What did I do? Did I do something wrong or did I miss something?' But I was making my payments. I was just going about my daily life. Then one day, boom. You see [your own house] for sale."

"Answers are good," I say. "But maybe they're not enough? You're owed emotional restitution," I suggest. "You're owed a house."

"I do think it would be nice for them to give me another house, because of the one they took," Tomeka says slowly. "That would make me whole. Replace what you took. They got plenty houses. They can spare one or two."

The Coalition for Property Tax Justice held an online forum earlier this year with over six hundred attendees to ask what form of compensation former homeowners most wanted. Cash compensation and property tax credits against future taxes emerged as the most popular, although the city has already denounced these as an unconstitutional lending of the city's credit. Alongside Council President Sheffield, the group has since asked the Michigan attorney general, Dana Nessel, to weigh in. Her opinion will inform the group's final proposal for a citywide compensation resolution.

But even if Tomeka ever receives compensation, her sense of loss might persist.

"It's almost like a death," Tomeka says of a house taken from her and given to me. "You don't never forget it, but you learn to move on."

Anne Elizabeth Moore is the author of *Unmarketable* (2007); *Gentrifier: A Memoir* (2021), an NPR best book; the Eisner Award–winning *Sweet Little Cunt* (2018); and other titles. She is a Fulbright Senior Scholar and has received support from the National Endowment for the Arts, the New York State Council on the Arts, the Ragdale Foundation, and the Yaddo Corporation. A new edition of *Body Horror: Capitalism, Fear, Misogyny, Jokes* is out from Feminist Press now.

UNADDRESSED

Bobbi Dempsey

Curbed, May 17, 2019

Officially, entire chunks of my childhood don't exist.

A few years ago, I applied for a freelance grant writer position at our school district in northeast Pennsylvania. The job mandates all potential employees or contractors undergo a state background check, which required me to list every address I've had since the 1970s and every person I've lived with during that time. My sister laughed and asked how many sheets of paper they allow you to use. We both knew, also, that there was very little official record of any of the places that make up my past.

I grew up poor, living in an estimated seventy places before I graduated high school. For many of these pit stops, there's no proof I was ever there. For me, and others like me, impoverished and lacking stability, entire chunks of my childhood don't officially exist. My family lived in a sort of "constant temporary" state. We moved almost nonstop. Often, this was because we couldn't afford rent. But sometimes it was also for our safety: for a long portion of my childhood, when my mother was trying to leave my father or after my parents' divorce when I was eight, my mother and siblings and I were trying to stay under the radar so we couldn't be found by my often violent father, who had routinely violated orders of protection.

Most of my immediate family was born in New York City or the coal region of Pennsylvania, and we moved around throughout the Northeast during my childhood in the '70s and '80s. My father had begun dealing drugs after a stint in the military; my mother worked low-paying jobs as a nurse's aide or retail cashier, or, better yet, found gigs that paid in cash. Our household income always remained low enough to preserve eligibility for welfare benefits—I was on public assistance from the day I was born until the day I graduated high school.

Our record proved confusing because we didn't use all of the markers of ordinary contemporary American life. For instance, we lacked a phone. Utilities were in the name of the family member who had yet to burn the power company. My parents never owned a car or held driver's licenses, so no DMV records exist. We didn't usually have a primary care doctor, so medical records would not help. Some of the ramshackle houses and buildings where we lived have long since been demolished, so the physical structure has disappeared, along with any proof that we were ever there.

In some cases, this lack of documented residences was deliberate. During the frequent cycles of crisis, it wasn't unusual for us to need to shelter in a place where we technically weren't supposed to be.

A friend or relative already living in that place may have been getting government benefits that would be jeopardized if unauthorized people joined the household. Or the landlord didn't allow children—at least not as many children as our family contained, enough to exceed the usual number of bedrooms, even with several of us sharing rooms. Sometimes, we split up because the homes we were staying in didn't have enough room for all of us.

On more than a few occasions, landlords were in on the deception. One "apartment" we lived in didn't have a kitchen, because the space was actually part of another unit that had been illegally subdivided. In our section of this off-the-books subdivision, part of one room had been turned into a makeshift kitchen with a portable plastic sink. There was a refrigerator in the cellar, but we avoided using it because you'd get a painful shock whenever you touched the handle.

In those cases, we or the landlord created a fictional address—or didn't use any at all—because listing the building's legal address, or an adjusted version of it, on official records might prompt local officials to investigate why two or more families were simultaneously using an address where only one legal dwelling existed.

When I applied for that grant at the Pennsylvania school district, I tried just listing information dating back to when I got married, but it was rejected. I ultimately gave up, because there's no way I could list *every* place I lived as a child. Even for those of us who were there, it can be a challenge to piece together the chronological and geographical sequence. The lack of official roots left me feeling unmoored.

That feeling has gradually abated over the years, but it's never fully left. I've lived in my current home more than twenty years. I was determined to break the family cycle, and committed to ensuring my children lived in only one home their entire childhood—a goal I successfully accomplished. Yet my husband recently discovered several boxes stashed throughout the house that I had left unpacked when we moved in. And occasionally I'll still jolt out of sleep in a panic, overcome by the feeling that I need to grab whatever I can as we rush to flee.

While there may be little or no proof of some of our former residences and our time inhabiting them, my siblings and I can recall each one. There was the apartment above a bar, where we had no refrigerator; in winter, we would leave milk on the ledge outside a window, hoping the temperature outside would keep it between freezing and spoiling. There were numerous places—surely not up to fire code—where several rooms had no windows.

The places that stand out most are often the ones where there would be few, if any, official records or vestiges of our presence.

Instead, we rely upon memories of what we experienced there—or in some cases endured or survived—as our proof, testament that we existed in that spot.

Bobbi Dempsey is a reporting fellow at EHRP and an editorial fellow at Community Change. Her work has also appeared in the *Washington Post*, *Harper's*, the *New York Times*, AARP, and other publications.

EVICTIONLAND

Joseph Williams

Curbed, January 24, 2018

My trip from the middle class into the ranks of the homeless began with a ticket of sorts. I came home one afternoon in 2013 from another fruitless job search to find a summons taped to the front door of my $2,000-a-month apartment in suburban Washington, DC.

Show up in housing court on the assigned date with the back rent, it read. Or be prepared to find another place to live.

I didn't think about it then—I was too busy trying not to freak out—but I was about to enter the world of eviction, a portal to poverty that is a largely unseen but growing part of the nation's housing landscape. What used to be primarily a scourge among the working poor is becoming a fact of life for the shrinking middle class.

I can't say I was surprised by the notice on my door that day. I'd been unemployable as a political journalist for almost a year, due to a series of events that began the summer before. The first domino fell in June 2012, when I suggested Mitt Romney, then the front-runner for the Republican presidential nomination, had problems relating to minority voters.

During a live panel discussion on MSNBC, I said Romney was "more comfortable" around "white folks" like himself—rich and conservative and unlikely to have two Black friends to rub together. Angry Romney supporters combed my Twitter feed and found a tasteless joke about Romney I'd thoughtlessly repeated, along with criticism of the racial climate at *Politico*, my employer at the time. (I was one of only a handful of African Americans working there.)

Outraged, activists in the conservative media called me biased and a racist; the Romney campaign rang up my bosses directly, demanding my head. I was immediately suspended, then fired a week later.

Just days after that, a Washington gossip columnist, checking out a tip, obtained a court file detailing how I hit my ex-wife in February during an argument. In court, I pled guilty to second-degree assault and received six months probation, paid several hundred dollars in fines, and was ordered to complete an anger-management program.

The salacious news—the Black guy who suggested Romney was a racist also beat his ex-wife—ricocheted around the internet, and my job prospects evaporated. I suddenly became unhireable, even for bottom-rung media jobs. The modest severance package I got from *Politico* drained away in a few months, along with my ability to pay my bills and child support.

Before I knew it, the rent was past due three months, going on four. Not long after that, the arrearage climbed to five figures, a serious problem I knew I couldn't ignore, yet felt powerless to fix.

Whenever I entered or left my apartment building, I held my breath and scuttled on tiptoe past the leasing office near the front entrance. It was as if I believed denial made me invisible, or that the increasingly urgent messages that Jen, the property manager, left on my voice mail, and the invoices she slipped under my door, would magically vanish if I ignored them.

The information on that yellow sheet, however, hit like a sledgehammer, smashing my imaginary antieviction forcefield. The county sheriffs would come soon to throw me out; I was pretty sure Jen and the building's owners would insist. I was renting on borrowed time, without the means to pay back what I owed.

It's a sharp reversal from the early decades of last century, when evictions were considered so rare—and the right to housing so sacrosanct—that entire communities would come out to stand with tenants in trouble, and an antieviction movement sprang up during the Great Depression. Now, property managers and large real estate companies have professionalized the forced removal of residents. Evictions have their own divisions within law enforcement agencies and a specialized arm of the court system.

Experts say gentrification is partly to blame: Real estate developers from red-hot San Francisco to up-and-coming Buffalo are cashing in on a booming urban rental and condominium market. Builders are ditching affordable housing for upscale apartments and condos with all the trimmings—granite counters, slate floors, stainless steel appliances, in-building rec rooms, coffee bars, and tenant-only gyms—that only the affluent can realistically afford, driving up housing costs for everyone in the process.

But a May 2022 study published in the *Proceedings of the National Academy of Sciences*—and coauthored by Matthew Desmond, a groundbreaking journalist who won a Pulitzer Prize for his reporting on evictions—found that an estimated 2.7 million households nationwide face eviction each year.

Meanwhile, the crisis of individuals and families swept from their homes due to financial instability is creeping up the class ladder. A *Yahoo News* article from April 2022 reported that some 8.5 million people were behind on their rent at the end of August, and 3.8 million of them say they're somewhat or very likely to face eviction in the next two months. That includes people earning up to $75,000 a year, which counts as a middle-class income in most places.

Eviction isn't just for the poor any more.

"We have these demographic shifts that are happening," says Mary Cunningham, codirector of the Metropolitan Housing and Communities Policy Center at the Urban Institute, a Washington think tank. "There's income stagnation, and there just isn't the [housing] supply needed to meet the demand. There's this rising number of renters, and people are coming out of the homeownership market. That's putting a lot of pressure on rents all across the income spectrum."

Yet policymakers in DC and elsewhere have seemingly put the issue on the back burner, and some doubt it's on the stove at all. President Donald Trump has not prioritized affordable housing, and Housing Secretary Ben Carson has been practically invisible since his Senate confirmation. Senators Bernie Sanders and Elizabeth Warren, the nation's most powerful economic-inequality avengers, haven't said much about affordable housing now that the 2016 presidential campaign is over.

Nevertheless, like my pretend-stealth comings and goings past the landlord's office in the weeks before I lost my home, ignoring what's become a national epidemic won't make it go away. It will only make things worse.

It's practically impossible to pinpoint how many evictions take place per year in the US. That's because housing and eviction laws, as well as public records statutes, vary from state to state. No one government agency is responsible for keeping track, not even HUD. In 1990, Senator Dennis DeConcini, an Arizona Democrat, introduced a bill to require HUD to establish a national eviction data center, but the bill went nowhere.

Redfin, a national realty data company, took a stab at quantifying the problem last year, compiling millions of pages of documents from the previous year.[1] But Redfin could find data for only nineteen states, or a bit more than a third of the country. The result: in 2015, roughly eight years after the housing crash that preceded the Great Recession, about 2.7 million people were kicked out of their homes.

Apartment List, another nationwide realty service, tried to measure evictions in October, using current and prospective renters who visit their website as a survey sample.[2] Collecting data from more than 41 million people, they found the crisis had grown since Redfin's assessment: an estimated 3.7 million renters have experienced an eviction.

The closest thing to an eviction data clearinghouse is the Eviction Lab at Princeton University, which collects publicly available data from states. Set up by Matthew Desmond, Eviction Lab is comprehensive enough that the US Census Bureau's American Housing Survey online page links to it. But there are holes in its data: some states, like Arkansas, don't make their eviction data public, while information from other states is incomplete.

That somewhat grainy snapshot reveals a perfect confluence of factors, says Robert Silverman, a University at Buffalo urban planning professor. Market forces unchecked by government economic policies—including flat wages, soaring living expenses, and college-educated millennials working entry-level jobs—have combined to push up rental prices across the board, particularly in desirable metro areas like Washington.

"Rents have been outpacing income growth, even in terms of other housing markets, like the mortgage market," says Silverman, a specialist in affordable housing and urban gentrification. Clamoring for upscale tenants, he says, "Landlords have been raising rents even though [household] income hasn't kept up with costs."

Factor in the post-recession "gig economy"—in which workers hold down a day job and a side hustle to make ends meet—and the conditions are near-perfect for an eviction boom. Freelance consulting or driving for a ride-sharing service after hours can help pay the bills, Silverman says, but moonlighting income can be inconsistent at best and unreliable at worst. Sometimes there's enough money to pay the landlord and the rest of one's creditors; sometimes one of the kids gets really sick or the car needs repairs, and the rent goes unpaid.

But the corporate landlords and real estate companies cornering the market on urban rental housing don't really care why the money's short; they only care that you don't have it, and they'd really prefer to rent to someone who does. Miss the rent often enough, for whatever reason, and the eviction machinery kicks in: a summons on your door, then an appearance in housing court.

And if you can't work things out in the courtroom, then a professional eviction crew, escorted by a law enforcement agency, will soon appear at the door.

When the date on my summons arrived, I headed to Montgomery County's modern, glass-and-concrete district courthouse in downtown Silver Spring, Maryland. Not knowing what to expect, I donned a jacket and slacks to make a good impression; more likely, it was another haughty act of self-delusion: *I'm middle class, with a white-collar career. I shouldn't really be here.* Even if my landlord, the past-due balance I owed, and the summons said otherwise.

When I got there, the assigned courtroom, number 303, was locked, and the hallway was crowded with my fellow scofflaws. Nearly all of them were people of color; judging by clothing and accented English, most seemed to be immigrants, blue-collar workers, or both.

That shouldn't have been surprising: "Evictions disproportionately impact the most vulnerable members of our society," according to the Apartment List report. Renters whose education stopped short of college, Apartment List says, are more than twice as likely to face eviction than the college educated—unless you're Black, like me.

Apartment List found that "black households face the highest

rates of eviction, even when controlling for education and income."
African Americans with at least a bachelor's degree are around twice
as likely to face eviction as whites, and about three times more likely
than Hispanics to get evicted.

That day in housing court, the judge entered the courtroom about
ten minutes after the bailiffs opened the door. Two by two, the liti-
gants marched up and stood before the bench, lawyer on the right,
debtor tenant on the left. Then, His Honor fired off a series of questions by rote: tenant's name, address, name of landlord, amount owed.
Each case took just a few minutes, start to finish; there were at least
two dozen cases' worth of people waiting for their turn that day.

As the hearing ground on, I kept thinking that a housing-court
case was less like a legal proceeding than a bizarre mutation of a marriage ceremony, with penury, not love or fate, uniting the two parties. Much like the groom in a shotgun wedding, the outcome of a
case—and the tenant's access to housing—hinged on whether he or
she could answer "I do" to two fundamental questions: Do you have
the past-due rent? If not, do you have a plan with the landlord to settle
the debt?

More often than not, the answer that day—including mine—was no.

Organizations do exist to help tenants facing eviction remain
in their homes. They range from government-sponsored agencies at-
tached to local social services offices and housing agencies to faith-
based outfits or nonprofits that use grants and donations to help
tenants pay back rent or keep the lights on.

The abundance of organizations and the lack of coordination
among them, however, can be overwhelming for tenants. And it's
a roll of the dice whether the agencies, usually private charities or
municipal-budget afterthoughts, are flush—particularly when lawmakers are usually more interested in cutting taxes (and choking off
revenue) than expanding the social safety net.

Two weeks before my day in housing court, I went to my local social services office, put my name on the waiting list, and subsequently
found myself in the cramped office of a Montgomery County social
worker. Maria, as I'll call her, was a petite woman with shoulder-length
silver hair, a warm demeanor, and the sort of earrings and bracelets

you'd find at an arts-and-crafts festival. She was empathetic but frank.

"Oh my," Maria said, trying to mask her alarm when I showed her an invoice of my past-due balance, which approached the yearly salary of a burger-flipper. "This is far too much for us to help you. Why didn't you come to us sooner when you first fell behind? We could have worked with you."

A block of ice melted in my gut; for an instant I saw myself in tattered overalls and a beat-up fedora, shuffling from my luxury apartment building with a hobo bindle on my shoulder. I mumbled to Maria something about not knowing that the county did this sort of thing—I'm from the middle class; I used to be a homeowner. I haven't ever really had to think about it.

"Well, even if I could give you some financial assistance, the county requires some kind of financial workout plan, so you don't end up in this situation again," Maria said. "And since you're unemployed, and no job on the horizon…"

I filled in the blank: "I can't qualify for a workout plan to get the money and show that I'll stay out of trouble."

"Yes," she said. "That's right."

I shouldn't have been surprised, says Silverman, the University at Buffalo housing specialist.

In areas where the real estate market is hot, "there's more incentive [for developers] to target higher incomes for new housing," he says. Construction cranes are sprouting like daisies across metro Washington, but they're building high-end units for upper-middle-income earners who've dropped out of the mortgage market and into rental housing. Not a lot of units are being built for middle-class incomes, let alone the working poor. That's not where the incentives or profits are.

Even in a city like Buffalo, "there's not a lot of construction to kind of relieve that pressure. And when new houses aren't built, affordable housing isn't always factored into the development project," Silverman says.

At the same time, he says, "middle incomes aren't growing like they used to be." That includes some of the new-economy jobs in the technology and service sectors. Those facts, he says, lead to a bitter conclusion.

"People who were middle-income in the past," he says, "might be lower-income now."

What I remember most about my eviction is how smooth, efficient, and surreal the process was.

Lacking the several thousands I'd need to stay housed and without even a nibble on the job front that would encourage a new landlord to rent to me, D., my girlfriend at the time, helped me make a strategic decision: Don't avoid the inevitable; lean into it.

So one Thursday evening in July, she and I boxed up the bulk of my belongings: dishes, books, photos, posters, winter clothes, spare bedding, knickknacks. I rented a storage locker two blocks away, then hunkered down, waiting for my fate.

It arrived the following Tuesday morning with several sharp, authoritative raps on the front door. On the other side of the peephole I saw two twenty-something Montgomery County sheriff's deputies—a man and a woman. When I let them in, I noticed the property manager and a dozen or so people lined up along the hallway outside my apartment, wearing identical red T-shirts stamped with a logo of some kind. They were holding thin black plastic garbage bags, the cheap kind I used to avoid, from the grocery store bargain aisle.

The professionalism of the move is an indicator of the exponential growth of evictions, Silver says. It makes sense: the quicker a landlord can turn over a delinquent property, the faster he can recoup his losses with a new tenant (and perhaps a higher rent).

Like HUD, the American Moving and Storage Association, an industry trade group, doesn't keep track of how often its members get hired by landlords to remove people from their homes. It also doesn't have an official position on the matter or a list of protocols for movers.

But after observing my own eviction up close, I came to a few conclusions. It's likely that the labor costs are offset by stuffing a soon-to-be-former tenant's belongings in plastic bags instead of packing them carefully in boxes. And, since the ex-tenant's stuff is going to the curb instead of to a new home or storage unit, there's no need for a moving van or driver. Ironically, several professional eviction companies in the Washington area use homeless people as moving crews for evictions, paying them a few bucks an hour—far below minimum wage.[3]

Eviction companies elsewhere even have ratings on Yelp.[4]

Having never experienced an eviction, I was taken aback when the deputies told me I couldn't stay on the premises to supervise, and one of them escorted me through my soon-to-be-former home as I gathered up toiletries and other last-minute personal effects. As I left the apartment for the final time, walking past Jen and the movers, I noticed their chatter had ceased, and no one would make eye contact with me.

Twenty minutes later, everything I owned was piled on the apartment building's vast loading dock. Within three hours, using a borrowed dolly, I'd moved most of my stuff to the storage locker I'd rented earlier, one dollar for the first month. Within a few weeks, after a couple rounds of house-sitting for vacationing acquaintances, I crash-landed in the spare bedroom of a family I barely knew, extraordinarily kind, unbelievably generous friends of a friend from my church.

We all thought the arrangement would last a few weeks, tops. It stretched nearly three years.

While policymakers on a national level haven't done much to stem the tide of evictions, some municipalities are taking steps on their own to address what they call an unseen element of the housing crisis. In New York City, Mayor Bill de Blasio has set aside millions to provide attorneys for everyone who needs one in housing court,[5] a promising experiment designed to keep people in their homes, while authorities in Milwaukee broke ground by conducting a yearlong study of housing and evictions.[6] Both cities have reached the same conclusion:

Helping people stay in their homes yields big dividends, not only for the city—which saves on welfare and emergency social services costs—but for tenants. A single eviction, studies show, can demolish a tenant's credit, undermine job opportunities, exacerbate homelessness and health, and make it far more difficult to keep one's place on the class ladder, let alone advance a rung. I finally got my own place this year: a single room in a split-level family home, all I could manage after getting a journalism job that pays me far less than I earned at *Politico*.

And I'm one of the lucky ones: I have a roof over my head, and home stability.

"Staying in a stable home is a part of that. What's on the [government policy] horizon isn't really well mapped out yet," says Silverman, the University at Buffalo professor. "Not a lot of concrete policy proposals out there that would talk about how that would happen."

CODA

Since I wrote this story in 2018, much is different, at least for me personally.

After a few years of renting that room for eight hundred dollars a month, I ended up in a one-bedroom apartment in a high-rise building, not far from where I was evicted in 2013. Then in 2022, I got a new job with a higher salary and rented a roomy townhouse in the same area, which I share with my two young-adult children and an adopted housecat.

The big eviction picture, however, has remained largely consistent, even amid a worldwide public health crisis.

In 2020, amid skyrocketing COVID-19 deaths, federal, state, and local government officials temporarily banned evictions to help stop the virus from spreading and limit the pandemic's economic fallout.

But in August 2021 the Supreme Court overturned the federal Centers for Disease Control and Prevention's national eviction moratorium, although it left state and local ones in place. A June 2022 study by Princeton University's Eviction Lab found that the remaining ones were uneven: most states paused just the eviction bureaucracy—court filings and hearings, for example—and only a handful of states froze evictions completely.[7]

The length of moratoria varied, too: While California banned evictions for more than eight hundred days, North Dakota stopped them for less than a month, according to Eviction Lab. And states began to roll back eviction protections—or restricted the protections that they initially offered—well before health officials had declared the pandemic contained.

Meanwhile, the rental housing market is still brutal, especially in large metro areas.

Here in the Washington, DC, suburbs, I pay just under $2,900 a month for a three-bedroom townhouse, which is statistically on par with the area, according to Rent.com. Their study found that, on average, a studio apartment in Silver Spring, Maryland, will set you back nearly $1,500 a month, while a two-bedroom apartment costs just north of $2,100 a month.

Those price tags are still significantly cheaper than crazy-expensive cities like New York and San Francisco, where one-bedroom apartments often top $3,000 a month, according to a July 2022 report in Bloomberg News.[8] But Bloomberg still ranks the DC metro area in seventh place, comfortably inside the nation's top ten most expensive rental cities.

In May 2022, President Joe Biden released a plan to create more affordable housing and published it on the White House website. It calls for federal investments and financial incentives to tackle the estimated 1.5 million shortage of affordable homes.

But Biden's plan has a five-year timetable, which won't help families facing eviction right now. It also calls on Congress to act, but there's no specific recommendations on what legislation he thinks lawmakers should pass.

One thing is clear, according to the proposal: while the shortage contributes to inflation, climate change, and other issues, "rising housing costs have burdened families of all incomes, with a particular impact on low- and moderate-income families, and people and communities of color."

In other words, the short-term outlook for eviction rates, and available, affordable rental housing is as bleak now as it was in 2018, and may not change for the foreseeable future. The more things change, it seems, the more they stay the same.

Joseph Williams is a writer in the Washington, DC, metro area.

37,000 US VETERANS ARE HOMELESS—I WAS ONE OF THEM

Alex Miller

Newsweek, November 10, 2021

In 2006, I served as a US Navy IT specialist aiding my ship's mission of finding and neutralizing pirates off the coast of Somalia. Two years later, I was homeless, standing in a line in Gainesville, Florida, that twisted around the block, so I could donate blood in exchange for twenty bucks.

Many of the men waiting with me looked almost as bad as I did—all of us homeless and hungry. My hair was matted, crusted from dandruff, and my eyes were bloodshot. My fingers tingled because of withdrawal from the antianxiety medications I wasn't getting from the Department of Veterans Affairs (VA). Between childhood trauma and my four years in the service, I relied on medications such as clonazepam, for anxiety, and Zoloft for PTSD, but the VA delivered my medication through the mail, and I hadn't had a stable home for some time—I was couch surfing, car snoozing, or sleeping in the back of the restaurant where I worked. With no permanent address, my meds never found me.

Sadly, my situation was far from unique. On a single night in January 2020, 37,252 veterans were victims of homelessness.[1] And the VA processes about 80 percent of veteran prescriptions by mail,[2] so when a veteran loses their home, they often lose access to the medications their life depends on.

Veterans bear the physical and mental scars of military service, yet when they return home, many of us face a society ill-equipped to offer proper care. Instead, once a year, our country celebrates Veterans Day with parades, services, and department-store sales. But homeless veterans don't need discounts; we need a system that protects us.

113

We need a comprehensive approach to care, one that ensures access to jobs, housing, medication, and treatments that holistically address their needs. Instead, so many veterans who leave the tangle of war end up on America's streets, still fighting daily for their survival.

This was the very fate I was trying to escape when I left the projects on Chicago's South Side. I came from the Robert Taylor Homes, infamous for their brutality, murder, rape, and drugs. On 9/11, I got swept up in the national patriotism that gripped the nation. At fifteen, I vowed to join the military to serve my country, knowing that if I died, at least it wouldn't be on the streets. At eighteen, I enlisted in the navy. I spent four years traveling the world engaged in goodwill missions, intelligence gathering, and assistance with other military branches.

But this regimented life wore on me. I saw firsthand the misuse of American military power, our imperialist treatment of developing countries, and the harm we inflicted on vulnerable people. It triggered a crisis of conscience and more trauma in my already depleted body. I was ready to return to civilian life.

I left under the impression that I could get any job I wanted. We heard it often—*vets receive preference in the workforce*—and high-skilled IT specialists like me held a special edge in the marketplace, I was told. I trusted that narrative. I applied to IBM, Google, Apple, and fifty other companies. I got one or two interviews, but neither led to a job.

I'm not the only one who has never seen this "military preference" play out in the job hunt. The truth hurts: That preference is a myth. Companies don't hire vets.[3] They worry about whether or not we'll be able to settle into normal jobs along with other stereotypes—that we all wear foil hats and fall back into flashbacks of war.

Three months after I left the navy, I ended up a broken, broke man. I had to leave my apartment in Virginia because of an eviction notice, a car I couldn't afford, jobs I couldn't get. I was embarrassed.

I'd go on to spend the next five years living without a home, without psychological treatment or steady access to medications, just trying to stay alive. For the first three years, I lived in the South—Virginia, Florida, Alabama—mostly couch surfing. I grappled with layers of complex psychological trauma and distress, but I wasn't getting properly diagnosed; the mental health treatment options in the South are very limited. Worse, like so many vets, I didn't know about the benefits I was entitled to, because the VA didn't tell me. I spent years wrangling with the callous bureaucracy of the VA: dropped calls, rude receptionists, misinformation about benefits. On top of that, I faced the daily indignities of joblessness, homelessness, and racism. As a Black man in the South, I felt smothered. I needed to get out. So when a friend in New York City offered me a place to stay, I saw my opportunity for a fresh start. A home. Treatment. A new beginning.

But he didn't tell me the offer was good only for a month. After that, he kicked me out and I began living on the Brooklyn streets in the dead of winter. I still remember wearing white Converse low-tops stuffed with plastic bags on the insides in January, because that was the only footwear I owned. The one pair of pants I owned, black Levis, was never not wet. My thin black jacket was holding up like rice under a faucet. I would frequently find myself with my new friend Jeremy, also a navy vet, drinking forties on a stoop in Brooklyn; if you're looking for ways to suppress your PTSD, malt liquor pairs well with self-hatred and regret. Inevitably, a cop would appear to harass us, an experience my fellow homeless vets and I grew familiar with, even after we identified ourselves as veterans.

It wasn't just the cops. Violence stalks homeless veterans at every turn. When I slept in shelters, I was often sleeping in cots next to ex-cons with any number of offenses; according to HUD, over 50,000 people move directly from prison into a shelter every year.[4]

Over time, I figured out how to work the VA's system. I learned how to be persistent, how to be the squeakiest wheel. And that helped me access my GI Bill benefits, which allowed me to receive the Yellow Ribbon scholarship, enroll in classes at the New School and find an apartment with a new friend. My persistence helped me network with other veterans to learn about programs, therapies, and group sessions that helped me rebuild my mental health. So many of us veterans are ignorant about VA programs and benefits because the VA fails to communicate with us, and often stonewalls us when we do inquire for help.

Programs do exist, but you have to know somebody. Or you need to call with the dogged persistence of a debt collector. It's absurd to expect this from those of us barely scratching out our survival.

Depressed veterans calling the Veterans Suicide Hotline have had their calls dropped or gone directly to voice mail, a failure so rampant that a bill called the Veteran Suicide Prevention Act was introduced last year.[5] This bill is to take a full accounting of all veteran suicides that have happened within the past five years preceding the passage of the bill. Included in the bill is a section that states that the VA "will report on the results of the review and make reports publicly available." This bill has never been passed.

Veterans are yelled at by VA receptionists, rushed through appointments with doctors, and, when we find ourselves houseless, the medications keeping us alive disappear into the mail system or sit unclaimed in pharmacies.

Instead of efficiency, scandals rock the department. In 2014, a scathing report showed that the department falsified medical waiting lists to cover up excessive wait times and delayed veteran care.[6] More recently, in 2019, a whistleblower asserted yet again that the department's official wait list contained just a fraction of the actual number of veterans waiting for care, which the department denied.[7] That same year another whistleblower told Congress that the VA ordered her to schedule fake appointments for veterans in order to shorten the wait list.[8] But the public shaming didn't lead to reform.

In recent years, nonprofits have stepped in to fill in the gaps left by the VA, like Call of Duty Endowment, the National Coalition for Homeless Veterans, and Stack Up.[9] These efforts offer hope, but I can't shake the fact that we have a VA funded by taxpayer dollars that is tasked with honoring the nation's veterans with dignified care—and it's failing at this.

I'm in a better place these days. I haven't been homeless in years. I recently moved into a new apartment and I've carved out a nice writing career. But I'm still healing. With the pandemic, access to mental health continues to be a struggle. Sure, I can get my meds now, but with so many other vets vying for attention from therapists, I've repeatedly been told that there were none available.

So I turn to those in my life for support. My writing group. A few friends. My cat. Eventually, I'll muster up the energy to make more calls to the VA, to seek out programs, to fight for my care. But it's sad that it's come to this. I left the military because I was done fighting.

Alex Miller, a reporting journalism fellow for EHRP, is a navy veteran and native Chicagoan. He's been published in the *New York Times*, the *Washington Post*, *Esquire*, and *Wired*. In addition, he has also been featured in the anthologies *The Byline Bible* and *The Chicago Neighborhood Guidebook*. He lives in New York and is writing a midgrade memoir about his experience of going to school for the first time at eleven years old.

WHY I CHOOSE TO LIVE HOUSE-FREE IN ALASKA

Joe Ford

The Guardian, January 14, 2019

> Homeless implies a moral failure while being houseless—lacking
> a permanent three-dimensional structure—is less stress on the
> planet and on my brain.

I am a sixty-four-year-old navy veteran of the Vietnam era and houseless in the tundra, somewhere around sixty-five degrees north latitude.
I have been scrambling around these parts since 2013, inhabiting a variety of iterations, from riverbank tent camps to cabins, buses, and RVs
and occasionally fancy lodges when I have worked caretaking gigs. I
live like this in protest of our consumer society. I find it more fulfilling,
more authentic, less stressful—on the planet and on my brain.

Feckless? Maybe. Shiftless? Probably. Irresponsible? Absolutely!
But homeless? I beg to differ. Homeless implies an individual mor-
al failure, which may indeed aptly describe one part of my character.
Houseless is simply lacking a permanent three-dimensional structure.

If you have a place to gather your thoughts and lay your head at
the end of the day, how is that not a home? My accommodations are
substandard if a house is used as a metric. But my tent keeps me and
my bedroll out of most elements in the spring, summer, and as far into
the fall as I can take it. I find sturdier shelter when the water I soak my
false teeth in overnight freezes and I have to chisel them free before I
can eat breakfast. Right now, I have a bus with a wood-burning stove
in it on loan for the winter, so I'm out of the elements until spring.

This ain't no city slickin', shopping cart, panhandling kind of
houseless. No dumpsters to dine at, no citizens to hassle for donations, no cops to dodge when you need to pee. Most days I see more
wildlife than humans. I spend more time traversing dirt than pave-
ment, more paths and game trails than roads and sidewalks. I hear

more of nature's notes than the white noise of civilization, and I can pretty much pee anywhere.

If you're not a moron, community members are not averse to doing you favors, giving you rides or putting you to work—labor can be a barter commodity. And most of these hillbillies are packing heat anyway, so it would behoove one not to be too stupid.

In general, stupidity out here in the frozen north usually carries severe consequences: campfires in a dry forest on a windy day easily get out of control; sloppy chainsaw, ax, or knife work, you could lose a finger or cut into an artery and bleed out; carelessness near rivers or ice could drown you; drinking water from a polluted creek will leave you very sick. Pick berries to eat oblivious to your surroundings and you could get eaten yourself (bears like berries, too).

People with a penchant for stumbling around drunk and stoned and sleeping it off curbside in the middle of the afternoon probably won't succeed out here. Discoveries of frozen houseless people regularly make local news headlines. If these folks can't make in an urban setting with services right around the corner, living in the woods miles from any help is not an option.

I'm vague about my location. I don't want a flock of freakin' hobos descending on the area like an invasive species only to discover, when the weather gets real, they weren't prepared and start dropping like the flies do on cold autumn evenings.

Hunting and gathering play a large role in the procurement of sustenance at my location. The activities reduce the degree of reliance on injected, processed, wrapped-in-plastic, crammed-into-coolers, industrialized food. We have meat on the hoof out here and I have no qualms about harvesting the resource sustainably. Plus, it's organic. This ain't a trophy hunt, this is food!

I do still have to rely on some factory food. On my monthly ride on public transportation to the local food bank thirty miles away, I'll pick up rice, pasta, cereal and milk, some canned goods, fruit, veggies, maybe some soup, plus peanut butter and welfare cheese (I hate how much I love that stuff!). I get fruit juice, too. If I add sugar and yeast to the juice it will ferment into a fairly stout libation in a matter of weeks.

All in all, though, I prefer a campfire-roasted porcupine that I killed and butchered (recently, one who had smacked my dog with his tail, embedding fifteen quills in the mutt's snout), slathered with high-bush cranberry ketchup, foraged chickweed salad with mushrooms on the side, a hot cup of stinging nettle tea to wash it down, and a handful of wild blueberries for dessert.

Bugs, sticks, sand, and assorted forest floor debris sometimes makes it into my vittles but, as the family I encountered in my travels through Canada some years back said when I pointed out that their kid was eating dirt, "It's clean dirt." And the bugs are protein! Anyway, I get to devour the feast creekside watching fish sex. No, it's not the latest Netflix series, it's actual salmon spawning in the water ten feet from my tent.

My living room floor gets a fresh gold carpet when fall colors take over and the tree branches go bare. Daylight starts fading fast closing in on the autumnal equinox and stays in decline till winter solstice, bottoming out at around five and a half hours here. So, I use recharge-able LEDs (a gift from a friend) to read and write by and a headlamp for more active endeavors like ice fishing or splitting firewood.

My toilet is a hollow cottonwood stump, and I bathe with a kettle of hot creek water. Some places along the highway offer showers but they cost money and contribute to ecocide, so I clean my crotch in the creek occasionally. But personal hygiene is not a priority. I have dirt under my fingernails, belly button lint, maybe some toe jam. I often smell like wood smoke from my campfires. My cologne: eau de burned alder. Instead of washing my clothing—layers come cheap from thrift shops—I air it out, hanging it on a tree branch for a snow-storm or two, then turn it inside out and put it back into rotation.

Cabin fever will kick in if you don't get out and move around, especially in the winter. I have a ten-year-old laptop and a mile hike to the library gets me some Wi-Fi and a battery charge. That and a tinny rechargeable battery-operated radio capable of pulling in the nearest NPR signal, which, like picking politicians, is the least of the worst, rounds out my engagement with the madness and spiritual corrosion of capitalism and the society it spawns.

I also go hiking, snowshoeing, ice skating, or cross-country skiing under a big moon. I can fall back into a snowbank with some home-grown and a pint o' schnapps and watch the northern lights or just get lost in the night sky.

Poverty can be a rough row to hoe. It has forced me to seriously compromise the lifestyle and the values I was raised to expect from my perch in a lilywhite midwestern suburb. During my lifelong descent of the economic ladder, which I attribute to my "don't care" attitude, I got a closeup view of all the unfairness, malfeasance, and destructive aspects of "the system." I was indoctrinated into it, and have gone from struggling to fit in to rejecting the game entirely and looking for alternatives.

As a result, my carbon footprint has shrunk. My presence on this planet leaves little trace, which is how I feel it should be. While that's pleasing to me, I also understand my withdrawal is meaningless in the grand scheme. The world needs systemic change. In my solitude and self-imposed isolation on the side of a mountain in an undisclosed location, I find it all mildly amusing.

Living on the edge of the fringe makes for an interesting experience. A bumper sticker on a four-wheeler that roared past me, destroying my Zen and shattering the stillness of the forest path I was traveling, read: "If you're not living on the edge you're taking up too much space." I smirk and can't help but agree.

Joe Ford is a writer and photographer in Alaska.

I WAS WRONGLY DETAINED AT THE BORDER—IT'S PART OF A LARGER PROBLEM

David Wallis

The Washington Post, May 18, 2022

When I tell strangers my name, people routinely respond, "Like the boss from *The Office*, right?"

No, I explain, he's W-A-L-L-A-C-E. I'm W-A-L-L-I-S. In the 1990s, after the celebrated novel *Infinite Jest* came out, I bet that my tenuous connection to author David Foster Wallace secured me some prized Manhattan restaurant reservations.

But any benefits of my commonish name vanished on a recent Sunday afternoon when I was returning home to New York following a four-day road trip to Montreal with my wife and twelve-year-old son. After we handed our passports to an agent at the Champlain, New York, port of entry, an alarm blared and the officer in the booth ordered, "Put your hands where I can see them." In a flash, at least four US Customs and Border Protection officers, hands on holsters, surrounded my Subaru. A blond-haired agent half my age who reminded me of a cross between Rutger Hauer and Opie from *The Andy Griffith Show* shouted for me to keep my hands up *and* get out of the car. That's impossible if you need to open a car door, which I tried to explain.

Gingerly exiting my car, I walked backward and then put my hands behind my back, following commands. The officer cuffed me as I looked at my shocked wife and little boy, wondering if I would see them again. The clink of the locking cuffs was an unforgettable sound. I scanned my memory for every possible misdeed. Was I bringing back too much Quebec ice cider? Were the Montreal bagels in the back seat banned agricultural products?

"Why am I being arrested?" I asked. The officer told me that I was not being arrested. It certainly *felt* like being arrested, as I was led into a holding room. A mustached officer told me that my name was the same as or similar to that of a wanted criminal. Some minutes later, I heard someone shout, "Okay, he's good," and off came the cuffs. I received not an apology for the false arrest but a pamphlet titled "Securing America's Borders: The CBP Screening Process" that includes this questionable claim: "We pledge to cordially greet and welcome you to the United States."

We tend to forget that we live in a surveillance state, just not a particularly sophisticated or efficient one. I covered the aftermath of 9/11 up close, so I understand that the US government must protect us from terrorists and criminals. I also get that borders are busy. CBP notes in its fact sheet that on a typical day it processes 491,688 passengers and pedestrians. But how is it possible that the US government, which can track a terrorist halfway around the world and deliver a Hellfire missile into his speeding car lacks the technology to differentiate between a law-abiding US citizen holding a valid passport and a wanted criminal?

I'm not sure why I was flagged or which watch list includes my apparently dangerous namesake or near-namesake, because neither CBP's director of media, Lawrence "Rusty" Payne, nor the agency answered questions about my detainment. I know, though, that federal agencies that manage immigration and our borders are far from bulletproof. A 2020 Cato Institute study concluded that Immigration and Customs Enforcement is "regularly issuing immigration detainers for U.S. citizens." The study examined a sample of 155 erroneous detentions and found that 15 percent were the result of mistaken identity.

In 2004, federal air security officials repeatedly questioned Sen. Edward M. "Ted" Kennedy because he was apparently on the no-fly list. A George W. Bush administration source told the *Washington Post* at the time that "the name 'T. Kennedy' has been used as an alias by someone on the list of terrorist suspects."

In 2015, mixed martial arts middleweight champion Rich Franklin was handcuffed, marched through Los Angeles International Airport, and held in a cell following a trip to Singapore because he had the same or similar name as an escaped or wanted felon.

Stephen Coulthart, an associate professor at the University at Albany's College of Emergency Preparedness, Homeland Security and Cybersecurity, estimates that a few hundred separate databases collect information on travelers. "The overall architecture is extremely complex," said Coulthart, coauthor of a 2021 policy paper, "Improving Big Data Integration and Building a Data Culture for U.S. Border Security," published by the Harvard Kennedy School. And he worries that "all these different databases, they don't speak well to each other. Because these different databases were set up in some cases with different protocols, maybe programming languages."

Jay Stanley, a senior policy analyst at the American Civil Liberties Union, fretted during a phone interview that since 9/11 federal government watch lists have become "big, bloated and over-inclusive." According to the ACLU, the federal watch list now includes about 1.6 million names. "There's every incentive to throw people on the list and little reason to throw them off," Stanley said. "Every person on Earth is a potential terrorist, according to our national security agencies."

"The fact that passports are such strong identification means that [CBP's] back-end system must be all the more problematic," continued Stanley, which "guarantees that innocent people will be treated as dangerous fugitives, and reflects a typical failure to balance bureaucratic security goals against the impact on innocent people."

Sylvie Nelson, fifty-six years old, can empathize. Nelson was born in Canada but is also a US citizen. Like many people who live near the border, she often travels back and forth between the countries to shop and stay at her second home near Montreal. In December 2009, she was heading home with her toddler son and six-year-old daughter when US border officers at Overton Corners, New York, handcuffed her and separated her, at least briefly, from her children. "They were still in their car seats. I was hyperventilating, as you can well imagine," she said. Border officers, she recalled in a phone interview, told her, "You need to calm down." Subsequently, Nelson, who was then head of her local chamber of commerce, was detained several more times and once held in a cell. She generally received polite enough treatment, but she recounted that an officer once told her husband, "That should teach you for going shopping across the border."

She learned during at least five detainments that she had been mistaken for someone who looked very different from her: "It was an African American man. I'm Caucasian and a woman. Two hundred and fifty pounds, and I'm not 250 pounds. Tattoos. I'm not tattooed."

Nelson said border officers recommended that she change her name or call ahead before traveling so they could conduct a "primary lookout override," which according to a CBP report assists "travelers who are erroneously designated for secondary inspections because they possess a characteristic similar to a person of interest," something of a manual purge of the incorrect information. But Nelson refused. "It's their problem," she said. "It's their antiquated system."

Only after she went to the press and contacted her representative in Congress, New York Democrat Bill Owens, who has since retired, did her border woes stop. In 2010, Owens received a letter from CBP officials that the agency had taken "positive steps" to resolve Nelson's quasi-arrests.

Chris Bronk, an associate professor at the University of Houston who has studied passport technology, called for CBP to increase the use of biometrics such as fingerprints to screen travelers. But Bronk, who served as a State Department official at the US-Mexico border in the early 2000s, also warned that even such systems have their limitations: longtime farm laborers might have worn down their fingerprints, for example—and hardened criminals could burn theirs off.

To lessen the chances of nabbing an innocent traveler, Coulthart urges CBP to provide frontline employees with more training in information technology. "CBP is struggling to develop a data culture," said Coulthart, who believes that the agency should establish an IT boot camp for recruits. He thinks officers would benefit from a better understanding of the data that they are using: "Just having some basic understanding of those systems is necessary for having some understanding of what they can and can't do."

During his State of the Union address in March, President Biden said that "if we are to advance liberty and justice, we need to secure the border and fix the immigration system." He added, "We can do both," pointing to "new technology like cutting-edge scanners."

For the time being, when it comes to border technology, cutting edge we're not.

David Wallis has contributed to the *New Yorker*, the *Washington Post*, and the *New York Times*, among other publications. He has edited two critically acclaimed books, *Killed: Great Journalism Too Hot to Print* and *Killed Cartoons: Casualties from the War on Free Expression*. He previously served as the managing director of the Economic Hardship Reporting Project.

I WATCHED WAR ERUPT IN THE BALKANS—HERE'S WHAT I SEE IN AMERICA TODAY

Elizabeth Rubin

The Intercept, October 25, 2020

I can't sleep anymore. I wake up in the middle of the night from hallucinatory dreams and don't fall back asleep. I'm obviously not alone with this condition. Sleeplessness and a kind of narcoleptic fatigue that I have all afternoon are gripping the country, actually the globe. Last night, I was locked inside a church and pulling the rotten, moldy, wood slats covering the windows to escape. I kept falling back onto the church floor and seeing bodies against the back wall.

Earlier this summer, as I walked past the hum of the morgue trucks parked outside our neighborhood hospital, I remembered my frequent pilgrimages to the morgue in Sarajevo as people searched for missing family during the war more than a quarter century ago. I can't believe it's that long ago. Watching what's happening around the country, images from the Bosnian war and from years of my past living amid other people's civil wars have crept into my daily and sleepless life. What were the precipitating incidents, what were the signs, when did rage and fear turn to violence, how did the fear defeat hope, was there some measure that could be codified? I don't think we're there yet. In fact, I can't believe we'll ever be there. But neither did they.

George Floyd's death, the video of his slow suffocation, his pleas for breath, his call for his mama as he lay dying under the knee of police officer Derek Chauvin ignited a rising-up against an entrenched and far better organized movement of white power, one that stretches back and back through our history. During one of the first Black Lives Matter protests in Brooklyn, I stood in a crowd wearing a mask and listened to a Black Episcopalian preacher give a sermon about peaceful anger. The next day, I was outside Barclays Center just before dusk with a crowd of protesters when another crowd arrived, having marched for miles from Bay Ridge. They stopped and one woman said they were going to pray, the evening Islamic prayer, and anyone could join or listen. They formed rows. A young man sang the call to prayer. The rest of the crowd—Black, white, brown—got down on a knee facing them. You could feel the surprise among the original crowd who had not expected the Bay Ridge Islamic Center's arrival. How to react? Time passed and the anxiety dissipated as the kneelers watched and listened and some raised a fist. Bay Ridge's Muslims were saying, Yes, we know well how the system wields power, sweeps through neighborhoods, crushes minorities. And we've joined forces before.

That night, the protesters stayed out after curfew; the police chased them, many were beaten, locked up. Groups formed to get people out of prison. You know the rest: Allies handing out water bottles, curfews, the chanting of names of Black men and women killed by police, police violence, clashes. And then, on the tails of demands for justice, the extremists flew in. In the streets of Portland, Oregon, the gun-chested, beefy, white power antimaskers and the Homeland Security dudes in riot gear ratcheted up the crisis, with unmarked vans whisking protesters away, with the Boogaloo Bois, the Boojahadeen, the Proud Boys, and antifa. In early June, helicopters were constantly buzzing overhead in my neighborhood in Brooklyn, and then at night the fireworks began. All over the city. At first, it was exciting, celebratory. I noticed Max, our six-year-old mutt, who could never get enough of the outdoors night or day, around dusk, his tail would drop, he'd lope to the dining table and duck under. If I tried to take him out after sundown, his feet cemented in place. Max wasn't alone. There was an epidemic of traumatized dogs. Canines sense an earthquake coming—why not war?

Max's fear started with the fireworks. And the fireworks set off more fears, conspiracy theories about government plots to drive people mad with sleeplessness, to stir anxiety in Black and brown communities, to send police fireworks squads into neighborhoods searching for "troublemakers"—code for protesters. You could find any and every theory, even that the fireworks were the prelude to war. Isolation, despair, insomnia, job losses, illness, curfews, police violence, looting—they breed conspiracy theories. It's the traction of those conspiracy theories that needs to be measured.

I lived in Sarajevo during the war, above the Catholic church in the old town called Baščaršija—"grand bazaar" in Turkish—with Vera, her husband Drago, and their traumatized dog, Blacky. Every time the phone rang, which wasn't often since the phones were often down during the war, Blacky flipped out. If you dared to venture forth and pick up the receiver, he'd grip your ankle with his teeth and yank. Everyday around dusk, an archipelago of shell-shocked dogs barked their agony across the city.

Vera, a poet and newspaper editor in her fifties, was convinced that war would never come to Bosnia. Even in 1991, the year before the war began, with the Yugoslav Army shelling towns on Croatia's Dalmatian Coast, with the Yugoslav army besieging the eastern Croatian town of Vukovar, Sarajevans did not believe that war would come to their beautiful city nestled in the mountains. War in Bosnia? No way, said Vera. It was too mixed up: Muslims, Orthodox, Catholics, Jews, all living together and intermarried. Vera was Croat. Vera's former husband was half Croat and half Jewish. Drago, a retired economist and bank director, was Serb. Upstairs in Vera's apartment building lived a Jewish Croatian Bosnian and his Muslim Bosnian wife and their mixed son. The whole building was like that.

Drago told Vera that she was naive. "The war in Bosnia," he said, "will be longer and bloodier than anywhere else." The two rarely agreed on anything.

Vera had been a baby in a bomb shelter in World War II. Drago had joined the partisans to fight the Nazis and their Croatian allies. He ended up in a concentration camp in Austria and nearly died of starvation. His sister happened to see his body thrown on a pile of corpses and saved him.

Drago always expected the worst. And so in early 1992, with war raging just across the border from Bosnia, Drago drove up north to his family farm where he'd once been mayor. Already, the Bosnian Serbs had declared autonomous zones and were preparing for an independent state. Drago heard that Ratko Mladić—the charismatic Bosnian

Serb military commander who would become notorious for leading the massacre of 8,000 men and boys in Srebrenica—was recruiting men for his separatist army. Drago urged the reservists he knew to resist Mladić and stay home, until a friend warned him to be quiet and leave lest he get thrown in prison or killed. On his way home, he saw irregular soldiers with beards and long hair wearing patches with crossed swords, a skull, an eagle. The Chetniks were back, reincarnations of the old nationalist guerrillas who'd formed an alliance with the Nazis in World War II to advance their dream of a Greater Serbia. Radovan Karadžić, the Bosnian Serb political leader, was a great admirer of the Chetniks. In their honor, he vowed that the Muslims of Bosnia would burn in hell if Bosnia declared independence.

Lately, I've drifted into Drago's camp. The images of bulging, bearded men with their ammunition bibs, wielding automatic rifles and a medley of white power symbols—swastikas, Confederate flags, nooses, patches of an arrow through a skull, and the words "death" and "victory"—just like a cabal of Chetniks. They mobilize like the wind thanks to their chat-frats. They message, "Any patriots willing to take up arms and defend our city?"—Kenosha, Wisconsin. They threaten to lynch and behead the governor of Michigan. Drago recently died, but I can hear him telling me, "Don't be a donkey." That's what he called me. A lot. Usually for missing signs of trouble, for not being vigilant.

In Sarajevo, whispers swept through schools, the hospital, newsrooms, offices. Serb friends and colleagues were suddenly off to Belgrade to visit family, or going to the countryside, or getting medical treatment, or just disappearing. Still few believed that war would come to Sarajevo. Between February 29 and March 1, 1992, Bosnia held a referendum on independence from Yugoslavia. A nearly unanimous "yes" prevailed. Except that the Serb-controlled areas of Bosnia boycotted the vote. In fact, they'd already declared a separate constitution.

On March 1, a Serb wedding party was heading toward the old Orthodox church in Baščaršija. Gunfire scattered the celebrants. The bridegroom's father was shot and killed. The Orthodox priest was shot. Sarajevans were disgusted but not surprised when the killer was rumored to be a local thug, nicknamed Celo, or "baldy."

Immediately Bosnian Serb leaders declared, You see? We were

right. Independent Bosnia means death to Serbs.

Up went the barricades manned by Serb paramilitaries. Students removing the barricades were killed. And up went the barricades manned by Celo and other criminals. Fairly quickly, the Bosnian government formed its own underdog army.

In April, Sarajevans still believed peace was possible. Because they wanted peace. Because they felt peace. They couldn't conceive that anyone would want war. Hundreds began marching in Dobrinja, the suburb created for the 1984 Winter Olympics. Hundreds turned to thousands and tens of thousands shouting, We can live together. They brandished photographs of the late Josip Broz Tito, nostalgic for his autocratic rule when everyone was a Yugoslav. They waved signs for sex, drugs, and rock and roll. This was Sarajevo. Fun town. Comedians. Musicians. Café hipsters. War was for those rural hillbillies. The protests carried on into the next day. Some 100,000 Sarajevans calling for peace. Then the shots rang out again. Bullets hit dozens of protesters. Fourteen were killed. The police figured out that Serb snipers were firing on the protesters from the Holiday Inn, the same hotel that would end up housing the international media for three and a half years of siege.

That day, April 6, Bosnia won international recognition of its independence. And the siege began.

The siege of Sarajevo, the longest in modern Europe's history, was brutal and twisted and yet so intimate. It's very intimacy made it so unthinkable that friends and neighbors could turn on each other. How could they? How could we? One Bosnian Croat writer and boxer I knew who stayed to defend the city told me that his best friend was on the other side with the Bosnian Serb army. During the day, they shot at each other. At night, they talked on the phone and wept. Ismet Ceric, the head of psychiatry at Sarajevo's main hospital, was Karadžić's boss for twenty years. He told me that the very day Karadžić ordered the shelling of Sarajevo from the mountains, he called Ceric's mother in Sarajevo. "He called to wish her a happy Bajram," Ceric told me, referring to the Muslim festival following Ramadan. Ceric then asked me, "Can you believe that?" Yes, sadly I could. Karadžić was so obsessed with Ceric that he followed his old boss around the city for the next three years with mortars and grenades. It was hard to say whether Karadžić wanted to kill him or taunt him, or whether Ceric thought there must be a Karadžić behind every near-miss.

When Karadžić told Serbs to evacuate the city, many refused, because they had nowhere to go, some because they refused to be refugees, and some because they believed in defending the old prewar Sarajevo even as the Bosnian army turned more and more Muslim. As hard as you tried to hold on to your identity as a mother, a doctor, an actor, a journalist, a policeman, that's not how others identified you. With a flip of a linguistic switch, you were reduced to Serb, Croat, Muslim, Jew.

What flips civil strife into civil war? A well-planned agenda, charismatic leaders, and fear. And perhaps one last ingredient that pulls together all three: the whittling down of history and all its complexities into a narrative of collective destiny—ours against theirs, us against them.

This summer some New Yorkers fled the city for the suburbs, the countryside, New England, California. The *New York Post* egged on the dystopian fears with headlines like "New York City Crime Wave Reaches New Heights." People have lost their homes, more are living on the streets. Storefronts and restaurants are empty. Overturned chairs and tables fossilized in the windows. My dentist in Manhattan told me that her colleagues want to buy guns. "What did you tell them?" I asked her. "That they should get them," she said. Her husband survived the war in Kosovo, he says they would be foolish not to have guns. A war photographer and friend told me that I should have an escape-survival bag always at the ready. He thinks us city people are idiots not to have guns.

An author and friend in Charlottesville, Virginia, tells me the feeling in low-income communities is that the mob is coming, and no one will protect them but their own guns. She says summer of 2017 in Charlottesville was our Fort Sumpter, the first generation of a virus that's morphing. When a group of Ku Klux Klan showed up to demonstrate, the police had their backs to them. Who were they facing down? The citizens who'd come to protest these avatars of violent white power. They chanted: The cops and Klan go hand in hand. And when the KKK left, the cops tear-gassed the anti-KKK demonstrators as if to say, "Yeah, we do." That was two years before George Floyd's death set off demands to defund the police. After all, who are they defending? The KKK? The

Proud Boys? The demonstrators? Onlookers? Their power?

FBI documents released recently give proof to the fact that right-wing extremists are infiltrating and recruiting the police. Daryl Johnson, an agent tasked with investigating domestic terrorism at DHS eleven years ago, was pushed out for his inconvenient findings that right-wing extremist terrorism is far more dangerous to the homeland than Islamic terrorists. Recent history in Las Vegas, El Paso, Gilroy, and Charleston just proves his point, a point he now makes in books, articles, interviews, to anyone who will listen. Hundreds of thousands of well-armed white power extremists are now fully out in the open. Their violent acts are enshrined in social media and heralded by the president. They have new charismatic leaders. They have a clear agenda. They have a narrative of historic grievances and a shared destiny: white power. They have their white supremacist bibles. Their conspiracy theories are sticking with acronyms like TEOTWAKI: The End of the World as We Know It. They could all be called the children of the Turner Diaries.

Residents in Erie and Union City, Pennsylvania, tell a *New York Times* reporter that people on both "sides" are ready for violence should the other candidate win. Biden and Trump supporters live side by side. Some in the same family. They all know each other. And they're all saying, Forget the courts. Trouble is coming to the streets. Because everyone's armed. Trump supporters say a Biden win would be a Marxist socialist coup—extreme-right rhetoric is now mainstream. Female Biden supporters like Mary Jo Campbell say they're scared to death. After Trump was elected, she and her friends started a club they called The Drinking Girls to meet, drink, plot, talk. During the pandemic, my women friends, and I'm pretty sure thousands of others, took to Zoom-drink sessions for similar reasons.

I keep looking at the portraits of Campbell and the other people of Erie captured by photographer Libby March. The faces—weary, drawn with anxiety, tough. They remind me of the men and women in central Bosnia, where the war hit first, where everyone kept an AK-47 or hunting rifle by the door. It's impossible to imagine neighbors and friends turning on each other. Until it's not.

I'm trying not to be a donkey, but being a Cassandra is extremely unrewarding. And annoying. A friend of mine who fled Iran when she was nine years old balked at my comparisons to Sarajevo. "The minute anyone compares completely different countries that share no history, I switch off. That is never going to happen here." I agree, in part. The United States doesn't share a political context or history with Bosnia. But then there's human nature, how we wield denial to survive, and tribalism when under threat, and how hard it is to turn off the worst of ourselves.

The two sides have come to stand for so much more than they can possibly hold and now face each other down like the forces of light and dark over Gondor. Only each side thinks the other is the dark. People who should be united by economic class are divided by skin color. The idea that one side is elitist and the other working class is a fallacy. Look no further than the elitism of the sitting president. Or the myriad working classes who compose the so-called elitist Democratic Party. Still, when we meet strangers, we know almost instinctively who is a Trump supporter and who is a Biden supporter. Who is other. Who is hateable, deplorable, dispensable. The language of othering slips so easily off the tongue in this fraught moment. We are in the throes of an inexorable rearrangement. History moves not like an arrow but a boomerang, Ralph Ellison wrote. And no one knows which way it will go. What is known is that none of us can escape from history.

I could leave off here. Except I prefer the endings of comedy, not tragedy.

My neighborhood park in Brooklyn has come alive as never before: It's an outdoor gym, an outdoor dance floor, people bring their exercise mats and a phone for their online high-intensity training or yoga class. People are kickboxing, jump-roping, sweating under the British prison ship martyrs' monument. I watch one-woman camera crews filming their friends for a TikTok video. Nightlife has also moved to the park: Picnics, small parties, a couple wrapped in a blanket because there's nowhere else to go. Every shape and color and size mingles in the park. I recently noticed that the hum and menace of a police generator and a police pole with stadium lights are gone. While ostensibly there to offer safety, the hum and glare stalked you, creating the menacing atmosphere of a dystopian film about surveillance, anomie, and the end of the world. Their absence has brought calm, respite, and festivity. And been replaced by nightly drumming sessions.

I loved Jerry Seinfeld for his real-New Yorkers-stick-it-out column, rebutting and lampooning a fellow New Yorker and comedy club owner whining on LinkedIn that the city is dead, his friends have fled, and he's moving to Miami. Imagine being in a real war with this guy, Seinfeld wrote.

The day after I read it, I was speaking to a friend who wrote one of the definitive books on the wars in Yugoslavia.

"We have to stay," I said.

"Of course we're staying," she said. "Where else are we going to go?" Then she said, "We'll be like the Sarajevans."

Even if Joe Biden wins, the divides ripping apart this country will not go away. But that doesn't mean we will go the way of the Balkans, find ourselves in Sarajevo's siege. That's the nightmare scenario. There are millions of people, most in fact, who want to find a way to bridge the divides and face the seismic shift that history is demanding.

In a recent dream, I walk into a party in Sarajevo. I plan to surprise Vera. We haven't seen each other in two decades. She's on the couch. She seems angry. "Why didn't you tell me you were coming, or is this just a coincidence, because you wanted to go to a party?" "No, no, no," I say, stunned by her anger. "I don't even know these people," I tell her. She hugs me so tight. We're both crying, in front of a roaring fire. The room turns to stone. The ceiling recedes, cathedral high. It's so dark. I take my daughter by the hand to show her the room where I slept without windows, but she is pulling me away, she wants to go talk to the kids outside. She says something about a new friend, Methody. Outside Vera's building I see a bent-over old man with long gray hair and a cane. It's Mr. Methody, the philosopher-father of the crowd. Everyone looks to him, but he keeps manifesting in different places. He whispers to me, "The structure of things is difficult. These are not normal times. The atoms and structures. It's not a time of normal cause and effect." Then he vanishes.

Elizabeth Rubin has reported from the Middle East, Afghanistan, the Balkans, Russia, Africa, and other parts of the world for the *New York Times Magazine*, the *New Republic*, the *New Yorker*, *Harper's*, the *Atlantic*, *Bidoun*, and *Vogue*, among others. Her journalism honors include the Livingston Award, the Bayeux-Calvados Award, and the Kurt Schork Award.

A FIERCE DESIRE TO STAY

Looking at West Virginia through Its People's Eyes

Elizabeth Catte, with photographs by Matt Eich
and poetry by Doug Van Gundy

The Guardian, May 8, 2019

To render a humane portrait of West Virginia and its people is to promise disappointment. The poet Muriel Rukeyser knew this as early as 1938, interrupting her own matter-of-fact description of West Virginia's plainness from *The Book of the Dead* to question her readers' expectations: "What do you want—a cliff over a city? A foreland sloped to sea and overgrown with roses?"

Matt Eich's photographs of Webster County, West Virginia, taken in July and December in 2018 in collaboration with poet Doug Van Gundy, contain similar questions.

If you look at Webster County on a map, you'll see more than five hundred square miles of forest nestled between rivers and mountains, and leaving the county requires a long crossing of one or the other. The county seat, Webster Springs, has just under seven hundred residents. The county is overwhelmingly white, and the per-capita income is just $12,284. This makes Webster County, with a median household income of $21,055, the fourth poorest county in West Virginia; 31 percent of residents are below the poverty line, including 40 percent of the county's children.

The county's most important link to the mining industry, a surface mine owned by Arch Coal, closed in 2012 and with it went 150 jobs. Timber, however, has long been the county's primary economic force. Over 93 percent of the county is forest, and timber companies own more than half of all private land, providing in return seasonal employment at five area sawmills. Much of the timber harvested in Webster

136

County is destined to become high-end furniture, the kind that mill workers and loggers can't afford.

Abandoned book, Webster County, West Virginia.

"They have no idea of the men and machinery, the sweat and labor, the diesel fumes and distance involved," Van Gundy writes, imagining the consumers of Webster County's bounty.

Timber is cleaner than coal mining, but most communities in

West Virginia have faced struggles connected to the totalizing nature of the extraction economy.

They are also attempting to go against the problem of image-making in the state, which is often about capturing the idea of West Virginia rather than its complexities. The most widely circulated version of the state is one that looks like it deserves to face its own oblivion, for its politics or economy or outdated modes of existence. But what if it doesn't look like that at all? What if it looks like ordinary things, like young love and fair weather, like clean countertops at a crowded diner?

There's a habit to simply go bleak, however, as places like Webster County depend on boom-bust industries not just for jobs, but for tax revenue that funds municipal services like schools and roads. And with a population that's been shrinking since the 1960s, the tax base created by property owners and small businesses is currently not enough to sustain basic government functions.

In 2016, Webster County found itself $1.48 million in debt to its regional jail authority, a sum that reflects the collision of old and new realities. Communities financially depleted by population loss and the decline of industry are now facing the devouring health crisis of opioid addiction. Claiming more than 20 percent of all fentanyl deaths in the entire state, arrests are up and elected magistrates favor harsher drug sentences.[1]

For more than seventy years, West Virginians have experienced both the economic push to leave and, for many, a fierce desire to stay. West Virginia is currently the only state shrinking from both natural population decline—there are more deaths than births—and out migration.[2] The presumed fates of people who live in places such as Webster County become anchored to abstract debates about who and where is worth saving.

What if, instead, images of West Virginia make it look like a place where people live? Not trapped in limbo, their fates sealed, but a place where roofs get repaired and wind chimes hung, a place that looks like other communities which, perhaps, are not so often visually consumed with implicit despair in mind.

In 1900, the Webster Echo celebrated its community as "rich in everything that goes to make a people happy and comfortable." Eich's photographs are piercing because they move against the grain to dignify people who still imagine that could be true. This West Virginia looks like a place where, instead of running out, life goes on.

—Elizabeth Catte

Reflections in a storefront in Webster Springs, West Virginia.

Half of the Story

I didn't grow up here.

Only been here a couple of months but I don't care if I never go back.
It looks like there's nothing to do here.

There's the river. There's the woods.

I fix up people's fishing and hunting camps—carpentry and electrical and that—enough to have something to do, enough to get by.
I live in that camper trailer over there. People are real friendly, but
they'll leave you alone, you know?

No drama.

The people I ran with lived on drama, died for it. Drama and drugs.
Of course, any drug you can get anywhere, you can get in Webster
Springs, but I mostly stay here: up the river where nobody bothers me.

Sometimes at this time of year, a little mist will hang over the river,
and the dust from the road will hang in the air, and the feeling sneaks
up on you that there isn't any world beyond the mouth of this hollow.

Outside of the Main Street Cafe, Webster Springs, West Virginia.

Hymn for Coal Smoke

Praise the antique odor—
wood smoke compressed and marinated
in subsea strata and mountain hillsides
to a richer, sharper smell: incense
burned on an ancient, animal altar.

Praise the thready column in chilly air—
slow to dissipate, almost an entity
in-and-of itself: black stone burnt
to yellow smoke and snow-
white ash.

Praise the sweat inside the scent—
sweetness of the human animal,
salt of its labor: blood
smell in the mineral
dark.

An elderly woman holds onto a post for support on the porch outside her home in Webster County, West Virginia.

Home Burial: A Love Poem

Please. Don't allow any strangers to lie
on this ridge, or any backhoes to dig
into this ground. I need you

to make a shovel-opened,
shoulder-pried grave for me when I go.
Box me, don't burn me: store me away

in a hillside I know like my bones.
Dig down to a clay floor so water won't get in
too easy: while I want to die

quickly, I want my body to linger as long as it can,
at least a century between box and bare bones.
There is no way you can bury me

without entering the earth yourself. You need to know
that worm's-eye view—feel the blade of the spade slicing
through roots of unknowable plants, see the rectangle

of trapped sky from the bottom of my grave.
Make certain it's safe enough, deep enough,
square enough to hold my eternity.

Once I'm packaged and lowered,
the preacher has intoned his boilerplate,
and you have heaped your plate with fried chicken

and pie, shovel me covered. After you do this
there is nothing I will not do for you. I believe
in the body, not its resurrection.

Fog on the mountains, Webster County, West Virginia.

The Personal History of Everyday Objects

Somewhere in a showroom in San Francisco or Seattle, a young couple
picks out their first nice dining room suite. They have no idea
of the men and machinery, the sweat and labor, the diesel fumes
and distance involved in placing this table in front of them to buy.

Jake-brakes judder a semi-truck to a stop at the only light in the county:
another load of hardwood headed to High Point
to be made into high-end furniture and shipped
all over the globe.

A white-haired woman with a walker uses every second
to clear the crosswalk, allows the truck to turn left
over the mountain bound for Summersville, Beckley,
points South.

It's a ritual repeated many times a day as the best timber in the eastern
  US—cut

into boards right here in Webster County, West Virginia, by men
who've spent generations in the logging woods and lumber mills —
    seeks out
its higher purpose.

The couple walks around the table a final time before deciding, trusting
it will match their hardwood floors, some of which
have come from the self-same hillsides
as the wood for the table.

They know it will look good spread with the Thanksgiving dinners
and everyday breakfasts they imagine preparing
with the four hands between them
for the family they do not yet have.

On the Night of the Fire

The Oakland Hotel, the town's last, abandoned
for a decade, proved the fire marshal right
by burning to the ground.

Embers winged in air, ash
drifting back to earth
as far away as the courthouse steps
and Elk River Road.

Theories swirled:
started by vagrants, meth-
heads, the mayor—
accident or arson.

The heat so great
siding melted from buildings.
Insulation dripped
from TV cables, telephone

wires.

Green leaves curled
into brown on oaks
halfway up the hillside.

People wandered from
their homes, drawn
to the light, until half the town
watched in pajamas and sweat
pants.

Dogs barked for hours
and hours afterward
just in case we
missed the message.

Sunset in Webster County, West Virginia.

Bergoo

Bergoo Mine #1 will not work,
Bergoo Mine #1 will not work tomorrow.

WDNE-AM, Elkins WV

These mountains have stopped
swallowing men & spitting
them back out, bruised by what
they've seen & done.
The men are gone
mines emptied
driftmouths mute.
Coal-camp names remain—
Bergoo, Parcoal, Diana—
stripped, half-sung
litany of used
-to-be.

Doug Van Gundy is a poet and musician from Elkins, West Virginia. He is the author of a collection of poems, *A Life Above Water,* and co-editor of the anthology *Eyes Glowing at the Edge of the Woods: Fiction and Poetry from West Virginia.*

Elizabeth Catte is a writer and public historian living in Virginia. She is the author of *What You Are Getting Wrong About Appalachia* and *Pure America: Eugenics and the Making of Modern Virginia.*

Matt Eich is a photographic essayist working on long-form projects related to memory, family, community, and the American condition. He teaches at the George Washington University, makes books under the imprint Little Oak.PRESS and resides in Virginia.

SECTION 3

Family

INTRODUCTION

Michelle Tea

What is family for broke folks? How does being broke break a family? For those of us who manage to break out, what happens to those we leave behind? For those of us who won't be inheriting wealth, those more likely to inherit a box of ashes but not the means to inter them anywhere (which has happened to my own mother upon losing both her father and husband; when she passes, I fear I will be charged with not only her cremains but the boxes of passed-away family members—and family members of family members—whose representatives on earth lacked the funds to stash them someplace decent for all eternity), family is fraught, spinning up feelings of guilt and obligation, helplessness and resentment, resignation, and love.

I was born and raised in Chelsea, an urban enclave just across the water from Boston. A city always receiving the latest wave of immigrants. My grandfather, Irish, dropped out of school to join the navy in World War II. In his eighties he finally received an honorary high school diploma from the government—far too late for it to make a difference in his life. The bitterness in his voice as he grumbled about this hurt my heart—a stoic man who worked a factory job till he retired, if he'd ever had dreams about a better life, I'd never heard about them.

My mom didn't go to college—nobody I knew went to college—and the insecurity about this was surely behind the mocking of collegiate-types, the sense that *those* people may be book-smart, but didn't know shit about the "real world," where you had to work a *real* job, one with a lousy boss and shitty pay that left your body broken and spirit smashed. In order to divorce my alcoholic father, my mom enrolled in the free nursing program Chelsea offered, getting a career a bit later in life, one that supported her until her COVID-forced retirement.

Poor families can be a paradox—both my sister and I were urged to be all we can be and, yes, aim for college, but when it came time to do that, nobody knew how. My parents were scared of bureaucracy, always certain there was something in the fine print to take advantage of the little guy. I learned this from them, and together, facing the paperwork of college, we were both stressed and anxious. They wouldn't sign a loan for me—the thought of owing all that money was terrifying. I managed to scrape together enough for a couple semesters, but then gave up. My sister, a hardier, more capable sort, managed our parents better and got them on board, but even she was dissuaded from applying to Harvard, a "designer school" that actually meant nothing, in the eyes of our family, despite her being brilliant, the valedictorian, and urged by her advisers to go to an Ivy League school. Our parents wanted us to do better—in theory. In reality, not only did they not know how to support this, they had inherited and nurtured a wounded psychology that actually demonized everyone above them on the economic rung. How, then, could they really launch their children into what felt like enemy territory? The various push and pull of love within poor families, the way that poverty and the outside world impact these bonds—these are only a few of the ways care was corrupted through the stressors of poverty.

The stories in this section of the way financial stress impacts familial ties will be enlightening for readers who come to it looking to learn how the other half lives. I count myself among that other half, for, though I have absolutely "gotten out," moved to a big city and achieved, some years, a middle-class income, I have within me those fears of falling through the cracks that so many raised broke never fully shake. Growing up within the poorer half of our country is my history; the scarcity issues I continue to work through is my present. Tearing through these thoughtful and varied pieces gave me those feelings of comfort and camaraderie seeing aspects of your own story can bring. In class-less America, where everyone, rich or poor, is adamantly *middle class*, it's always a relief to see the experience of economic struggle discussed frankly. But the pieces gave me another feeling, too—the surfacing of my constant companion, casually dubbed *my scarcity issues*. The familiar trill of panic I consciously breathe down multiple times a week, the energetic answer to the refrain, "Am I going to be okay?"

I'm a writer constantly on that hustle Robert W. Fieseler documents in his 2020 HuffPost essay about the fallout of touring his tremendous book *Tinderbox*, as if he could afford to do such a necessary thing. I've been caught in such loops—*must spend money touring book or else no one will buy book and I will never make money ever!* It makes me reflect upon Annabelle Gurwitch's 2019 essay about taking unhoused young people into her home for the *LA Times*, when she states, "If the city can't accommodate artists from economically diverse backgrounds than only the privileged will get to create."

And have pets! In Bobbi Dempsey's 2018 *Guardian* piece, which investigates what happens when the pets of the poor have a medical emergency, she writes, "Pets are yet another thing that are used by people as an excuse to poor-shame, essentially telling indigent people that they aren't worthy of the companionship of a loving pet." I wondered as much before having my own son—did I have a right, as a broke person, to become a mother? But family is essential. Its hold on us, and the problems unique to broke families, is explored here to moving ends.

I'll never forget the host of a radio show who had invited me on to talk about a book of working-class stories I'd edited asking, "Why should we care about these people? If they're so smart, why are they poor?" In a culture that looks down on poor people, it makes sense that broke folks imagine they might be middle class; no one wants to be a loser. But the reality is, over 140 million American families are impoverished or low-income, says the Poor People's Campaign, who carry on Rev. Dr. Martin Luther King Jr.'s quest for economic justice. And most American families do not fit into the heterosexual, nuclear model conservative forces insist upon, either; the 2002 census had only a scant 7 percent of families falling into that mom-dad-child paradigm.

Bearing witness to the following stories brings us deeper into the truth of what it means to be an American family today. These pieces conjure compassion and empathy, as well as anxiety and frustration. How have we humans not found a better way to live together? How bad will it have to get, for how many people, before the old ways crash and something newer, kinder, more thoughtful emerges? Those are questions for us, the readers. For these writers have done their job: sharing the face of low-income family, with its legacies both ragged and rich.

Michelle Tea is the author of over a dozen books, most recently *Knocking Myself Up: A Memoir of My (In)Fertility.* She has been awarded honors from the Guggenheim Foundation, PEN/America, the Rona Jaffe Foundation, and other institutions.

DON'T BE THIS WAY FOREVER

Text and images by Jordan Gale

A crucifix at a rural cemetery, through the front windshield of a car in Eastern Iowa, 2019.

I was born and raised about two hours west of the Mississippi River, in the relatively small city of Cedar Rapids, Iowa, in a single-parent home. Throughout my childhood, I can remember that, more often than not, it was difficult to get by. That, and the stress associated with it, was hard on my mother, and on me. I learned from an early age that we were poorer than others, and considered lower class to some. I remember growing up angry at the fact that I had to struggle in life, more so than others did. It's still an emotion that I have to suppress. I resented the space I was born into, fearing I'd never leave Iowa or make a life of my own. These emotions ultimately caused me to perpetuate self-destructive tendencies as a young adult that I saw frequently in my mother and within my community at large. That realization only deepened my anger, anxieties, and feelings of stagnancy.

I first picked up a camera when I was sixteen years old. My art teacher lent me her old 35 mm so that I could participate in my high school's darkroom class. I fell in love with developing film, being alone with that process and the ways in which a physical photograph could hold intent and emotion. My family could never afford the needed equipment or fees to participate in sports and other extracurriculars, so I gravitated toward my art classes—the only subject that could hold my attention. There had to be a job I could do in photography out in the world, I thought. The idea of making pictures in an artistic way and living a sustainable life doing so seemed like a way out, a life that I could be proud of.

Self-portrait in my grandmother's bedroom. Cedar Rapids, Iowa, 2022.

I enrolled into the University of Iowa as a first-generation college student. I had saved up some money to buy my own camera and took it with me wherever I went. I had no real direction or intent with any of my pictures, but I was always shooting and developing images until I had hundreds of my family, friends, myself, and the landscape. My imagery varied and told no real story at first glance, but at some point the images clicked in my mind. I noticed that the moments I had captured were based on the dissemination of my inner emotions and experiences. My eye would perk up when a moment aligned with a past experience: my adolescent resentment, my frustrated curiosity of why things had to be this way.

This photo series has taken on many forms over the years. At heart, it is a visual diary seeking to confront my past and my tumultuous relationships in and with my hometown. It spans roughly over a decade, from when I left high school through subsequent visits home. The act of making pictures in this space has been a cathartic process, aimed toward better understanding past actions and emotions while attempting to mend the frail relationships I keep returning to.

My mother, Lynne Gale, smoking a cigarette in the bathroom, Cedar Rapids, Iowa, 2018.

My grandma, Evelyn Saldana, sewing at the dinner table in Cedar Rapids, Iowa, 2015.

Jordan Gale is a photographer based in Portland, Oregon. His photographs examine human relationships, community, and American politics.

WHEN MY FATHER CALLED ME ABOUT HIS UNEMPLOYMENT

Lisa Ventura

Slate, December 23, 2020

> I cheer the new benefits. I also know exactly who will continue to bear this burden.

I'm sitting in my living room writing progress notes for work—I am a New York City housing case manager—while navigating Connecticut's Department of Labor website in a different tab. I'm filing for unemployment for a fifty-seven-year-old car mechanic for Chevrolet, who was just furloughed after two years. The process takes about three hours, the beginning of a weekly routine to receive checks that won't even cover the man's bills.

And with that, my own twenty-case workload now includes one more unofficial client: my father.

I'm not alone. The skills some of us have navigating bureaucracy are suddenly necessary for the survival of millions of people who never needed them before the pandemic downturn. So many children of parents like mine have become the translators and saviors of their aging mothers and fathers with no skills for this.

My own father's education stopped at eighth grade in the Dominican Republic. A first-generation immigrant, he speaks mostly Spanish. And I have the human services and administrative skills, which I got as the first in my family to go to college. My father lacks the language, knowledge, and computer access to even attempt applying for pandemic-related unemployment and other benefits on his own. While I cheer the new $900 billion COVID stimulus package approved by Congress to include three hundred dollars more per week for laid-off workers like my father—and many of my friends as well—I know it means I will be busy saving him through paperwork for another few months at least as well.

My resentment isn't only with the system. When I was a kid, my father was never around. He and my mother divorced when I was five years old. My mother, brother, and I moved in with my grandmother in a one-bedroom apartment in Washington Heights. My father would disappear for months at a time, calling occasionally to check in or to say he would be picking my brother and me up on the weekend. We would then excitedly wait for his call to say he was on his way, or better yet that he was already downstairs ready to take us to McDonald's. More times than not, the call never came.

My father does not have the words to tell me how proud he is of me for beating the odds, for succeeding despite his little involvement in my life, for making do while my mother provided for my siblings and me with the help of public assistance. He is a prideful Dominican man, finally renting his own apartment after years in rented rooms. I know that while he now requests my help—embarrassed, no doubt—he did not make an effort to attend my college graduation or any momentous occasions.

Yet today, as a grown-up, a housing case manager, I know I must help my father through this continued social crisis. I navigate the system all the time, so I know how these things work. My father does not have these survival skills. And I worry he's at risk in other ways. An avid cigarette smoker who is constantly feeling chest pains or experiencing breathing problems due to the nature of his job, he is at a greater risk of serious illness from this virus. Plus, he is single. Although he has a sister nearby, he does not get along with her, so there is no one else but me.

When I file for his benefits, I use my own email address because I know I will receive all the correspondence to translate and clarify for him. I have him send pictures of all the furlough paperwork, along with his Social Security and permanent resident card numbers. I read through unemployment paperwork. (I cannot assist him financially myself because I, too, am pressed for cash, with school loans, a mortgage, and two young children at home, whom I also coteach while my partner works thirteen-hour days.)

It takes a few days for the application to be approved, and in the meantime, he contacts me constantly to see if I have heard anything back from unemployment, unlike the days of my youth when I would wait weeks for him to call just to be taken to McDonald's. He asks if I can call the hotline to follow up and make sure his application was completed properly. I tell him that during the pandemic this process can take longer than usual. I attempt calling anyway to appease him but cannot get past all the automated machines.

Once the application is finally approved, I am then in charge of filing his claims every Sunday thereafter. Every Saturday evening or early Sunday morning, he reminds me to file his claims to get paid the coming Monday.

The benefits, when they do come, have been barely enough up until now, a mere four hundred dollars a week to pay for rent, utilities, groceries, cell phone, and cable, and to wire money to my older siblings in the Dominican Republic—my sister, who has four children and no job. At the Chevrolet dealership, he made about twenty-two dollars per hour, or thirty-three dollars an hour when working overtime.

As the pandemic continues, seemingly indefinitely, I have trained myself each day to be more empathetic. As much as I want to hold on to my grudge for my father's shortcomings, I also know that COVID-19 could take him or anyone at any time, and in the meanwhile I need to give him the grace or forgiveness he deserves. I also fear he might be left without an income yet again. Unable to stay home because of restlessness, boredom, and a diminishing savings account, he might decide to go in search of work, placing his life at risk to stay alive.

For now, he is able to scrape together some money that, combined with potential payments from the new stimulus package, will provide him with enough to pay his bills. But only if I keep doing this paperwork. I love my father regardless and know he loves me, although he does not tell me often.

CODA

Unfortunately, my father never returned to the dealership where he was being paid a steady salary with benefits. Once the unemployment checks ran out and the COVID frenzy died down, he had to figure out ways to make ends meet. Since then, he's found consistent work at an auto body shop doing what he does best. However, he does not have any benefits and so he must continue living with uncertainties—

without medical insurance or a retirement plan. Neither of us knows what lies ahead, but even under those uncertainties, he just takes it day by day, expressing he's content enough with having a roof over his head and cars to occupy himself with.

Since writing the article, our bond has strengthened, and we've continued visiting each other during holidays and special occasions. I felt terribly once I shared my truth regarding the resentment I felt toward him. In hindsight, however, I acknowledge it was necessary to reshape the narrative I repeatedly played in my head. It made me realize it was never too late to forge a more nurturing father-daughter relationship.

As for myself, after what felt like a debilitating panic attack, I decided to resign from my position as a case manager to nourish myself emotionally and physically with the intention of becoming a stay-at-home, full-time writer-mom. So far, the resignation has proven to be exactly what my mind, body, and soul needed. It was finally clear to me that I was burned out, there was no other solution but to leave without a plan in place. I, like my father, am living a life filled with uncertainties but my writing life keeps me afloat. Perhaps, this is also how my father feels while doing the thing he loves most.

Lisa "Rubi G." Ventura (she/her) is a Washington Heights–bred, Black Dominican poet, essayist, teaching artist, and author of *Con qué papel me envuelves la luna?* Lisa has been published by Dominican Writers, *Raising Mothers*, and Economic Hardship Reporting Program in conjunction with *Slate*, as well as NatureCulture's, *Writing the Land* anthology. She was interviewed for the *Nation*'s *Going for Broke* podcast and documentary series as well as *Refinery29*'s Somos. Lisa is a VONA 2022 alumna and featured poet for the Morris-Jumel Mansion, and her work has been showcased by the Bronx Academy of Arts and Dance, the Billie Holiday Theatre, Bold Voice Collaborative, and IDEA Cultural.

I TOOK IN A HOMELESS COUPLE—WOULD YOU?

Annabelle Gurwitch

Los Angeles Times, September 2, 2019

The first few nights that two strangers spent under my roof, I couldn't sleep. I stashed a rusty hatchet under my bed. The blade was so dull that the best I could have hoped for was that it might cause a tetanus infection. What had I been thinking when I invited a young homeless couple—and their pet rabbit—into my house?

This June, I participated in Safe Place for Youth's Host Home Program, short-term "interventions" for unhoused young people, ages eighteen to twenty-four. In December, stuck in LA traffic, my ears had pricked up. Marlene and Michael Rapkin were on the radio describing an inspiring three months they'd spent as two of Safe Place's initial cadre of hosts.

"Welcoming the stranger" is one of my core Jewish values, and I'd helped with the annual homeless count. I knew the problem was serious—one in ten young people in the US experience homelessness in a twelve-month period. But could I take in someone off the street? What with a recent divorce, my kid's stint in rehab, and college expenses, I'd been renting out a guest bedroom to make my monthly nut. But when a tenant canceled, and I learned that Safe Space offered a small stipend to offset hosts' household expenses, I challenged myself to "walk the walk" of my social justice values.

In its host training sessions, Safe Place provided helpful prompts advising us that "youth will sometimes make choices we don't agree with" and that our guests were most likely without shelter "through no fault of their own." Its get-to-know-you host-guest picnic was not unlike a Match.com mingle, and afterward, I offered to house any of the youths I'd met *except* that heavily tattooed couple. She had the word "cured" in bold block lettering on one cheek and "More Love" above her brow; his forehead read "Less Hate"; alas, a skater beanie obscured "Less."

So what if we'd agreed that hot coffee is vastly superior to cold caffeinated drinks, these two looked ... sketchy. Plus, I wouldn't feel safe being outnumbered. And the rabbit—my cat deems anything furry dinner. Then I learned that Keyawna and Jesse had been living—sweltering—in their 2008 Kia. I've complained that my marriage broke up because my spouse and I shared a bathroom. The least I could do was help keep that bunny alive.

Before my housemates arrived, I scrubbed the guest bathroom and put out the good sheets and towels. But I also hid my jewelry and the sterling silver flatware in my bedroom closet. The couple showed up hours late.

"Irresponsible," I thought.

"Unorganized," I told my friend Judith, who promptly reminded me that I'd once been three hours late for a lunch date.

Right away, my inner circle fretted for my safety. "Text me before you go to bed," urged one message. I made light of my fears by keeping a running tally: "It's been twenty-four hours and my house hasn't burned down!" Meanwhile, Keyawna and Jesse occupied themselves with suspicious activities like preparing salads, unloading the dishwasher (unprompted), feeding the predatory cat, calling their mothers, and joining the congregation of a church.

They didn't owe me their story, but they wanted to share it. They'd grown up in the Rust Belt, where one in five children are raised in poverty. (Alison Hurt, executive director and founder of Safe Place, says most of the young people she serves are "children of the working poor.") Between them, Keyawna and Jesse had experienced home foreclosures, utility shutoffs, transiency, and the economic blow of family members with health problems. Each had forfeited a college scholarship, partly out of a desire to contribute to their families' strained finances and partly to pursue a future in the capital of creativity.

Safe Place likes to match hosts and guests with shared backgrounds. I, too, had come to LA to further my artistic pursuits. I, too, had dropped out of college due to my family's financial woes. I funded my relocation by selling stocks I'd been given as a bat mitzvah present from a family friend; they'd worked minimum-wage, manual labor jobs.

Keyawna had arrived first. She lucked out, landing a job as a personal assistant and a house-sitting situation. But the job ended, Jesse joined her, and they lost their savings paying up front for a nonexistent Airbnb rental. I'd hit LA with the advantages of industry contacts, a few local ties, and deeper pockets. They knew no one and faced a much tighter housing market. In 1989, I paid $750 for an apartment that today would go for $2,800. Soon Jesse and Keyawna were couch surfing, and then, the car.

"Why don't they get service jobs?" a friend asked. I had an idea why, having tried and failed to help my own kid get a summer dishwashing job. In 1989, I easily scored a steady hostessing shift, but Jesse and Keyawna were subject to the vagaries of the gig economy. Their attempts to put together first and last month's rent, and a security deposit, by "juicing" Lime electric scooters and Postmating proved unsuccessful.

Still, that phrase "through no fault of their own" floated through my head. They'd *chosen* expensive LA. But if the city can't accommodate artists from economically diverse backgrounds, then only the privileged will get to create. I was also certain face tats were job killers, until Keyawna explained that they fit their "brand," and most were Jesse's designs. He's a visual artist; she's an aspiring rapper and soul singer.

At one point, Jesse showed me a picture of his parents. "In case you wanted to know," he said. What he meant was, in case I wasn't already convinced that he was loved, lovable, loving. I'd bounced around a lot when I moved to town, but I never felt compelled to prove my humanity by showing a picture of my parents to those who hosted me.

During their last days under my roof, I invited Keyawna into my closet so we could ferret out clothing for a music video she was shooting. In clear view of my jewelry and silver, I was abandoning every last "us" and "them" I'd been clinging to. Every boundary I'd set was crossed. (She told me later they'd hidden their valuables from me too.)

Six out of the six youths in Safe Place's inaugural Host Home Program ultimately landed in permanent housing, and there's every reason to hope Keyawna and Jesse will too. They are currently living with another Safe Place host family. The model is so promising, the Los Angeles Homeless Services Authority is helping to fund its expansion here. With approximately 500,000 single-family homes in Los Angeles, if only 10 percent of homeowners participated, we wouldn't see any young people living on our streets.

After Keyawna and Jesse left, I found bits of pulpy bunny litter lodged in the nooks and crannies of my home and a note thanking me for changing their lives. But it was *my* default otherizations that got reset, *my* assumptions that were corrected. I never did ask Keyawna why she had "cured" inked on her cherubic face, but I hope she stays that way. Although I expect to remain tattoo free, Jesse's "More Love, Less Hate" combo does hold a certain appeal.

Annabelle Gurwitch is a *New York Times* bestselling author of five books, a Thurber Prize for American Humor Writing finalist, and an actress. Her writing frequently appears in the *New York Times*, the *Washington Post*, the *Los Angeles Times*, and *Los Angeles Magazine*. This essay, which was awarded an Excellence in Journalism citation by the Los Angeles Press Corp, is included in a longer form in her most recent collection of essays, *You're Leaving When? Adventures in Downward Mobility*, a *New York Times* Favorite Book for Healthy Living 2022.

MY MARRIAGE WAS BROKEN—THE CORONAVIRUS LOCKDOWN SAVED IT

Robert Fieseler

Huffpost, April 18, 2020

"They turned the lights off yesterday, in the apartment," my husband, Ryan, said when he picked me up from the airport. I saw his hands trembling on the wheel. "I didn't want to ruin your happiness."

I'd just returned from New York with a surprise win at an awards ceremony for my debut book, *Tinderbox*. This was nearly a year before the COVID-19 pandemic overtook America. Awards don't equal money. We had none. I put my hand on his shoulder. He knew I was sorry but didn't want to hear another apology.

My words got us into this mess: My book had eaten our relationship. It was a critical hit still netting accolades—but it hadn't earned royalties. It claimed our 401(k). Then it exhausted our lines of credit. We went from living check to check to living day to day. Ten dollars became a saving grace.

When we got home, Ryan went into the bedroom and wept audibly. I tried to hold him there, to comfort him, but it was no good. My arms shielded him from nothing. I set my new award across from me, on the shelf in our living room, and I stared into the statue's sphinx-like face occasionally lit by the headlights of passing cars.

After more than a year of that game—fronting prosperity while touring the book basically for free—I found Ryan one evening sitting in the kitchen with a whiskey. He told me he had to beg his parents for more money—a shameful, pathetic thing in this country. He told me I'd been selfish with my book career, which monopolized my time and didn't pay the bills. He said he used to trust me with our finances and now needed space.

I started crying, terrified, knowing what he said to be true. He cried seeing me cry, and I asked if we were separating. It turns out we were—functionally if not legally. He took the dog, the one I'd raised since puppyhood, and his computer, the one he used to retouch photographs and earn our income while I traveled the country giving lectures and readings. He went off to stay with his parents in rural Kentucky, and I remained in self-isolation in New Orleans. Then COVID-19 hit.

How did we get here?

I had dreams of publishing a book that mattered, which required four years' research on the typical modest advance awarded to debut authors—$22,500, the second half delivered almost a year late and without interest in 2018. The effort sapped our finances and pushed us to the brink of starvation. According to the Authors Guild 2018 Author Income Survey, most who define themselves as full-time book authors earn a median income of $20,300 per year. The *lucky* ones skate beneath the federal poverty line, presenting themselves as charismatic members of the intelligentsia when they're actually paupers. One-quarter of all published authors, according to the same survey, would predictably earn zero dollars in book income last year, like me.

The media industry, in contraction since the late 2000s, already existed in perpetual purge, sweeping full-time journalists and their costly benefits from payrolls. Ayn Rand won. Only titans matter. With the COVID-19 downturn, this dynamic will likely accelerate, converting more full-timers into shit-out-of-luck freelancers, who will join the swell of twenty million-plus Americans filing new jobless claims.

Every author in publishing is, by contractual definition, a freelancer; when contracts end, you're out of work. Amid the ever-present fear of surface contamination, fewer readers want reading materials delivered to their doors, and books are being delayed as nonessential or not sent from Amazon warehouses. As indie bookstores plead through GoFundMe campaigns and authors launch titles using Zoom, publishers fear that each release will become the literary equivalent of stillborn.

Ryan and I appeared to be at the end of our "first marriage" when COVID-19 struck. We both woke up, alone, more than five hundred miles apart. And then he called. It was St. Patrick's Day weekend, right when Spain closed its borders.[1] He said he was scared. This is my fault, I told him. He said he missed me. I asked if he was so fed up that he needed to shelter out the pandemic in separate places: "Are you mad enough to risk dying apart?" He paused a long pause, and I thought he was going to ask for a divorce. But no—I'm stupid lucky. He asked me to join him and take refuge with his family at their remote place in Kentucky.

After a harrowing ride to the airport, with the Uber driver hacking phlegm, I texted my husband, "I love you." Armstrong airport looked like the last scene in *12 Monkeys*, with crowds of people laughing and hugging and handshaking and high-fiving while a virus had an orgy. Ryan promised to pick me up in Nashville, and my flight left the gate with half the cabin empty.

After we landed, I caught sight of my husband in the car and nearly fainted from relief. He smiled and winked at me. His hazel eyes shimmered. I'd still want to date him if we met as strangers. Before I hopped in, I stripped my outer clothes in the arrivals line and place them in a trash bag. I tore off my mask and latex gloves and tossed them in a nearby can. Then I "deloused" in our back seat with sanitizer. More than disinfecting, I kept thinking, the madcap process felt akin to Blanche DuBois trying to wash her life's disgrace down her sister's bath. "Thank Goddess!" Ryan exclaimed as he pealed out. "I'm so glad you made it." When we got to my in-laws' house, I did a final decontamination with soap and water in the freezing outside shower.

Imperceptibly, we started living by plague rules, and plague rules usurp the usual pantomime of class respectability. Plague rules turn the tables and place life over livelihood, while the opposite is usually true. Artists do well by plague rules, which remove all guarantees and say anyone living is richer than anyone dying. They ask the big questions—not "Where's your savings?" or "How big of a nest did you make?" but "Who do you love?" and "What did you make of this game of existing?" With your last cough and breath, it doesn't matter if you packed your nest like pharaoh packed his tomb. Nothing in the nest is going with you, and nothing in the nest is going to save you.

I was of the generation that believed all the Eminem bullshit about taking your one shot—one opportunity to seize everything you ever wanted in a moment. You white-knuckle the risk and hope everything pays off like a magic trick. When I published, my mentors warned me never to let an audience see me sweat; because success or failure can't be random in showbiz—the instant someone gets the whiff of a book in commercial peril, they'll fault the work and sideline the writer. Ayn Rand smiles from the grave. Titans rule. Third prize is you're fired.

This is what you do if you've wanted to write and publish a book that matters since you were five years old but were born in the middle of Midwest nowhere: You hide the hustle. You affix a smile and hide the damage where no one sees it, where only he can see it. You fail your husband when you should have failed your book.

The day Ryan kissed me again, after a morning hike, was the same day I applied for a $1,000 grant from the PEN America Writers' Emergency Fund—a charitable lifeline for impoverished authors that recently expanded to help those affected by COVID-19. By chance, that day also happened to be our second wedding anniversary. Before I pressed "send" on the online submission, I asked my husband if it was okay to spill our broke-ass story to the PEN folks. "Yes," he said. "It's time we stop lying for your publisher, for your pride." As the novelist Zora Neale Hurston once wrote, "If you are silent about your pain, they'll kill you and say you enjoyed it."

My husband put his hand over mine. We pressed "send" together, and our rings clinked. "It's all bullshit," he said. "The way they treat artists . . . and the shit people do to feed themselves. The way the rich and their companies can break us." We stood and kissed. It was the long kiss of a couple that kissed for fifteen years and then stopped kissing for two weeks. In a capital world, a paper-thin dollar became the one barrier we couldn't overpower. But that was before a deadly disease, which broke the markets and brought us back together.

Robert W. Fieseler is a National Lesbian and Gay Journalists Association "Journalist of the Year" and the acclaimed debut author of *Tinderbox: The Untold Story of the Up Stairs Lounge Fire and the Rise of Gay Liberation*—winner of the Edgar Award and the Louisiana Literary Award, shortlisted for the Saroyan International Prize for Writing. Fieseler is presently working on his second queer history book, which was a finalist for the J. Anthony Lukas Work-in-Progress Award. He graduated co-valedictorian from the Columbia Journalism School and lives with his husband and two kittens in New Orleans.

P.S. 42

Celina Su, with a photo by Annie Ling

The Believer, April 24, 2020

Livingroom detail in the home of Mrs. Fung, who is a homebound resident of a tenement building on Pell Street in Chinatown.

That's what I remember now: That you couldn't escape. That she was really cool, with bell bottoms and long hair. She was trained in open classrooms. [These bright fluorescent lights, a link to the outside world.]

She gave us extra math tutoring during what would have been a lunch break. They didn't have the missionary syndrome (coming down here to save "the poor Chinese people"), a white savior complex. That you make your own choices. With guinea pigs, frogs, baby chicks. [The school bell rings.]

We played crab soccer, because there wasn't enough room for regular soccer. We would line up against opposite walls, ready on all fours. Roll call: 1, 4, 5. That they emphasized good sportsmanship, not to tease. That we would crawl out on our backs, backward like crabs. [Rolling back on the office chair.]

The time I was put in the closet for being defiant during music class. That was when I realized I don't scare easily. That I admired the wroughtiron vents on the coat closet doors. [Returning a wave to a student, bending down to meet his eyes: *Hi!*]

That during parent-teacher conferences, my mother brought wonton soup for all the teachers, because she knew it was a long night. That when I didn't get a reader, she gave the teacher a piece of her mind: *Just because my daughter's last name is Wong, doesn't mean that you don't give my child a reader, that you ran out. No such thing.* [An emphatic nod. She was a real tough cookie.]

That I got a reader. On cold winter days, a twenty-five-cent knish shaken with salt in a paper bag. That it was the best thing. That I learned to read and write. [A sheer purple curtain, tied to the side in a knot.]

Roll call: The knish man, the pickle man across the street. Mr. Plaskowitz, Mr. Carrow. Ms. DiSilvestro. Ms. Moringelli, Ms. Crane. Ms. Wong. Presente. That's why I came back. I want to be here.

Celina Su was born in São Paulo, Brazil, and lives in Brooklyn. Her first book of poetry, *Landia*, was published by Belladonna in 2018. Her work focuses on everyday struggles for collective governance; her current book project centering radical democracy, *Budget Justice: Racial Solidarities & Politics from Below*, is forthcoming from Princeton University Press. Her writing includes three poetry chapbooks, three books on the politics of social policy and civil society, and pieces in journals such as *n+1*, *Harper's*, the *New York Times Magazine*, and elsewhere. Su is the Marilyn J. Gittell Chair in

Urban Studies and a professor of political science at the City University of New York.

Annie Ling was born in Taipei and is based in Chinatown, Manhattan. Her work is in the collection of the Museum of the City of New York, and the National Museum of Iceland. Her solo show, "A Floating Population," at the Museum of Chinese in America, featured more than eighty images spanning four years of work. She is the recipient of a NYFA fellowship and a director's fellowship from the International Center of Photography. Annie also holds an MFA from the Yale School of Art, where she was awarded a Critical Practice Research Grant, and was a fellow at the Center for Collaborative Arts and Media. www.annielingphoto.com.

MY SISTER IS A RECOVERING HEROIN ADDICT—I CAN'T FIX HER, BUT SHE ALSO CAN'T FIX HERSELF

Elizabeth Kadetsky

Vox, November 19, 2015

My sister, Jill, is brilliant—a Phi Beta Kappa and a graduate, like me, of New York City's Stuyvesant High School. She regularly scores over four hundred in Scrabble and can race through the Sunday *Times* crossword. She reads and writes in four languages, plays Beethoven's Emperor Concerto on the piano, and devours classics and contemporary literature. But none of that has protected her from a life of drug addiction, mental illness, and homelessness.

"How come you're different?" my mother once asked me, meaning, "Why wasn't I afflicted by addiction as well?" Our mother's mother, Jill's and my "Grandmaman," was toxic in body and mind, a bottle-of-bourbon-a-day alcoholic. Perhaps addiction was a recessive gene in our family. "I'll think about tomorrow," I told my mother, who also never suffered from addiction. I don't think either of us had an answer apart from genetics.

I USED TO WANT TO BE JUST LIKE MY SISTER

Jill's lifetime of drug use has shaped not just her life but much of mine.

Jill went to junior high at a fancy prep school in Manhattan where drugs were ubiquitous. She experimented—and introduced me to drugs. For me, the next day's recovery seemed to take up too much time. Instead, I enjoyed Jill's war stories—how the soil in a planter box came alive one time after she took belladonna; how a friend's hair turned to lightning rods one time while Jill was tripping on acid. Still, people mistook us for one another; I remember how proud I felt one time when I was in junior high and Jill in high school, and a mutual acquaintance ran up to me in Central Park with a joint in her hand and hugged me. "Jill!" she cried.

"You're all drunk and tripping," our mother ranted one time when we were both in high school, upon walking in on the two of us during a party in our living room hosted by Jill. Our mother lifted her arms in the air, shook her head dramatically, and retreated to her bedroom. Our mother often said she thought we'd grow out of our self-destructive behavior. She also said she was thankful we were doing drugs at home and not out on the streets.

I REALIZED SHE HAD A SERIOUS DRUG PROBLEM

The fact of Jill's addiction came into focus for me when I was in my late twenties and she was about thirty. It was the early '90s; the echo of Kurt Cobain's guitar had migrated to New York City, and heroin was de rigueur at the Lower East Side clubs. A talented guitarist and singer, Jill haunted that scene. I enjoyed going out with her and even tried heroin once—though in my case I threw up, fell asleep for twenty-four hours, and missed work for a week.

After that, I limited myself to observation. There was a dealer in the basement of a bodega on East Twelfth Street, Jill told me; you went underground through a tunnel and entered a bathroom, where you knocked on a medicine cabinet; the mirror swung open and a hand emerged offering a baggie of dope. At the El Sombrero Mexican restaurant on Ludlow Street—"the Hat"—you could smoke H in the bathroom and sit forever at a table where you'd see other acquaintances also nodding and never ordering food.

Some people exist breezily in such a world without ever succumbing to the temptation for everlasting euphoria or escape—me, for instance. But for Jill, drugs perhaps salved some wound. At a Thanksgiving during that era, Jill went seemingly blank for an extended moment, her eyes shut, the contents of her plate spilling to the floor. Soon after that, we visited our father and his second family up in Boston, and Jill went out and returned with two six-packs and slurred speech. I knew what other family members seemed to be denying or ignoring or, in the case of our mother, blatantly rejecting. When, one time, I tried to talk to my mother about it, she accused me, "Why are you so hard on Jill?"

AND I DISCOVERED I DIDN'T WANT TO BE LIKE HER ANYMORE

Like little sisters everywhere, I'd admired my older sister and emulated her. Perhaps this was why I took her fall so hard, why I felt abandoned. Like our mother, Jill was exotic—ballsy and gorgeous. I'd adopted not only her quirks and mannerisms but her worldview. I copied her emotional fragility—the meltdowns, the weeks of consuming sadness. Like Jill, I harbored anger and resentment. Our father was often the target, for favoring his children by his second wife, for making us feel shame for our second-class position in our family. I borrowed Jill's general aura of detached, sometimes humorous fatalism.

But then one day, Jill vented on the telephone to me about our father. It occurred to me that if it wouldn't kill Jill, bearing her disposition would certainly kill me. I needed to stop thinking about what was wrong in my life and focus on the positive. I wanted to stop brooding. I wanted to heal.

In 1995, Jill had a series of outbursts at her job in book publishing, and her supervisor asked her to take a mental health leave. Jill claimed the leave was unwarranted, and she quit instead. I'm not sure Jill considered the possibility she had mental health issues at all until 1997, when at age thirty-four she entered counseling for addiction during her first attempt at recovery. She began speaking of her issues with chronic pain and depression.

After that, Jill moved in with our mother and joined a methadone maintenance and counseling program at Bellevue Hospital.

Later, there were more telephone rants, Jill's fury sometimes directed at me. She began taking benzodiazepines, which when mixed with methadone can bring on an opioid euphoria and, like heroin, addiction. When I asked her to seek more help for her drug use, she called me self-righteous and superior. I was making a living as a writer; Jill was still unemployed. She said she resented my success at life, that I made her feel like a loser. I worked hard to avoid guilt or a creeping sensation that I was implicated in her downfall or should fall alongside her in solidarity. I tried to nourish rather than diminish my drive to succeed. I believed she wished me failure.

I began to see Jill only when I visited my mother. There were ups and downs. She apologized, began consenting agreeably when I made suggestions but often without actually taking them. She'd flare up again.

I wonder what I would have done differently if I'd accepted the reality of her depression earlier. I imagined I was helping each time I begged her to attend recovery or when I did the research to discover good programs or ways to pay for them. I attended Al-Anon and learned that one must strike a balance between detaching and enabling, that one should strive toward a stance someplace in the middle, of loving strength. For me, the pain of the situation led to frustration and distance. Perhaps I would have found a more elegant middle ground if I'd accepted from an earlier age that I was not Jill, much as I wanted to be. Freeing myself from that thinking would have allowed me to see the more important truth: that Jill was not me.

THE DEFINING MOMENT

Things were unstable if predictable in our family, Jill continuing to live with our mother, until one day in June 2011. I got a call from someone who'd been buzzing over an hour at the apartment in Long Island City, Queens, shared by Jill and our mother—who had by now been diagnosed with midstage Alzheimer's. I rushed over. Inside, our mother followed me as we entered their shared bedroom. Jill was in a deep sleep on her bed with blood on her wrists; my mother sat down on the adjacent twin bed and looked over with an expression of confounded worry; she stared at me, stared at my sister, frowned, asked me what was going on.

I reached out to touch Jill's shoulder, my body operating as if in slow motion. She shook awake, which startled me and—for a second, anyway—allayed my panic. Had she taken pills, I thought to ask her. Jill spoke as if from underground. She'd cut herself with a broken glass at the sink, she said. She was tired. I didn't understand what it was like to be her, she added, and then she went back to sleep.

This defining moment would reverberate in our family for years to come, but it was weeks, even months, before I grasped that. Perhaps she was right that I'd mistakenly thought I understood her. I managed to get a call out to Jill's counselor at her methadone program at Bellevue. Over the course of the day, Jill and her counselor made plans to admit Jill at Bellevue's mental health ward for depression. Her counselor deemed her attempt to "take her life" with pills and a broken glass not serious—but it was a warning.

The problem was not resolved, but I moved on to the more imminent need: making arrangements for home care for our mother now that Jill would no longer be home with her to watch her. Though, really, who had been watching whom?

As it turned out, Jill's plan couldn't avert the next disaster. The next morning I was back across town, and Jill went out to do an errand in preparation for her hospital stay. By the time she returned home, our mother had gone missing. We couldn't locate her until a doctor at the ER at Elmhurst Hospital in Queens called that night to say she'd been there since the afternoon. My mother hadn't been able to provide her name or address, but the doctor recognized her from a previous stay. The hospital's care team, finally able to reach me, informed me what I already knew: our mother couldn't safely stay at her apartment.

For Jill, bad luck had led to bad choices had led to more bad luck one too many times. My mother would move to an assisted living in Brooklyn. Neither Jill nor I nor our mother could afford the apartment. Our mother would have to give up her home—Jill's home, as well.

Because of her drug use, Jill had either kept her distance from other family members or alienated them, as she had me. Our mother's illness had brought me closer to Jill again. But at that crossroads in 2011, taking her into my home was out of the question: I didn't have the space, Jill didn't want to move in with me, and most, though I loved my sister, I didn't trust the addict.

Jill's place of residence became her bed at the Bellevue mental health ward. She was forty-seven.

JILL'S HARROWING YEARS
IN NEW YORK CITY'S HOMELESS SHELTERS

Jill was not discharged from Bellevue until September 2011, after a delay of several weeks while her counselors worked with her to find her "a bed"—as a free spot to live is euphemistically called for the homeless. The next several months passed tumultuously for Jill, but my own focus was elsewhere: Our mother was dying.

Our mother's assisted living began sending her almost weekly to the various hospitals in Brooklyn for issues untreatable by their nonmedical staff; those issues often revolved around their desire to have her medicated. While I attempted to advocate for our mother and refuse additional drugs for her, Jill moved from Bellevue to a one-month rehab in Poughkeepsie. She was discharged with a referral to a so-called three-quarter house called Narco Freedom in the South Bronx,[1] whose operators have since been sent to jail and indicted on charges of taking kickbacks and perpetrating Medicaid fraud.[2] The house offered its own Medicaid-funded methadone maintenance program and counseling, and in fact required its residents attend it—which was the nature of the fraud. Jill didn't discover this until she arrived, however, and, wanting to continue her positive relationship with the counselor and program at Bellevue, refused to shift her Medicaid funding. Her only alternative was to leave.

Jill next checked herself in at the city's intake shelter for women in Jamaica, Queens, and two days later was given a permanent shelter assignment at the Park Slope Women's Shelter, which is sandwiched into a section of the beautiful and historic Armory on Eighth Avenue. A third-floor apartment across the street is listed for sale today at $1.15 million. The Department of Homeless Services' annual performance rankings praise a handful of women's shelters, and Park Slope Women's ranked fourth out of twenty shelters for single women that year. Still, come winter, Jill told me that life was just too hard in the shelter, and she was finding it hard to stay off benzos. She was addicted, she said, and wanted to detox and reenter a long-term rehab. She went back to Poughkeepsie, then a month later returned to Park Slope Women's, and it wasn't another few months before she called me again to tell me the same thing. She was depressed, life was too hard, and she was thinking about going back to the rehab.

Then in October 2012, Hurricane Sandy struck. Jill had been in the shelter system a year, and our mother, too, had survived those months in institutional living. Both were in crisis. It was as if chaos swirled in every corner of the sky above me. I sealed all my windows and got under the covers.

At about midnight my mother's assisted living called me to say they'd moved all the residents to another assisted living further inland in Brooklyn. Then another call came saying that my mother, disoriented in the new location, had refused to cooperate and had been sent to Maimonides Hospital in Brooklyn. I called Maimonides, and she wasn't there. I located her two days later, at Methodist Hospital in Brooklyn, ten blocks from Jill's shelter in Park Slope. Except Jill wasn't there—she'd disappeared, too.

Jill didn't turn up again for four weeks. A bank account I managed for her went stagnant, showing one ATM withdrawal near Poughkeepsie the night before the storm, and then nothing. Our father had kept his distance from Jill after several telephone tirades and one drug arrest; he was in the habit of expressing his concern by giving me money for her here and there, and by calling me and asking why Jill couldn't just get a job. Now even he began calling daily to encourage me to track Jill down. Part of me knew she'd gone to rehab, but part of me thought she'd been swept up in the storm, and part of me thought she'd gotten depressed and dived in the ocean with heavy boots on.

Jill called a month later, having returned to her permanent shelter in Park Slope. "Oh, sorry, I thought I told you I was going to rehab."

"I thought you were dead."

"I'm sorry."

Those were the easier days for Jill, if not for me. My phone and email records from the time show that I let my job suffer as I made contact after contact trying to help my mother and Jill.

Our mother never left Methodist. Even as I fought with the staff to resist her overmedication, she fell one night, sedated, while an attendant helped her from bed, and she broke her hip. Rehab went slowly. Jill visited her daily, and then one night the hospital called to say our mother had contracted fatal pneumonia. According to the doctor's prognosis, our mother had three to ten days of life left barring interventions, which she'd refused in her advance directives.

Jill and I took turns sitting with our mother. One day during our death watch, I bought a pocket radio at the Radio Shack across the street on Seventh Avenue, so our mother could listen to her favorite classical music. Her last words came during Mozart's bassoon concerto in B flat major: "That's nice."

Not long after, Jill relapsed again into benzodiazepine abuse and left the shelter in Park Slope to enroll, once again, at a rehab. After she was discharged, she ended up at a different shelter, one that was ranked third from the bottom of twenty shelters for single women. And for good reason: Over her nine months there, Jill described urine puddles and stacks of garbage at the elevator doors on each floor, particularly on weekends when the facility was short-staffed. Guards, counselors, housing aides, and desk clerks were hostile. Mail was intercepted or lost, including the all-too-common yet arbitrary notices to submit new qualifying documents in person at the Medicaid office.

One day, Jill intentionally missed curfew in order to get her shelter assignment switched, and succeeded in receiving a new assignment in Crown Heights. This proved equally dysfunctional, throwing hurdles in the path of survival at every turn. Jill's locker was burgled one day while she was attending her program at Bellevue. She lost all her medications, including antidepressants; Neurontin, for pain; and Seroquel, for sleep. She went to her clinic to ask for replacement prescriptions but was denied because of her history of pill abuse. She called to make an appointment with her psychiatrist and was told she could walk in, but when she walked in, on a weekend, she was told she needed an appointment. She went to the hospital emergency room but was told she'd have to admit herself for several days of observation before they'd consider a new prescription, and also that in the hospital they'd discontinue her methadone temporarily. Jill therefore went without, and became, not surprisingly, depressed.

The consequences were significant. The shelters are charged with helping residents locate permanent housing, but they require cooperation from their residents—for instance, residents must keep appointments for housing interviews, collate materials for their housing files, and stay abstinent. For the shelter resident facing such obstacles to everyday functioning, this is not easy. That week, Jill missed several housing appointments. She also overslept and missed her Saturday pickup for the weekend's methadone.

I'M WALKING A FINE LINE BETWEEN
ADVOCATING FOR MY SISTER AND ENABLING HER

By this time, I'd shifted my stance of detachment—but how to know where to draw the line to avoid enabling? I began to intervene for her. I called a friend who worked for an advocacy for mental health and asked for help getting Jill's Medicaid turned back on. I helped her recover prescriptions; I gave her warm clothing and last-minute cash; I organized her paperwork for an as-yet-unfiled Social Security Insurance application.

One time, she asked for cash because she was in a "life or death" emergency. I didn't ask for details—I didn't want to know. Was there a dispute over drugs? Did she score a Xanax because it was all so stressful? I gave her the cash. Later she explained that she'd overslept that Saturday and missed the window for her weekend-long supply of methadone. She faced withdrawal and a reprise of her chronic back pain. She'd needed the money to score heroin.

Now, was the H really necessary to ward away the withdrawal? Was there really no better solution? Should I have intervened further to create a better outcome? To what extent do I let her make mistakes on her own, or can I even prevent them?

I CAN'T FIX IT—AND JILL CAN'T FIX IT ON HER OWN EITHER

I do know I can't fix this myself. It's funny, because it's something I've often told Jill over the course of our lives: "I can't fix it"—as if to convince both Jill and myself that I, the so-called functional sister, am nevertheless not capable of solving the world's problems. "I can't fix it," I used to tell Jill when our mother, still living in her apartment, would leave her keys in the oven, put cookies in the cat bowl, leave the stove on with the cat litter box on top of it. She'd brush her teeth with Lysol, defecate in the shower. As our mother's Alzheimer's progressed, I hired a home care aide, and the aide showed up late one time.

"What am I supposed to do?" Jill ranted at me. "I can't live like this."

"I can't fix it," I said.

I do wish I'd had greater perspective earlier on. I wish I'd convinced our father, as I finally seemed to after the Sandy episode, that just "getting a job" after fifteen years' unemployment was not going to solve Jill's problems. I wish that the city's homeless services system put fewer roadblocks in the path of worthy recipients of aid, and that that worthiness wasn't judged on specifically the metrics that the homeless person is not able to reach.

What's most difficult for me is accepting that Jill can't fix things on her own either, that she has neither the tools nor the resourcefulness to take on the Sisyphean challenge before her. If I were in her situation I would act differently, but she is not me. The differences are too stark now to ignore this. No one runs up to us in Central Park with a joint anymore mistaking one for the other. I'm that university professor who argues with her son's daycare about the sugar content in breakfast cereal; Jill is the one who gets her cereal for free at the homeless shelter. Her four years in New York City's shelter system have shown me more clearly how her lifelong mental illness makes it impossible to take charge of her troubles.

The key seems to be some middle pathway of availing herself of the support on hand while also helping herself.

That negotiation seems connected to a conversation Jill and I often repeat about whether addiction is a condition or a choice. Lately, I've come around to a point of view that accepts her as her own person and not a mirror of myself, that understands "choice" is not as simple for her.

She seems to be accepting a view that incorporates more personal responsibility. "I need to stay stopped, one hundred percent," she wrote me recently. "Not even once in a while. That's what I've managed to put together. About two months so far with no use. Hurray for me! I'm just tired of Xanax. I don't need to be tranquilized or high. And things always work out better for me when I'm clean."

CODA

Rereading this essay, I see the chaos tearing through the container of the rational narrative I constructed—the world around us was disintegrating as our mother put cookies in the cat bowl and brushed her teeth with Lysol, and Jill sent me humorous texts that masked her despair. Keeping sane in such insane circumstances is a challenge for anyone, but it's clear now that the challenge was greater for Jill.

After five years in the shelters, Jill did succeed in filing for and obtaining disability through SSI, and gaining a spot in a "supportive living" arrangement managed by Catholic Charities. A fantastic aunt to my eight-year-old son, Jill seems to remain liberated from drug addiction, and lives in an owner-occupied duplex on a pleasant street in Woodside, Queens, that she keeps immaculate.

She contends with a dysfunctional roommate and caseworkers we find to be inadequate. Often, her medical prescriptions become un-fillable, subject to the quixotic decisions of ER personnel or the spotty availability of Medicaid-funded appointments. I continue to receive calls from ER staff, counselors, and legal staff to whom I must rationally explain that, indeed, Jill has been subject to circumstances that sound utterly irrational but are actually real.

I often come back to the question of whether Jill's addiction and the struggles that arose from it were the results of a mental health condition or simply the choices she made. I believe the answer is neither—and both. A more fitting dichotomy might involve the personal versus the collective. Many people come to the world with mental health challenges, or acquire them due to trauma. Our society has let these individuals down and compounded their woes by providing such meager support for them.

Elizabeth Kadetsky, a three-time Fulbright fellow to India, is author of a *The Memory Eaters*, a memoir of loss, nostalgia, and longing in the face of her mother's Alzheimer's and her sister's homelessness. *The Memory Eaters*, published by the University of Massachusetts Press in 2020, was winner of the Juniper Prize in creative nonfiction and was named a top pandemic read for March 2020 in *Buzzfeed*. Elizabeth has work recently published in *Chicago Quarterly Review* and *American Scholar*, and she coedits the nonfiction section at *New England Review*. She is the author of three previous volumes of fiction and nonfiction and many works of journalism and personal essay, which have appeared in the *New York Times* and elsewhere. She is an associate professor of creative writing at Penn State and can be found at www.elizabethkadetsky.com.

IN THE PANDEMIC, COOKING CONNECTED ME TO MY ANCESTORS

Elizabeth Gollan

Catapult, June 14, 2021

Sometimes life gives you a sourdough baguette toasted with fresh ricotta cheese and homemade cherry preserves. Oysters. Handmade cheese from far corners of France.

It's not hard to eat well, or cook well, on an unlimited budget. At other times, life gives you old lemons from the discount bin at Carnival Foods, on Beverley Road where the Rite Aid used to be. When that happens, give it back pickled lemons, lemon cake, lemon ices.

Turning simple ingredients into exquisite food is the stuff of fairy tales, fashioning culinary dross into gold; it's a magical power, a kind of alchemy. You are suddenly in the realm of the ancestors, the old country, or, sadly, in America and many other countries right now.

When the pandemic began last March, I had the funny sense that I had been through this before.

Except it wasn't me who had been through it. My ancestors had, and I took strength from the thought of them facing their own difficulties.

My family came from Poland, Romania, and Russia. Our memories started, in earnest, on this side of the ocean. All of us— great-grandparents, grandparents, aunts and uncles, and cousins— lived within a one-mile radius in Buffalo, New York. Our traditions are not discussed further back than my great-grandparents, because no one wanted to remember the war.

My grandparents crafted their own traditions out of the forbidden. My maternal grandfather, Irwin, would take us grandchildren out for steamed clams at Santasiero's, a simple Italian restaurant by the Niagara River, where we'd have the kind of food that sailors or working men would eat. My grandparents were flouting the traditions of their kosher parents by doing this: religious Jews don't eat clams because shellfish are considered unclean bottom-feeders.

My paternal grandfather, Murray, came to the United States in 1912, when he was two years old, from a small town on the border of Russia and Romania. Whenever the mood struck them, he and my grandmother would take us out for lobster dinner, riding through the city in his mint-green Cadillac Eldorado. Our destination: a North Buffalo place with walls decorated by nets, lobster traps, and buoys. It was called the Royal Pheasant, though I thought it was the Royal *Peasant* until I was in my thirties. Even now, I have to consciously correct myself when I recall its name.

On the way home from the Royal Pheasant, we'd stop to pick up treats for his mother, my great-grandma, Nana Jenny. She liked chocolate turtles and coffee ice cream from the turquoise-and-orange Howard Johnson on Delaware Avenue, the building shaped like a plastic chalet in Switzerland despite being here in Buffalo.

At eighteen, I started to hang out in New York City and felt free, finally, from Buffalo. I lived there some summers, reading Kafka and eating elephant-ear pastries at The Hungarian Pastry Shop on Amsterdam Avenue. There, I befriended a Polish refugee named Henri, who inscribed my copy of a Tatyana Tolstaya book: *For Elizabeth, who is like someone from Warsaw.* I had never been to Poland (still haven't), and my relatives rarely spoke about the past other than my mother's occasional mentions of her grandmother Henny ("She chewed on chicken bones because she loved the taste! She cooked mushroom stock for days!"). Still, I knew what Henri meant.

As the years went on, I forgot about that inscription and stopped eating elephant ears. I married, had babies, and cooked for my family. As a plant-based private chef, I brought dishes made of barley and lemons to Wall Street and other illustrious addresses. I thought only of the foods I grew up with on Jewish holidays, when I would make potato pancakes or kasha varnishkes, but I put the stories of chewing chicken bones away on a shelf in my mind and more or less forgot them.

When those babies had become young men, and the pandemic hit, the stories that once seemed mythical now came into focus. If my grandma could make soup from practically nothing—my mother recalled a giant stockpot of mushrooms, onions, salt and pepper, and "maybe paprika," in the age-old tradition—I would do the same. *I am not alone,* I thought, reaching for cabbage off the shelf of the food co-op while the state of the world looked more and more uncertain. All my ancestors felt near to me then. I could almost sense them beside me, as if the spattered index cards they'd left behind, with recipes written over blue lines, had come to life.

What was ours is cabbage. Rugelach, borscht. I pickled turnips and lemons, as if this would bring us home, and wrote menu plans for my husband and sons. In a frightening world, we still ate dinner at six, and we still ate well. It's hard to sustain fear in the face of a just-baked plum cake with almonds. Possible, of course, but harder.

I knew this drill from more than just ancestral memory. Six years ago, we moved to New York with two children and without any savings or jobs. Once, I found money on the street and could afford three bags of groceries at our co-op. I don't remember exactly what I bought, only that it really went far: precious olive oil, small yellow onions, chopped tomatoes in boxes, garlic. Some food to cook. Who could ask for anything more? I thought.

But you can't count on finding money. That night, after a delicious dinner, I read Enid Blyton's *The Secret Seven* to our nine-year-old, trying to stay connected to the plot and keep it all straight, who stole the diamond, why they were running, trying not to wonder what we would do when rent was due in four days.

During that time, I felt strange in the cookie aisle, staring at the $4.99 Newman's Own Mint Oreos I knew my kids would have loved. Things you don't buy when money gets too tight: anything bottled or packaged; anything brand-name, even if it includes Paul Newman's handsome face. Especially not his handsome face.

You scooch past things like that, which would last only twenty minutes in the hands of a man and two preteen boys. I grew lean and finally had the figure of my dreams: don't ask me how I did it, but I finally lost the ten pounds almost every woman in America seems to think she should lose. But if you ask anyway: in addition to not having any extra food, be too nervous to eat normally and walk every chance you get, especially near trees. In this way, you stay connected to nature and to some fundamental rhythm. Plum cake, branches of any tree, and an open sky: all was okay for the moment, and the stacking of moments makes a life.

Before last March, my co-op shift was part of my rhythm, ten people around a table bagging fruits and nuts. I could rely on it, the soothing, repetitive work of scooping rose petals, almonds, pine nuts, and loose Darjeeling tea into two-inch plastic bags. Once, someone dropped a box of two hundred organic Medjool dates onto the floor (valued at $111.30). Two fell; the rest, wrapped in layers of tissue, didn't even graze the floor. A co-op worker said, "We can't sell these by law. Throw them away, or take them home, if you like." Organic Medjool dates were staunchly in the unthinkable category, next to those fancy mint-chocolate cookies.

A box of organic Medjool dates is a fortune. I brought it home, lovingly put them into giant glass mason jars. For months after that, we savored them like delicacies fit for royalty.

I served the dates with roasted almonds and red wine on old china, lit those little silver tea lights, one hundred for five dollars at the Dollar Store. We always ate by candlelight, even when I was afraid to run out of matches.

This is my secret trick, one of the many treasures culled from those years, before new degrees and jobs brought us more. Anything at all that makes you feel rich, you do it. Think it, imagine it. Put it at the front of the cabinet so you keep on seeing it, until the day when the coffers are full. Magnify your richness, if you can.

Our landlords decided to sell their house last September. We spent six months looking for a new place. We looked in Bay Ridge, by the water. We looked around the corner from our last apartment, at a brick duplex with a rickety black porch over Dahill Road, near Carmelita's Flower Shop and a Bengali pharmacy. We could drink our coffee on the porch, we told each other. Instead, last January, we moved next door and downstairs. Our new landlord (and old neighbor), Freddie, and his wife, Charlotte, are in their seventies, and from Hungary. The apartment is cozy, patched together with a handmade wooden kitchen that makes it feel like you are on an old ship. They live upstairs, and we feel cozy. They murmur to each other in white plastic chairs outside our bedroom window in the morning, taking the sun.

We do member shifts at the Park Slope Food Coop again (shifts stopped in the pandemic) but they no longer occur on the same day each month, with an unchanging squad of members. Now, shifts are scheduled online, on whichever day works, a new group of people each time. "They broke the rhythm," I think. It's different to see the same crew every month. This shift is almost imperceptible, but its real; the erosion of a little tribe. Boxes of Medjool dates still line the shelves, but there are gaps, shelves full of boxes of apricots and figs. It's due to transportation or shortages, my shift leader said.

When the New York Department of Education lifted its mask mandate, my son said that only the really good-looking kids at his high school had taken theirs off. Many kids stayed hidden. Since they had started high school during lockdown, they'd never seen one another's faces, nor their teachers'. I tried to imagine the unveiling, or being taught by a teacher whose face you can't see. I cried, and then I baked a plum cake, a pot of leek soup, and preserved a jar of lemons. We sat down at six and lit the candle. I didn't eat steamers with my grandpa Irwin by the Niagara River, or drive in my grandpa Murray's long, green Cadillac not to know what to do. I imagine my great-grandma Jenny eating Howard Johnson's coffee ice cream from a white china bowl the size of a pack of cards; making the most of every bite, really tasting it.

VICHYSSOISE AND BE FANCY (POTATO-LEEK SOUP)

Serves 8

$4.50 per pot; 56 cents per serving (organic ingredients priced at Whole Foods)

Ingredients

- 3 medium leeks
- 2 medium russet potatoes
- Olive oil (extra-virgin, cold-pressed)
- Sea salt
- Water
- Pepper
- Nutmeg
- Parsley

Equipment

- Heavy pot
- Wooden spoon
- Hand mixer

Directions

Cut the leeks in half vertically, and wash them well in cold water, including the insides.

Cut the leeks into one-inch pieces and place them in a bowl.

Wash the potatoes, and cut them into one-inch pieces. Place them in a separate bowl.

Gently heat three tablespoons of olive oil in a heavy pot.

Add the leeks and a sprinkle of salt, and sauté with a wooden spoon until translucent and sweet smelling, about three to five minutes.

Layer the potatoes on top of the leeks.

Add cold water gently down the side of the pot, trying not to disturb the vegetables. Place a lid over the pot, turn the heat to medium-high, and bring it to a boil. Then reduce the heat and simmer for approximately twelve minutes, or until the potatoes are soft. Turn off the heat and blend the vegetables completely in the pot with a hand mixer.

Add one-quarter cup water, or enough to create a brothy and smooth soup when stirred. Add salt and pepper to taste. Drizzle with olive oil and garnish with nutmeg and finely chopped parsley.

Elizabeth Gollan is working on a book about her work as a caregiver and personal chef and the political and cultural meaning of those professions.

THE UNDERGROUND ECONOMY OF UNPAID CARE

Julie Poole

Yes! Magazine, July 12, 2022

In August 2021, when my sixty-two-year-old mother said hello on FaceTime, she was holding the side of her jaw, grimacing. She was in anguish, but kept repeating, "I'm okay, I'm okay."

At the time, my mom was living in Bellingham, Washington, two years into providing unpaid live-in care for her father-in-law (my step-grandfather, whom I reluctantly call "Grandpa," despite not having much of a relationship with him). He was suffering from debilitating cancer and heart disease. But providing home care to him came at a price to my mom's health, safety, financial security, and family. The job was all-consuming: she quit painting and gardening, which she loved, and she grew isolated from her own children and grandkids during the COVID-19 pandemic.

My mom's experience is not unique. She is among the roughly one in five Americans who provide care to an adult or child with special needs. Of the estimated 48 million people caring for adults, about 41.8 million provide unpaid care, just like my mother. While the work of unpaid caregivers is deeply undervalued, paid home care workers struggle too. Roughly two million people make up the home care workforce, which is 86 percent women, 60 percent people of color, and 14 percent immigrants. According to the National Domestic Workers Alliance, nearly 20 percent of these workers live in poverty, with and average hourly wage of $12.12 and annual earnings of $17,200.

In 2019, Grandpa had asked for my mother's help in exchange for room and board. The offer came just when she was on the brink of homelessness. But keeping up with the demands of caring for Grandpa meant she put her own health needs last. She hadn't seen a dentist in years, and her jaw pain traced back to an abscessed tooth that eventually would have to be pulled, along with three others. It was the first in a series of health issues that would eventually land her in the hospital.

In addition, the home environment began to feel unsafe for my mother. Shady visitors would show up at the house to do odd jobs and steal stuff. Grandpa also hoarded newspapers, and my mother worried about the potential fire hazard the stacks could create.

My mom's needs—for her health, finances, and personal happiness—have always taken a back seat. Raised in a strict Catholic family, she grew up believing women were supposed to care for others, whether blood relatives or not, and not pursue careers or dreams. When doctors found a tumor in my father's brain, my mom, then in her early twenties, set up a hospital bed in our dining room and tended to him for five years until he died. She later remarried, but her second husband stole her life insurance payouts, used them for drugs, and turned abusive. She got a restraining order, which he repeatedly broke. After selling our house, we spent three years moving around—living with family, in hotels and rentals, and in a tent—until my stepdad died and my mom felt safe enough to settle down and purchase a home.

In her forties, she returned to unpaid caregiving, first for her father, who had a heart attack and died six months later, and then for the last four years of her mother's life, and her mother had Alzheimer's. Then, my mom's then-boyfriend revealed he had cancer, so she cared for him until he, too, died. By her fifties, my mom was living below the federal poverty line, had lost her house, and had begun staying with relatives. She cared for grandkids and worked short stints as a housekeeper at hotels and nursing homes. She survived on a minimal government annuity check, the bulk of which went toward credit card debt and storage unit fees. In 2019, when relatives could no longer house her, she thought about living in her car, until she lost that too. That's when her late husband's father called.

My mom overheard Grandpa tell people he rescued her from homelessness by offering her room and board. While taking her in was a kind gesture, my mother was providing him with round-the-clock care—a job that paid caregivers in the state of Washington receive a living wage for. According to ZipRecruiter, paid live-in caregivers in Washington make more than the national average, which is about $17–$18 an hour, $35,360–$37,440 annually, and that the room provided is required to be clean and habitable. Every night, my mom tripped through the sea of clutter just to reach her bed. She kept her belongings in plastic storage bins in the bathtub.

The cost of caregiving can be devastating, especially for those with fewer resources. According to a 2021 study, 42 percent of unpaid caregivers have experienced job loss or reduced hours. In June 2020, when Colorado nursing student April Kimbrough learned her twenty-three-year-old son Da'Corey was diagnosed with a rare kidney cancer and had six months to live, she faced a terrible choice: keep her job at a hospice call center or accompany her son to his treatments.

"No mother should have to ask herself, 'Do I go to work, or do I sit by my son's side?'" Kimbrough said. Her employer didn't offer paid family leave and denied her requests to work remotely when her son needed chemotherapy. Ultimately, she lost her job and ended up living in her car. Kimbrough shared her story as part of the campaign to pass Proposition 118, which, starting in January 2023, will mandate paid family and medical leave in Colorado. But it's a benefit that came too late for Kimbrough. In May 2022, her son died.

"The system we currently rely on is built on the backs of the unpaid support of family caregivers . . . [They are] the invisible workforce that the government has just relied on," says Nicole Jorwic, the chief of advocacy and campaigns at Caring Across Generations, a caregiver advocacy group. Caregivers contributed an estimated $470 billion in economic value in 2017 but face rising financial strain. The 2020 AARP study found that of the 1,392 unpaid caregivers sampled, 28 percent had stopped saving, 3 percent filed for bankruptcy, and 2 percent were evicted or had their homes foreclosed upon.

Meanwhile, only a small portion of caregivers qualify for public support through the recipient's health insurance program. Medicaid programs offer Home and Community Based Services, which provide home health care, medical equipment, and physical therapy, as well as case management, home meal deliveries, transportation, and adult day care—necessary services that help people stay out of nursing homes. If an elderly recipient qualifies for these services, their benefits can be allocated toward compensation for their caregiver. While other non-Medicaid programs offer limited and short-term home care services, Medicaid is the largest funder and the principal way family caregivers can get paid.

But the national average wage for these caregivers is twelve dollars an hour. Eligibility for Medicaid services varies state to state, is income-based, and has income caps so low—$841 month in some states—they hover under the national poverty level.[1] If over 41.8 million people are unpaid adult family caregivers, and only 3.7 million elderly recipients receive HCBS through Medicaid, there's a good chance many people are not getting the benefits they qualify for, either because they aren't aware that financial help exists, because the process is too daunting, or because there's a national waitlist that averages more than three years long.

Barriers to care like these mean many family members step in, receiving no compensation in return. In my mother's case, Grandpa didn't qualify for Medicaid, which by default meant she didn't qualify for payment as his caregiver, because his income was too high. He received a pension and US Department of Veterans Affairs benefits, and had assets, including a house and three cars. She also didn't qualify to become his caregiver through the VA, because his medical conditions were not a direct result of his time in the service. Last, she missed out on accruing Social Security benefits that would have been available to her at age sixty-two had she been working an on-the-books job.

Meanwhile, my mother grew increasingly scared of the people loitering in and around the house. She installed a lock on her bedroom door to protect her belongings. A paid worker would likely have had somewhere to turn, an agency supervisor, possibly a social worker, but my mother had no advocate, and even a visiting social worker never pulled her aside, out of Grandpa's earshot, to see if she was okay, because she wasn't the patient or the client.

Christina Irving, the client services director at the Family Caregiver Alliance, says caregivers aren't on the radar of social workers and case managers, but they should be. "If caregivers aren't given a voice in care planning or conversations about health, then we're missing a lot," she says.

Today, caregivers are able to obtain support through organizations such as the Family Caregiver Alliance, the National Family

Caregiver Support Program, and online support groups, such as The Caregiver Space, which has a 7,900-member Facebook group. Jorwic notes that when caregivers share experiences, momentum builds, and legislators are forced to listen. Unpaid family caregivers start to see the work they do as worthy of payment. In cases where the care recipient doesn't qualify for Medicaid, Irving suggests that families draft Personal Care Agreements so family caregivers' financial health and well-being are better maintained.

For years, advocacy groups have been fighting systemic injustices within what's called the "care infrastructure." Organizations such as the National Domestic Workers Alliance, Caring Across Generations, and MomsRising want to see lasting and substantial changes: expanding Medicaid Home and Community Based Services, Paid Family and Medical Leave, affordable and quality child care, and wage increases for paid care workers, who are often also providing unpaid care for their own families. A robust movement has been forming around the #CareCantWait coalition.

Recently, California lawmakers moved to nearly eliminate monthly income and asset limits by July 1, 2022, which means more people will qualify for home- and community-based care. "Eliminating restrictive financial requirements," Jorwic says, will prevent older adults and people with disabilities from having to "spend down all of their personal assets before they can get the services they need, or remain in a state of poverty to keep them." Jorwic adds that this is something advocates will be pushing for on a federal level. "Everyone will need these supports, or will know someone who does."

In December 2021, I received a text from my sister that my mother had been admitted to the hospital. She had difficulty breathing and acute anemia from stomach ulcers. The doctor told her that had her blood cell count been much lower, she could have had a heart attack or a stroke, both of which are considered growing risk factors among family caregivers during the pandemic.

She told her father-in-law's extended family that she was no longer able to take care of him and moved into my younger brother's one-bedroom cabin in the woods to recover after her hospitalization, which was hours away from her doctors and other necessary services.

The change of scenery helped, however. Living in a wooded area with deer, coyotes, and foxes inspired her to return to landscape painting, the dark circles under her eyes have faded, and she's paying more attention to her own health.

She now says she will never return to caregiving, however, and her housing situation remains precarious.

I teased her over FaceTime that maybe she should start online dating now that she had access to Wi-Fi, and maybe even fall in love (but only with someone in supremely good health). She shook her head no. She told me that all she wants to do is paint and garden and, for the first time in her life, think about her own needs.

"I'm happy where I'm at," she said, smiling. "I'm ready to fall in love with myself."

Julie Poole is a writer living in Austin, Texas. She received a BA from Columbia University, an MFA from the University of Texas, and is a professional track journalism student at Moody College of Communication at UT.

THE WORST PART OF BEING POOR

Watching Your Dog Die When You Can't Afford to Help

Bobbi Dempsey

The Guardian, November 9, 2018

> Oreo and Mitzi were sick—but since we couldn't pay thousands
> of dollars immediately, we couldn't get the care they needed.

A few years ago, my sister Marylin's peekapoo—a playful and affectionate dog named Oreo—went to the vet for minor bleeding in her mouth. Any issue involving blood is always of concern, but Oreo was only eight and in otherwise good health so it wasn't alarming. Maybe she had eaten something that had irritated her digestive system, we had assumed.

The vet prescribed Rimadyl, an anti-inflammatory medication often prescribed for arthritis and other conditions.

Within a few hours, Oreo's condition only worsened. She couldn't eat and was obviously in distress. From there, things got alarming. She became disoriented, unable to stand or walk without falling. Then hemorrhaging started. Yet the cause of her sudden decline proved a mystery.

We called local vets, hunting for one that could see her right away. That's when we discovered a cruel fact of life for pet owners of modest means. If you can't hand over a bunch of cash immediately, you often have no way to get your pet the medical care they need. Even in the worst emergencies.

Like most animal lovers, I think you can't put price tags on the lives of our beloved four-legged friends. Unfortunately, that's exactly what being a poor pet owner forces you to do. My state, Pennsylvania, ranks among the most expensive for emergency veterinary medicine. If your pet has ever eaten something they shouldn't (and whose pet hasn't?) consider yourself lucky if it didn't cost you a fortune. The

196

average cost of "foreign body ingestion," a common pet emergency, is often more than $1,500.

The American Veterinary Medical Association suggests that financially challenged pet owners talk to their veterinarian about payment plans or deferred payments, look into low-cost clinics, and check for charities that might be able to help—all of which we did, to no avail.

I've heard plenty of comments along the lines of: "If you're poor, you shouldn't get a pet." One person in a local Facebook group—in a discussion where someone was asking about affordable vet services in the area—chimed in with his opinion that if you cannot dedicate at least $1,000 a year for vet care, you shouldn't get a pet. Pets are yet another thing that are used by people as an excuse to poor-shame, essentially telling indigent people that they aren't worthy of the companionship of a loving pet.

The harsh reality is, veterinary care is a business, and just like any other business, its clients must provide that revenue. But even pet owners who have the best-laid plans initially—perhaps even with a dedicated savings account for vet expenses—can run into unplanned circumstances. They can lose their jobs, experience a sudden medical crisis, or any other troubled situation affecting their ability to afford vet care.

In the case of my sister, despite her poverty she was determined to have a dog and to save her when she was ill. We started by calling a few vets who had treated Oreo, thinking they'd be the most understanding. Each one explained that we would need to pay the full cost of the visit upfront, plus any necessary treatment, which they estimated to be a minimum of several hundred dollars.

Like most low-income and working-class people who live in Pennsylvania coal country, my sister and her husband live paycheck to paycheck. At that time, Marylin had been recently forced to leave her job as a cashier due to breathing difficulties (she's now facing a double lung transplant) and her husband worked at a local furniture store.

For many months, they barely had enough to cover their bills. Coming up with hundreds of dollars on the spot proved impossible. Credit cards are also a rarity in our family due to shaky credit, no credit history, or lack of sufficient income, so putting this on plastic wasn't an option.

All this meant Oreo suffered into a second day. At this point, she was lying on the kitchen floor, wailing. It was agonizing for the whole family. My niece, Crystal, sobbed as she lay on the floor next to Oreo, trying in vain to comfort her. In despair, my sister begged the vets' offices, and even offered to let them garnish her husband's paychecks.

Still no luck.

As a Hail Mary, they rushed Oreo to one local vet's office, hoping that seeing the dog's distress would move the staff to waive their normal payment policies given the dire situation. As Oreo bled heavily all over the waiting room floor, the staff informed my sister that they couldn't do anything unless she could bring someone who could get approved for a credit line of at least $1,000.

Oreo, clinging to life at this point, entered the third day of suffering. She would look at you in desperation, like she was pleading with you for help. Growing increasingly listless, she barely even had the strength to whimper.

We expanded our search for a vet and called every one of them within an hour of my sister's home, our panic growing. We weren't even sure if Oreo would survive a car trip that long but we were determined to try.

The only emergency vet hospital within forty-five minutes of us demands payment immediately when you walk in the door—before they'll even take your pet back to the exam room—so that wasn't an option. The immediate "just to get in the door" payment is $150, but they warn you that even just an initial round of tests could easily run you several hundred dollars or more. They can't even give you an estimate for the total treatment cost until they do an evaluation and tests.

By this time, we had faced the ghastly reality that Oreo was probably too far gone to be saved, so we also reluctantly contemplated the idea of putting her out of her misery, despite her relatively young age and our desire to save her. However, even for euthanasia, all of the local vet offices require immediate payment at the time of service. Costs vary, but euthanasia typically can run to two hundred dollars or more.

As it approached day four, we finally found a vet more than a half hour away who agreed to examine Oreo. They weren't sure if there was anything they'd be able to do for her at that point, but at least they were willing to give it a try. But right after we spoke to that compassionate vet, Oreo passed away in Crystal's arms. It was a heartbreaking end to an excruciating few days.

This spring, I had had a disheartening case of déjà vu as my mother's beloved pomeranian, Mitzi, faced health issues we couldn't afford to treat. At thirteen, Mitzi had been plagued by an assortment of health problems (including food allergies) for years, but we'd been able to keep those mostly under control with a combination of treatments and a diet that we cobbled together as my mother's budget allowed. Her only form of income was a meager Social Security check, but every available penny she had would go to Mitzi's food and care.

But when Mitzi started having seizures and other signs of potential neurological maladies, I was struck by dread, because I knew where this was heading. The vet informed us that the diagnostic tests alone could easily cost close to a thousand dollars. And if anything showed up, the expenses would escalate from there. Even if she could afford the tests, my mother realized it was pointless to have them done, because realistically there was no way she would be able to afford any necessary treatment.

My mother is a widow whose serious health issues—including advanced Parkinson's disease—leave her unable to leave home except for doctor's appointments, so Mitzi served as her constant companion and a source of comfort. Still, Mom reluctantly accepted the inevitable and tried to prepare herself that Mitzi's death was near.

Wanting to avoid a repeat of Oreo's slow, painful death, we vowed that when it became apparent that Mitzi was in pain or her quality of life was declining, we would have her put to sleep humanely. Even that cost was beyond what my mother could scrape together at the time, but fortunately I was able to put aside enough to cover the basic costs of euthanasia.

A few weeks later, after Mitzi had a particularly bad night in which she suffered a series of seizures, I took Mitzi to the emergency vet hospital in the middle of the night to have her euthanized. It was still emotionally tough, but at least we knew she hadn't suffered unnecessarily due to financial factors.

What can be done in other cases like Oreo's or Mitzi's?

Organizations like the Connecticut-based not-for-profit organization Pet Assistance can be one answer. They provide help, often in the form of advice and referrals, to longtime pet owners facing unexpected bills for emergency vet care.

Some Humane Society locations and other pet organizations offer "wellness clinics" providing free or low-cost vaccinations, spay/neuter assistance, and other routine services, but these are available only in certain areas and generally don't cover extensive procedures or emergency care.

But those options aside, why do so few veterinarians offer sliding scales to pet owners in need? Why don't the many well-funded animal-friendly organizations establish a source of funds to help indigent pet owners cover their animals' medical costs?

Without more available resources to help desperate pet owners, given the current state of wage stagnation more and more animals will be suffering and dying, needlessly.

Bobbi Dempsey is a reporting fellow at EHRP and an editorial fellow at Community Change. Her work has also appeared in the *Washington Post*, *Harper's*, the *New York Times*, AARP, and other publications.

NOMEN EST OMEN

Mitchell S. Jackson

The Believer, September 2, 2020

> Their names. Names they got from yearnings, gestures, flaws, events, mistakes, weaknesses. Names that bore witness.
>
> —**Toni Morrison**, *Song of Solomon*

Say these names: Stretch, The Honey Bee, Tank, 2 Ounce, The Mayor, Mack Truck, Big City, Slice, Juice, Fresno Mike, South Central, Tennessee, Famous, SAL, Greedy, Yella Tay, D-Stoud, D-Reid, D Third, Jo Jo, T.B., P-Strick, K-Dub, B-Brooks, T-Ross, T-Bone, L.V., A.D., T.T., Toine, Blass, Fat Fred, Tancy, Fluffy, Bookie, Biggie, Slash, Da Natural, Monkey Mike, Peek-a-Boo, Chicken, Jay Bo, Ray-Ray, Big Red, Playground, Chocolate, Love, Smooth, Foo-Foo, Eastwood, Big Smurf, Lil Smurf, Tuna, Da Bell, Scarface, Jay-Ray, Brain Damage, D-Bo, No Toes, Pooh B, Blazer, Rabbit, Neck, Cool Nutz, G Nuts, Ghost, A-Bone, Champ, Pep, Cluck, Toddy P, Moon, Charm, Fast Eddie, Fast Livin, Slow, Kenny Mac, Maniac Lok, GeeChee Dan, Choo-Choo, Double F, Silk, Goggles, To the Left, Everything...

We could add my ephemeral handle of Kupchak to the list. In the days of yore, young buck me would lounge with my stepdad and his brotherpatnas in an attic room while they puff-puff passed and watched sports. In those days, that's what most of the men in those sessions called me: Kupchak. The namesake of that fleeting moniker was former NBA player Mitchell Kupchak. Though Kupchak was a stellar college player, and won two NBA titles, he was not an NBA star. In fact, it's a strong bet that dude wasn't my stepdad's nor any of his brotherpatnas' favorite NBA baller. It's also true that in those days, I had neither evidenced any great aptitude for the game or confessed aspirations of biddy ball stardom. Nor did Kupchak and I resemble:

201

he being a six-feet-nine white man and I being a pint-sized Black boy. On the real, my stepdad christened me Kupchak for no reason I can surmise other than the man and I shared a first name.

In the Middle Ages people were known by their first names alone: Pate, Larkin, Jude. In England, surnames weren't added until the tenth century when Norman William the Conqueror (a fine epithet if ever there was one) usurped the throne in the infamous Battle of Hastings. Back then, surnames were often created from a patronym, for example, generations ago, one of the white men who would come to enslave my forebearers was the son of a man named Jack or Jackson; were also derived from character traits, e.g., a tall man might become Jack Long; were also derived from location, e.g., Jack from London became Jack London; were also derived from a trade, e.g., Jack Carpenter. The gradual change of surnames becoming hereditary commenced around the mid-fourteenth century, and the first names that did were the ones connected to craft since a person often followed their father into a trade.

Nicknames AKA appellations AKA sobriquets AKA handles AKA monikers, follow a kindred christening rubric. And akin to medieval times, one cannot (or better yet should not) name oneself. Around my way, a nickname must be bestowed—and in most cases, must be bequeathed *and* earned.

Sometimes between the conferring and the reaping, a nickname follows the Latin proverb attributed to playwright Plautus: "nomen est omen" (the name is a sign; your name is your destiny). It becomes what, almost a millennium later, the editors of *New Scientist* magazine coined as "nominative determinism," that is, a name-driven outcome. The editors used the term to describe how a person's name influences their profession of choice, but the term has since been expanded to include "key attributes of life." And what could be more key than a nickname that dictates the decisions that equal one's fate?

In what we dubbed the NEP (North East Portland), names again and again became our destiny. Take for example one misguided night friends and I were celebrating a snow day off from high school by sitting on a porch and guzzling brews. The crew included two of my basketball teammates (yep, I ended up playing) and another dude who was a scat back on the football team and also a gang member with a handle that should've been spelled with a Q but was spelled with a K, since for Bloods, C's were straight verboten. Good and loaded, we all decided the sensible thing to do was fetch our girlfriends. The plan was to swoop the girls and meet back on the porch. We returned that night, girlfriends in tow, by the agreed time. All of us, that is, except for K. We waited until our worry that something had gone awry with K threatened to overwhelm us. We marched down the hill to K's house and knocked on his back door, malt liquor reeking on our breath and swooshing our underdeveloped brains. K's mother answered and we stuttered a bit and asked for him. "Oh, no," she said. "K left here while ago. Him and ____ got into it and he shot at her in the house." "He shot at her in the house?!" we repeated, our eyes widened to the size of beer caps. K shooting at his girlfriend in his mother's house was both unbelievably ludicrous and undeniably plausible. Though I never asked him where his name came from, I was certain K's AKA had something to do with his physical speed *and* his temper, and reasoned it working as a harbinger—even if I didn't yet know that word.

Back then we all lived in what we called the hood. It's also been called ThetrapThestreetsTheblockThesetUrbanAmericaAghettoAslum . . . It exists of course in all the usual urban places that command our popular imaginings. However, I can also attest that it exists in cities like Madison, Wisconsin; Little Rock, Arkansas; and Wichita, Kansas. Scholars and social scientists sometimes call them depressed communities, and though their particulars may differ from state to state, you can bet they all share ubiquitous deprivations and vicissitudes, denizens denied the whole damn pyramid of Maslow's needs, and beaucoup dudes with nicknames.

In those places, a nickname becomes a means to combat those hardships—what the owner of that name knows, even if they can't prove it, are systemic assaults on their well-being. It becomes an avenue for reinvention, a means of claiming visibility in a world chockfull of erasures. Please believe, this ain't me contending all nicknames lead to prison or death or other dire consequences. Let the record show that K rerouted what looked like fate in his youth. There are appellations aplenty which've inspired heroism, academic achievement, athletic feats. I once knew a dude who was such a phenomenal athlete that somebody named him Baby Jesus. Post his baptism as such, he leaped so high and from such great distances that I swore he was indeed anointed. But as I said, I've seen it work the opposite way as well. A dude is christened, say, Devious or Stitches or Spider and in no time flat, owns a rep for apoplexy and bloody fisticuffs, has committed an armed robbery or assault, has shot someone or been shot, murdered someone or been murdered, which is to say, their AKA became an invitation, an appeal, a beckoning, a motive, a fortune, transmuted into a prison that far too often ushered them into a literal one.

In forty-five years of living, I never received a nickname that stuck. Years after me ceasing and desisting Kupchak as a sobriquet, I was named Action Jackson by one of my high school patnas. Bad as I wanted a moniker, I knew almost at once that Action Jackson wasn't it. It was an unimaginative name for one. For two, that patna was the only person on earth who used it. For three, it never inspired me on the court or elsewhere. For years, I mourned the fact that I was known in the neighborhood simply as Mitchell or Mitch. These days, though, I'm grateful for my lack of a nickname, for never feeling pressured to achieve someone else's vision of me, for never feeling confined by the expectation of a name. Oh so thankful for what I now know as the gift of freedom to become.

Mitchell S. Jackson's debut novel *The Residue Years* received wide critical praise. Jackson is the winner of a Whiting Award and teaches in the Creative Writing Program at the University of Chicago.

SECTION 4

Work

INTRODUCTION

To Make Work Visible, Again and Again

Kathi Weeks

Ann Larson's account of working at a grocery store during the COVID pandemic deftly captures the strange invisibility that many service workers experience. The class blindness on the part of the consumer public, the disappearing of low-wage workers from media reports about work, and the fear on the part of workers themselves of falling—without a safety net—into destitution, produce a form of social distancing that, as Larson astutely observes, "has been occurring since long before the onset of the pandemic." These blind spots and social divisions make the kind of "ferocious solidarity" that Molly Crabapple reports the New York Taxi Workers Alliance managed to realize both more difficult and more vital to achieve.

Karl Marx provided a valuable lesson about how to confront this ignorance about the working conditions of the majority, in his case, under the conditions of industrial capitalism. The key, he argued, was to find out what happens *after* the two parties agree to the terms of employment. That contractual process, which takes place in the public space of the labor market "in full view of everyone," is seen to involve two free and equal individuals, one a would-be employee and the other a prospective employer, who agree to freely exchange labor for wages to the benefit of each party.

But once we follow the employee from the marketplace into "the hidden abode of production" of the privatized workplace, on whose threshold, Marx wryly observes, "there hangs the notice 'No admittance except on business,'" we can see the realities of class society begin to take shape. The formerly free individual employee who was endowed with rights and was equal before the law, is transformed at the work site into the employer's subordinate. It is precisely this

206

inequality and unfreedom, a product of the employer's right to command, control, and benefit from their employee's labor, that is the true secret of both exploitation and profit-making.

One likely reason why the sphere of production was so less visible than the "noisy" realm of the market in Marx's day is that in front of the factory, his paradigm site of employment, there was literally a "no trespassing" sign. But in the current landscape of postindustrial service work the stubborn invisibility of low-wage work is more puzzling because so much more of it takes place in full view of the consumer public. Delivery workers, Uber drivers, retail workers, taxi drivers, cashiers, restaurant workers, adjuncts, grocery store workers, and other service workers whose experiences are recounted in this section, may not be out of sight in the way factory workers can be, but they remain somehow out of mind—a kind of ideological blindness that may be harder to challenge than simple invisibility. The term "disavowal" is one way to describe this disappearing, this hiding in plain sight of the realities of so many jobs.

Another example of this unseeing, which is the essence of class blindness, comes from accounts of what it is like to move down the occupational and income ladder. John Koopman's piece describes the experience as a matter of falling or sliding into invisibility, as becoming a "nobody." This is yet another form of social distancing. When someone is no longer reflected in cultural representations, when they seem no longer to merit even a story line in the American dream of middle-class work and consumption, sympathy, let alone solidarity across class and occupational divides, becomes more difficult to muster.

One strategy for teaching people how to see is to report personal accounts of the conditions of these low-wage, part-time, unbenefited, insecure, physically taxing, emotionally draining, and chronically stressful jobs, together with the rising debts, rents, transportation and health-care costs that help to ensure that workers' noses are kept to their grindstones. But given the dense layers of ideological mystification that shroud low-wage work, these realities of mass employment, along with the inspiring instances of workers' acts of individual and collective rebellion against these conditions, must be continually—and also loudly and vividly—revealed. In her piece, Gloria Diaz asks whether or not "a piecemeal living of part-time work, no benefits and looming student loans is as good as it will get." The answer depends on our ability to organize. Fundamental to this organizational work is the kind of struggle that the authors in this section wage so eloquently: to make visible the real experience of income-generating employment under capitalism.

Kathi Weeks teaches in the Gender, Sexuality, and Feminist Studies Program at Duke University. She is the author of *Constituting Feminist Subjects* (second edition, Verso, 2018) and *The Problem with Work: Feminism, Marxism, Antiwork Politics, and Postwork Imaginaries* (Duke UP, 2011).

HOW THE TAXI WORKERS WON

Text and images by Molly Crabapple

The Nation, December 13, 2021

On September 19, a group of cab drivers organized by the New York Taxi Workers Alliance rolled up to the corner of Broadway and Murray Street in downtown Manhattan, parked next to city hall, and declared they would not leave until the city fixed the crushing debt that had driven many of their fellow drivers to suicide. They held a press conference, hung an SOS banner from the nearby beaux arts subway entrance, set up some folding chairs, and sat down to wait.

I stopped by the encampment at midnight to find eight drivers trading jokes on the lonely concrete of the Financial District. Augustine Tang invited me to join them. Thirty-seven years old, with the characteristic swagger of a native New Yorker, Tang had inherited his father's taxi medallion—the badge that gives cabbies the right to operate—along with $530,000 of debt. He was one of the group's most eloquent spokespeople and also one of the youngest. His companions were all older, men who had spent decades behind the wheel—like Mohammed Islam, from Bangladesh, who owed $536,000, and "Big John" Asmah, from Ghana, who owed $700,000. At an age when many people are contemplating retirement, these drivers instead faced a future of fourteen-hour workdays that would bring them no closer to freedom as well as harrowing financial burdens they would pass on to their kids.

But these drivers also knew a way out, which is why they had decided to camp outside the gates of city hall.

In late September of 2020, the New York Taxi Workers Alliance had drawn up a plan to cap drivers' loans and limit their monthly payments. The city ignored it, just as, for years, it had brushed off NYTWA's protests against medallion debt. This sit-in was an escalation—an attempt to force New York City mayor Bill de Blasio's hand.

Inspired by the drivers' struggle, I kept coming back, night after night, then week after week. I listened to their stories, drew their portraits, marched in their picket lines, and ultimately joined their hunger strike. Despite their defiant assurances of victory, I could not shake the sense that I was witnessing the doomed last stand of yet another group of working-class New Yorkers who would be crushed by the hedge-fund Bretts who run this city.

Instead, on November 3, NYTWA announced that the city had adopted almost every detail of its plan. The drivers had won.

"This victory means everything. It was beautiful to see the unity between the working people," Tang later told me. "We've had cabbies that don't own any medallions show their gratitude for our fight. We've had strangers outside of the industry crying with us after we won. Working people just want working people to succeed."

The drivers' victory was a testament to the unifying power of collective labor action. Ninety-four percent of cab drivers are immigrants, and 95 percent are men, but there are few other commonalities among them. Cabbies represent almost every race, religion, and country of origin, and they speak over 120 languages. They spend their days isolated in their cabs, competing for a dwindling number of fares. Yet for decades, NYTWA—a 21,000-member union of cab, livery, and rideshare drivers—had brought them together around their common plight. Now, through relentless work, shrewd organizing, and ferocious solidarity, cabbies had moved the city.

Kuber Sancho-Persad holds his father Choonilal's taxi light over his head. Choonilal died in 2017, and Kuber inherited the debt.

Hughes Isaac was once an internationally touring musician, and wrote a memoir, Humming Man, about his time as a cab driver.

Chime Gyatso bought his medallion for $570,000 in 2009 and was a regular at the protest camp. "The city threw us in the Hudson river," he said.

Molly Crabapple is the Puffin/EHRP Fellow. She is an artist and writer whose inspirations include Diego Rivera and Goya's *The Disasters of War*. She is also the author of *Brothers of the Gun*, an illustrated collaboration with Marwan Hisham. Her animated short film *A Message from the Future with Alexandria Ocasio-Cortez* has been nominated for an Emmy Award.

MY PANDEMIC YEAR BEHIND THE CHECKOUT COUNTER

On Working amid Paranoid Customers, Hungry Shoplifters, Sick Coworkers, and People Who Just Need a Bathroom

Ann Larson

The New Republic, March 5, 2021

A few weeks ago at work, a man came in the door, crouched down, and shit on the floor. Colleagues who witnessed it happening were shocked but not surprised. This kind of thing—incidents having to do with the universal human needs to eat, empty bowels, and keep bodies warm—happen often enough at the grocery store where I work.

People living at the encampment a few blocks away often come into the store to shop, steal, thaw out frozen limbs, or relieve themselves. Store bathrooms are accessible with a code that is given out only to paying customers—a policy that has resulted in unhoused people, or really anyone who doesn't have money, waiting outside the door so they can grab it when someone exits. I'm guessing what happened with the man who dropped his pants had something to do with that informal system—maybe no one opened the door from the inside in time.

The episode caused a split inside the store, a divide between those who thought of it as a personal affront and those who thought of it as an unfortunate consequence of circumstances outside of the man's control. When my colleague, a security guard, told me about it, I told him, "Everyone has to shit somewhere." It was my way of defending the man. My coworker shook his head. "Jane had to clean it up," he replied.

He was drawing a line between us and the man; it also occurred to me that his response was a kind of solidarity that applied only to those of us working in the store. Cleaning up feces was not part of Jane's official duties, and since most of us have boring, dirty, low-wage jobs, protecting ourselves from added labor is a high priority. We had to be united against that kind of thing, and in my colleague's version of what happened, the unhoused man was on the wrong side of the divide because he had made our lives even more miserable and degrading that morning.

Low-wage workers are far from the only people who draw lines between ourselves and those we regard as dangerous. There's a genre of writing that's developed in parallel to the pandemic, call it the COVID explainer, that basically performs the same function. Last November, the *New York Times'* Tara Parker-Pope published a piece called "How Do I Make Thanksgiving Shopping Safer?" It was full of helpful advice for customers who wanted to enjoy a Thanksgiving meal but who were worried about catching COVID-19 while buying turkeys, sweet potatoes, and cranberry sauce.[1] The reporter recommended going to the store during nonpeak hours—forget Saturday afternoons—wearing a good mask, frequent hand sanitizing, and getting in and out quickly.

The article was similar to one that appeared a couple of months later after a new, more contagious strain of the virus had started spreading. In *Vox*, Julia Belluz published "Still Going to the Grocery Store? With New Virus Variants Spreading, It's Probably Time to Stop."[2] In the piece, the reporter described new dangers to shoppers and recommended some precautions: "If we want the pandemic to end as fast as possible, we need to pump the brakes right now . . . that means avoiding optional gatherings with other people—even grocery trips . . . 'Shopping for five minutes in the grocery store is a lot better—six times better—than shopping for 30 minutes,' said Tom Frieden, the former director of the Centers for Disease Control and Prevention."

I know that pieces like this serve a real purpose, but all I could think about while reading these articles was: What about those of us who work in grocery stores? We can't spend less time indoors or limit our gatherings with large numbers of people because those are the activities that we are (poorly) paid to do. If we didn't do them, there wouldn't be grocery stores for *Times* and *Vox* readers to worry about going to. But I don't think we're part of the presumed readership of publications like these: affluent, likely white-collar with a newly remote job; staying home because they can afford to; the kind of person who encounters service workers but does not do service work and can't imagine that they ever will.

In addition to exhibiting a class blindness which forgets that grocery stores have to be run by someone, some media reports on the
pandemic have veered into describing a world where working-class
people don't even exist. *Vox* advised readers to "pick up groceries at
the curbside" instead of going into the store, as if the desired items
just assemble themselves.

The *Times* reporter's way of disappearing low-wage employees
from a scenario that actually features them was even more striking.
"Some stores," she wrote, "sanitize the carts several times a day as part
of their regular cleaning procedures." This is correct. At my workplace,
shopping carts are sanitized after each use. However, they are not sanitized by the "store," but by people who are paid between ten and twelve
dollars per hour to do so.

My point in all of this is that while everyone needs access to grocery stores, especially during a pandemic, some people have to work
in them, and some people don't; some can afford the goods inside, and
those who can't sometimes rely on stores having accessible restrooms.
Grappling with this fact may be key to building a more equal world,
one in which solidarity doesn't end at the grocery store door or with
Vox advice columns. Creating such a world would mean not just ac-
knowledging that such differences exist but ending them.

A good percentage of customers at my store know that my colleagues and I are doing a dangerous job that they are grateful not to
have to do themselves. Some even take time to say thanks. But gratitude is not the same as solidarity. In fact, it may be its opposite. Gratitude allows a profoundly unequal situation to continue as long as its
beneficiaries are nice about it.

Not everyone who shops at my store is nice, though, and some
aren't even grateful. These days, my colleagues and I are just as likely
to be treated as vectors of disease as treated as essential workers. From
my place behind a check stand, I have regularly observed customers
whose nervousness emanates from across the room. Some shoppers
stiffen up as they approach a checkout lane, as if they are preparing to
enter the gauntlet: physical nearness to a working-class person who
has probably spent all day next to other working-class people.

One customer even sniped at a bagger, an eighty-year-old woman who was working my line. "Stop touching my groceries!" he yelled. When she walked away in frustration, he turned to me and said, "We're in the middle of a pandemic," as if I needed to be reminded. I don't think it would have helped to inform him that, before a customer purchases a grocery item, it has already been touched by multiple people, including those who work in my store between 10:00 p.m. and 6:00 a.m. unloading trucks and stocking shelves. For people like him, in that moment, the world is already divided up neatly and correctly into people who have to work at grocery stores and people who don't. These days, his main goal is avoiding contagion during the brief moments when he shares a space with us.

In some ways, I don't really blame him for that. There is no way to social distance in a grocery store. My colleagues and I are frequently and unavoidably in close contact with each other and with our customers. A recent study by the *Journal of Occupational and Environmental Medicine* summarized the toll at one store in Boston: "One in five (21 out of 104) workers tested positive for SARS-CoV-2, indicating a prevalence of 20 percent at that point in time," the study authors wrote.[3] "This was significantly higher than the prevalence of the infection in the local community at the time." Shoppers are not wrong to fear that my colleagues and I are infected. We are a danger to our customers, and they are a danger to us.[4]

Higher rates of disease are one reason media outlets are offering advice about how to stay safe in grocery stores. For our part, my colleagues and I express solidarity with each other in another way: we try not to stress each other out. This is more important than it may seem. One day, I was working a few feet away from a college student named Madison. She approached me, her hot pink mask pulled tightly around her face, and said that she had just received a call: Her recent rapid COVID-19 test had come back positive. "Go home," I said and waved her off. How many minutes had I and others spent in her presence? I wasn't sure. Had Madison suspected that she was sick? If so, why didn't she stay home?

My annoyance at Madison didn't last. Her approach to working during a pandemic is widespread in our store. Until actually contracting the virus, my colleagues and I just keep going about our duties. There is no reason to get all worked up about what might happen until it does, especially since everyone in our store—customers and employees—is required to wear a mask, and all staff members have been provided with hand sanitizer and access to a handwashing station.

Still, policies about sick leave and when someone might qualify for it are not always clear. When Madison returned to work a few days later, I asked a manager about her status. "Has she tested negative?" The manager just shrugged. The process by which she had moved from a positive test back into her check stand was mostly a mystery. But it hardly mattered. The Christmas season was upon us, and we were being overrun with holiday shoppers.

Laughter is another coping mechanism that doubles as a kind of solidarity. Our capacity to infect each other has become a running joke. During the night shift, employees organize themselves into groups to get rides home. (Most of us don't have cars. We can't afford them.) People begin asking: "Who has a car tonight?" The word gets around. "Bobby is dropping me off tonight," I said to my colleague Katherine one evening. "You should ask him if he has room for you, too." By closing time, Bobby had a full car of grocery store workers newly released from their jobs. I rode in the front, and three others squeezed into the back. "We're all getting COVID tonight!" Bobby announced as he started the engine. We all laughed.

This type of solidarity occurs because the store provides an institutional framework that makes it possible. As the defecation incident revealed, though, the sense of togetherness doesn't apply beyond our workplace. Collective coping mechanisms do not contain the seeds of a broader political awakening. One reason is that most people are totally consumed by the necessity of earning enough money to pay the bills. It can make the world feel very small. Another, at least in my store, is that my colleagues and I are surrounded by desperation and a need that surpasses our own, and that presents us with a vision of social collapse that we are more interested in keeping at a distance than in connecting to our own lives. This is a type of social distancing that has been occurring since long before the onset of the pandemic.

We create this distance in other ways: In addition to serving customers, one of the things that employees at my store do is help catch thieves—and there are a lot of them to catch. The reason for a recent spike in theft at grocery stores is not hard to discern.[5] The Census Bureau recently reported that as many as one in six adults in the United States do not get enough to eat on a regular basis.[6]

As one response to a mass hunger crisis, security guards at my store sit on a balcony above the main shopping concourse where they scout for thieves. Scuffles between guards and people trying to leave without paying—stuffing dinner rolls into their pockets or candy bars into their purse—are a regular occurrence. Many of my colleagues willingly participate in the chase. This feels to me like another way our solidarity is tested, and limited.

Part of it is coercive—catching shoplifters makes us seem like better employees. But I don't think that can explain all of it. Many of us are one or two missed paychecks away from having to pilfer groceries ourselves, but among my colleagues, a widely held view about those who steal still goes something like this: "I work this terrible grocery store job. And anyone else could do that, too, if they wanted to make an honest living." From the point of view of the not-quite-destitute, food thieves don't deserve solidarity.

The question of solidarity and who is privileged enough to be able to express it is a theme of one of the most well-known American short stories ever written—one that just happens to take place in a grocery store. John Updike's 1961 "A&P" is narrated by Sammy, a cashier in a store north of Boston. The tale takes place in the summer, when three young girls walk into Sammy's workplace. Wearing nothing but their bathing suits, they attract a lot of attention. The nineteen-year-old is transfixed. "All three of them stopped in the cat-and-dog-food-breakfast-cereal-macaroni-rice-raisins-seasonings-spreads-spaghetti-soft-drinks-crackers-and-cookies aisle," Sammy says. "I watched them all the way." By the time the girls reach Sammy's checkout stand with snacks, the manager has noticed the trio, too. He comes over and loudly declares that they are indecently dressed, which is against store policy. Everyone in the store is gaping at the girls now. Sammy is appalled at his manager's attitude. "Policy is what the kingpins want," he thinks to himself.

As soon as the girls leave, Sammy confronts his manager: "You didn't have to embarrass them," he says. The boss snorts, "It is they who were embarrassing us." In an act that is equal parts youthful bravado and solidarity with the girls who have already disappeared from the scene, Sammy quits on the spot. He leaves the store with his former manager's dark warning ringing in his ears: "You'll feel this for the rest of your life." Once outside, Sammy turns to see the man who uttered those words behind the register "checking the sheep through."

I have come to think of Sammy's decision to walk away from his grocery store job as a method of protecting himself from the grimy feeling of being implicated in an injustice. He knew that saying "I quit" in that moment was one of the last times he would be able to risk his own livelihood to speak up for someone else. As adulthood and the need to make his own way in the world loomed, Sammy would not be able to afford to be in solidarity with just anyone—especially not with three strangers that he would never see again.

For my colleagues and I, no such solidaristic "I quit" moment is available. What is available is chasing down shoplifters—an act that at least breaks up the tedium of our jobs and makes us feel like the good guys. Our solidaristic instinct is not shaped by an understanding that we have more in common with grocery store thieves than with the corporate owners who want us to stop them. It is shaped, instead, by the more tenuous and insular hope that the next workday might not be as long and boring as the last and that maybe, if we're lucky, none of us will have to clean up shit.

Our version of solidarity, of wanting everyone with whom we work to suffer a little less on the job, requires regarding food thieves and unhoused people as potential threats.

But I can picture something different, though a lot would have to change first. We need to think and act collectively to fight for new social policies that would make new, more expansive forms of solidarity possible. But such an effort is hampered by the world we already have, in which looking out for yourself, your family, and the person working next to you in the grocery store is the best most of us can do. It's what we have been taught all our lives.

The sort of changes necessary here are vast, but I want to add something to the discussion about what policies would help address economic inequality in the US, Medicare for All, a federal jobs guarantee, and mass debt relief among them. To those good ideas, I want to add another: a real redistribution of labor. What if people who don't normally work in grocery stores had to pull a few shifts in order for us to have grocery stores? I'm not talking about everyone in the neighborhood picking up a weekly shift at the local food co-op. I'm talking about a much more fundamental change.

David Graeber introduced us to the concept of bullshit jobs, those "pointless" roles that capitalism produces for the sole purpose of "keeping us all working." For him, the ruling class has convinced us that "anyone not willing to submit themselves to some kind of intense work discipline for most of their waking hours deserves nothing." Graeber's proposal is that we get rid of the useless jobs so that everyone is free to work less and enjoy their lives.

While not disagreeing with his broad point, I do wonder if "submitting themselves to some kind of intense work discipline" might actually be a good thing for some people, specifically those "salaried professionals" who Graeber names as having benefited from the bullshit jobs regime. Maybe a key to ensuring that all jobs are less horrible and better paid is not so much in separating the pointless from the essential but in making sure that "corporate lawyers," "financiers," "lobbyists," and the like have to finally spend some time doing the ones that count.

Instead of eliminating bullshit jobs, what if we focused on an upward redistribution of the shit jobs so that millions of people who have been doing them forever can finally take a break?

Think about the social policies that might suddenly find more widespread support if such a system of labor redistribution were implemented. How many more affluent people would be in favor of doing whatever was necessary to end homelessness if they had to clean up the messes that arise from the problem of not having access to a bathroom?

I propose that a key to social change that lasts is assuring that, if there is shit to clean up, those who have contributed so little for so long are the first to be handed a dustpan and a mop. That's solidarity.

Ann Larson is an organizer and grocery worker. She cofounded the Debt Collective and coauthored *Can't Pay Won't Pay: The Case for Economic Disobedience and Debt Abolition*. From time to time, she teaches writing in the Honors College at the University of Utah.

FROM ACADEMIC TO ASSEMBLY-LINE WORKER

My Life of Precarity in Middle America

Gloria Diaz

In These Times, January 8, 2019

What does failure smell like? To me, it reeks of rotten potatoes.

After twenty years of trying, unsuccessfully, to piece together a living from adjunct teaching and freelance writing, last summer I took a job at Saratoga Potato Chips, LLC, boxing chips at their Indiana factory.

My first morning on the job, I knocked over an entire pallet of boxes stacked nine feet high. Later, on the multipack assembly line, I scrambled to keep up like a panicky Lucy Ricardo at the candy factory.

Finally, I was sentenced to chip inspection. I was led to the line with no instruction, so I made up my own rules. I decided that if I wouldn't want to eat the chip myself, it would go into the trash.

The chip inspection room, with its three fryers, was probably close to one hundred degrees. But even in the heat, we were not allowed water at our stations. Occasionally there would be a five-gallon Igloo cooler with blessedly cold water. But the cooler was rarely refilled. As I gazed at it longingly, it seemed to mock me with false promises.

Located in the Rust Belt city of Fort Wayne, the factory seemed like another country. Managers and fellow employees assumed that Spanish was my first language because of my skin and hair. The Puerto Rican half of me was showing, giving me a chance to practice my limited Spanish.

Flyers near the time clocks announced, "Tomar fichas sin autorización es robar. robar fichas llevará al arresto." (Taking chips without authorization is stealing. Stealing chips will lead to arrest.)

None of this was supposed to happen. Growing up in Indiana, I had always heard, "If you want a decent job, you'll have to go to college."

222

My mother, who had dropped out of school, had suggested I become a teacher. But terrible experiences in middle school and high school made me never want to go back, not even as an authority figure.

I had an alternate plan: I'd go to beauty school, graduate, do hair, save my money, go to college, major in business and start my own salon. But in beauty school, I discovered I was allergic to permanent wave solution. The director of the school said that even the fumes might cause me to break out. So I quit. I think if I had to do it all over again, I'd just put some gloves on and stick it out.

I eventually did go to college, majoring in English. When I graduated in 1992, I started a career in journalism, working at a small-town newspaper in Huntington, Indiana. I wrote two feature stories a week, took photographs and informed readers of births and weddings. After three years, I figured I was ready for the big time and applied to one of the two papers in Fort Wayne. But I wasn't hired, and I didn't have the money to move away in search of other work. My writing career stagnated, consisting for years of freelance writing and part-time work for the local weekly entertainment journal.

In 2006, I got part-time work at the local community college, first doing note-taking, then teaching as an adjunct instructor. I've taught there off and on ever since.

I was a humor/general interest columnist at the *Fort Wayne Reader*. For fourteen years nonstop, my column, "Buenos Diaz," appeared twice a month. It also made me a Grade Z local celebrity. People seemed to enjoy it, so that was a kind of success. But in late 2018, the *Fort Wayne Reader* folded. The very last column I wrote was a review of *Bohemian Rhapsody*. In 2014, I went back to graduate school for a master's degree in writing studies. But after graduating in May 2017, I was still unable to find a full-time teaching position.

After attempting to scrape by on adjunct teaching and retail jobs, I finally returned to the world of temp agencies. Last June, I was between teaching gigs, and I needed to find more work fast.

This is a common predicament. Reeling from state budget cuts and propping up top-heavy administrations, universities have turned increasingly to the cheap teaching labor provided by nontenure track faculty. More than half of college faculty today are adjuncts, but the jobs are notoriously precarious and low-paying—a 2014 survey eventually found that the median income is just $22,000 a year.

The trend toward low-wage, insecure jobs has been proceeding in blue-collar and service industries for decades. Many are surprised to see it now afflicting the bearers of advanced degrees; adjuncts have been called the "fast-food workers of the academic world." But I'd point out that in order to make ends meet, some adjuncts may actually find themselves pulling shifts as actual fast-food workers—or fried-food inspectors, in my case.

Sorting through chips for nine dollars an hour, I made just a dollar more per hour than when I started at my first newspaper job more than twenty years ago.

There was also considerable loneliness in my new world of potato chips. My station isolated me from everyone else. If I was desperate for water or to use the bathroom, I had to wait until the fryer operator was in sight and wave him down.

"Necessito agua" or "Voy ir al baño," I would say with a smile.

For about three of the weeks I was working in the factory, my car was out of commission. It needed seven hundred dollars in repairs, money I had to save up while I worked. That meant I had to spend another three hundred dollars on Uber rides just to get to and from work. I felt too bad asking my friends to shuttle me there at 6:00 a.m. It just added to my feelings of failure.

Each day after work, I considered drinking or doing drugs to escape it all, but I didn't. All I could think about was going home and taking a shower, grabbing some chocolate and a glass of ice water, and laying on my bed with a portable fan running full blast at me while I watched YouTube.

In mid-July, I got a small reprieve. I had a successful interview at the University of Saint Francis in Fort Wayne, my alma mater. As an adjunct professor, I make about eight hundred dollars a month teaching at the university and another four hundred dollars at the community college—hardly enough to get by, but more than I made inspecting snack food. I quit the factory in August.

This wasn't the life I had envisioned for myself: part blue-collar worker, part professional, unable to fit in fully in either realm. I wonder if a piecemeal living of part-time work, no benefits, and looming student loans is as good as it will get. Sometimes I feel fraudulent. My master's degree sits on a bookshelf with clutter on top. I am proud and ashamed at the same time.

Now that I'm back in the classroom, I'm honest with my students—perhaps too honest. I tell students that I have to teach classes at other schools, I tell them about the factory jobs I've had, how I drive for Uber and Lyft, and how I often work seven days a week but still barely scrape by.

I still believe in the value of education as its own end. I get great satisfaction from helping students get through an assignment that they thought they couldn't tackle. But anyone still selling an advanced degree as the path to prosperity should seriously rethink this view—maybe while spending the summer inspecting potato chips.

(Editor's note: In response to queries from *In These Times* about working conditions described in this piece, Saratoga Chip Company CEO Peter Margie said that drinking water is not allowed near the chips "in accordance with good manufacturing practices and food safety requirements." He also said that the company "has had previous unscrupulous employees that stole chips on a large scale" and that company policy permits staff to take home two bags of chips per week.)

CODA

I quit Saratoga in late summer 2018 to return to adjunct teaching at Ivy Tech Community College and my alma mater, the University of Saint Francis. In late February 2019, I moved to Xiamen, China, to teach English. I had a unique front-row seat for the COVID-19 outbreak, and published articles in *Thought Catalog* and *Chaos+Comrades* about what life was like in China before, and dealing with the aftermath. I am back in the classroom as a full-time lecturer.

***

Gloria Diaz has written professionally since the early 1990s. Her work has appeared in *Bust* online. She has self-published three books of short fiction. *Served Cold: Tales of Revenge and Redemption* is available on Lulu.com. *Anything for Georgetown and Other Stories* and *Tickle Your Fancy* are collections of erotic fiction published under the pen name Janell Elizabeth Meyer, and are also available on Lulu.com. Previously, she freelanced for WhatzUp and wrote a humor/general interest column, Buenos Diaz, for the *Fort Wayne Reader*. She finished her second novel, combining humor with erotic fiction, which she describes as *Bridget Jones's Diary* meets *Fifty Shades of Grey*. Ms. Diaz is a native of Fort Wayne, Indiana. She writes about her life in China at nowaylaowai.home.blog. She lives in Xiamen, China.

ONCE UPON A TIME, WAITRESS WAS A UNION JOB— COULD HISTORY REPEAT ITSELF?

Haley Hamilton

Slate, September 20, 2022

It was August 2019, and while the Red Sox weren't having the best season, every bar within walking distance of Fenway Park got absolutely crushed on game days: lines around the corner before we opened, lines three and four people deep on all sides, a service-ticket printer that ran nonstop. There would be a quick lull just after the first pitch that, depending on the home team's performance and the day of the week, could stretch into the third or fourth inning, but there was always a second wave of insanity—sometimes a third— that could take us straight into last call. On Saturday nights, when the last tabs had been closed and the final guests had either left or been forcibly removed at 2:00 a.m., I would look at the dirty glassware lining the entire bar, the chaos of the drink-building wells, and the bottle of tequila my coworkers and I would absolutely finish before we clocked out, and try to do the math for how long it was going to take us to clean up.

I'd usually follow that with more tequila while stewing about how utterly insane it was that I needed two jobs to sustain myself financially, how it should be illegal to pay anyone—even those of us making good money in tips—less than eighteen dollars an hour in a city as expensive as Boston, and finally, how just seventy-five years ago, I wouldn't have had to deal with any of this—at least not on my own: it was something my union rep would have taken care of.

It's easy to be unaware of the organization history of servers and bartenders because, well, restaurant workers are seldom studied: as a group, we aren't often taken very seriously, or at least haven't been in the past forty or so years. There was a time, however, when hospitality industry unions were some of the most powerful and robust labor organizations in the country.

Unionization in the service industry is increasingly in the news today, as employees at Chipotle and several Starbucks locations, as well as Google's cafeteria workers, have successfully organized and begun the work of negotiating contracts with their employers. It's incredibly exciting to witness workers for these massive corporations organizing and collectively bargaining for increased wages and better working conditions. But it's also important to recognize that this, much like the cocktail renaissance, isn't a new development so much as a return to the deeply entrenched values and practices of what is now a different era. We aren't so much fighting for something new as reconnecting with part of what was, not that long ago, the status quo.

The first hospitality industry union formed in 1866, just after the end of the Civil War, and went by the name of the Bartenders and Waiters Union, Chicago. Later dubbed Chicago's Local 57, the organization was largely made up of recent German immigrants. With the end of the Civil War came the development of the cross-country railway system, which drastically changed the hospitality industry. Before, American hotels and restaurants had been patronized by the odd band of travelers; after railway construction, they were mandatory, for both railroad workers and people taking advantage of new interstate mobility. By the 1890s, roughly a quarter of a million people were working in kitchens, bars, and hotels, and many of them were attempting to organize and join the newly formed American Federation of Labor, which today is the American Federation of Labor and Congress of Industrial Organizations, or AFL-CIO, the largest federation of unions in the United States. In 1891, the Waiters and Bartenders National Union was approved and launched as a member of the AFL.

Later called the Hotel and Restaurant Employees and Bartenders International Union, and then, finally, HERE, or the Hotel Employees and Restaurant Employees Union, the organization started with 450 members and grew slowly. In 1899, membership had not passed 1,000, but by World War I, HERE membership was over 65,000. Prohibition once again knocked membership down as the entire hospitality industry was torn apart, but HERE nearly doubled its membership in 1933 when the Volstead Act was repealed, and had over 400,000 members by 1940. That number climbed by fifteen million in the mid-1950s.

The benefits of unionization were clear, and federally protected: The National Labor Relations Act was signed in 1935, codifying workers' rights to organization, strikes, and collective bargaining. In an industry that is still often marked by sixteen-hour shifts, wage theft, and reports of sexual harassment, belonging to a union meant the possibility of having guaranteed minimum earnings, bargaining power, and protection. But, as historian Dorothy Sue Cobble wrote in her 1991 book *Dishing It Out: Waitresses and Their Unions in the Twentieth Century*, in the 1930s, '40s, and '50s, even as manufacturing workers gained protections, "the five-day, forty-hour work week remained a dream for most culinary workers." Hospitality workers were explicitly excluded from the 1938 Fair Labor Standards Act (it wasn't until the early 1960s that a majority of restaurant workers were paid extra for anything over forty hours). Even so, unionized bartenders and servers worked far fewer hours than those who were nonunion, and they had longer lunch breaks and received holiday pay. By 1960, nearly 100 percent of the 97,000 organized culinary workers in California received paid vacation.

So, what happened? How did we go from nearly one-quarter of all hotel and restaurant employees being members of a union—receiving some benefits from organization, even if they weren't eligible for certain protections—to the haphazard and controversial union organization going on in the hospitality industry today? Why are so many bar shifts 3:00 p.m. to 3:00 a.m.? Where are our paid vacation days?

In the heyday of the 1940s and '50s, hospitality industry unions "called the shots because of their economic and political clout," according to Cobble's book. If a business tried to circumvent union standards or hire unaffiliated help, the affected local could, through strikes and boycotts, shutter that establishment in weeks. Once employers "adopted union standards and hired only union help," however, "the union protected their business interests by attacking 'unfair' competition and by encouraging patronage of union houses." Unionists were contracted to help stabilize business and "maintain the efficiency and profitability of the establishment where they worked." Disputes between the unions and employers were rare because unionists "placed less emphasis on the protection of individual members and more on the mutual interests of the overall industry and the occupation."

By the 1980s, none of this mattered, and there are a few major factors to blame. When unions started to gain true power in the 1930s, there was, of course, backlash from those who would make less money by being contractually obligated to pay their employees a living wage. At the end of World War II, there was considerable recoil against organized labor as the US government settled into the conservatism of the McCarthy era. The Taft-Hartley Act of 1947 declawed many unions, regardless of their trade affiliation.

In the restaurant industry, specifically, the power of organized labor declined as the nature of the country's restaurants shifted from thousands of small, independent establishments into chain outlets. In *Dishing It Out*, Cobble writes that in 1931 "fewer than three percent of the nation's restaurants were chain operated; in the 1980s, McDonald's alone accounted for 17 percent of restaurant visits." As soon as nonunion competition had a toehold, skepticism about the benefits of working with the unionists spread. Unorganized restaurants had lower labor costs and therefore higher profit margins. Once a few nonunion restaurants successfully established themselves in a community, they were all the proof restaurant owners under contract with unions needed that there was another, cheaper, way to operate.

The final nail in the coffin of organized hospitality labor was the general cultural shift of postwar America. While part-time and temporary laborers had always made up a significant segment of service industry employees, by 1970, a majority of servers and bartenders worked on a part-time basis, up from about one in eight in 1940. Technology played a part, as well, as a larger proportion of restaurants became focused on speed and convenience over personalized, interactive service. All these factors (and the grotesque power of the National Restaurant Association, which is another story altogether) combined to kill both the power of restaurant unions and the idea that working in hospitality can be a skilled trade. That feeds the idea that those of us working for tips in bars and restaurants don't deserve improved working conditions and ought to just *get a real job, already.*

But there's hope: a majority of hotel employees are still unionized today (in 2004 HERE merged with UNITE, the Union of Needletrades, Industrial and Textile Employees, and exists today as UNITE HERE, a 300,000-member organization); there is growing interest in and a successful push for unionization in both chain and independent restaurants; and there are alternative-style labor organizations, collectives of workers and activists focused on enacting legislative change, that are working to secure the kinds of rights and protections that once required a traditional union contract.

"What's happening right now, especially with a lot of younger workers, is that they're being exposed not just to unions but to *organizing* and the idea of standing up for yourself, even if they wouldn't even use the word 'organizing,'" said Saru Jayaraman, who is co-founder of Restaurant Opportunities Centers United; current president of One Fair Wage, a national coalition of activists seeking to increase the minimum wage and end the tipped subminimum wage that still exists in a majority of states; and director of the Food Labor Research Center at the University of California, Berkeley, "There's a lot of different forms of organizing going on right now," she said, "and we really do ourselves a disservice by only looking at examples of unionization in the traditional model. Workers across the board are recognizing their worth."

The pandemic has certainly been a catalyst for the renewed interest in organized labor, particularly within the restaurant industry, because for so many of us, there's little left to lose.

"For so long, the worst thing in people's minds that could happen was losing your job. And then they did. Everybody lost their jobs in March of 2020, and they realized, 'Wait—the worst thing I thought could ever happen just happened, and I'm still here. Maybe I could go do something else, maybe what I'd put up with for so long wasn't something I should ever have put up with,'" Jayaraman said.

The fight is happening via traditional organization as well. There has been successful unionization among restaurant workers in Austin, Texas, where on August 5 workers at Via 313 pizzeria filed for a union election, the first step toward officially unionizing, and won, as did workers at Tattersall Distilling in Minneapolis in August of 2020.

Both these collectives have yet to move into the contract bargaining phase with their employers, but the process has begun.

The farthest along in their journey are the employees of Colectivo, a chain of cafés and coffee roasters in Wisconsin and Illinois. Their fight began two years ago in response to what they described as a lack of safety protocols and consideration for staff during the pandemic, and they are now at the table negotiating their first contract with their employers. The unionized baristas, café workers, and warehouse employees are members of the International Brotherhood of Electrical Workers Local 494 and Local 1220, the electrical workers unions of Milwaukee and Downers Grove, Illinois.

"We're willing to sit down with anyone who is interested in learning to unionize," said John Jacobs, assistant business manager with Local 494. "On the surface it's like, *how does that work—the electrical industry and coffee?*" he said, which was exactly my question. But the IBEW covers a lot more than construction; there are a lot of different facets of electrical work. Ultimately, like most unions, the brotherhood's focus is on working conditions, and their expertise is in negotiating contracts. "These folks did not like where the company was going in forcing them to come into work during the pandemic and the staff's needs were not being listened to. That's the work we do," Jacobs said.

Ryan Coffel, a Colectivo barista and union organizer with IBEW Local 1220, said it has been a symbiotic and collaborative relationship from the start, industry differences aside.

"From the start, IBEW just said, '*Yes, all right, what can we do?*' We've learned how to do this in the café environment, which is pretty different from showing up at construction jobsites, and it's working," Coffel said.

The Colectivo union started in secret, first over Zoom calls and in private social media groups, but soon spilled over into in-person, on-the-job organizing—workers talking to coworkers and picking up shifts at different café locations to spread the word. When the vote to unionize passed in 2021, an estimated 400 to 450 Colectivo employees joined the IBEW.

"The thing that makes organizing in the service industry so difficult is feeling like it's not possible," Coffel said. "The biggest hurdle to get over is just the anxiety of reaching out to organizations. Call any labor organization. They want to help you, too."

We may never return to a time when one nationally recognized union represents the rights and interests of restaurant workers, but maybe that's okay. If I die on a hill, it will be while screaming about how being a bartender or a server is one of the most real jobs you can ever work; how fifteen dollars an hour plus at least 20 percent in tips is honestly the only fair wage for this kind of work today; how if you don't plan to pay your kitchen staff thirty dollars an hour you probably shouldn't open a restaurant. It is frustrating, to be sure, but it's becoming less so, because thanks to the work being done by the Starbucks 7, the Colectivo workers, IBEW Local 494 and Local 1220, One Fair Wage, the Restaurant Organizing Project, Restaurant Workers United, and the hundreds of workers out there organizing on every level, I know there are people on that hill with me, in solidarity.

Haley Hamilton is a Boston-based writer and bartender. Her writing has appeared on *Eater, Catapult, Bustle, Truly*Adventurous, Mel Magazine,* and elsewhere.

WHY I CHECK THE "BLACK" BOX

I Learned Racial Ambiguity
Was Not Something I Could Afford

Lori Teresa Yearwood

Slate, December 8, 2020

I have light-brown skin the color of coffee mixed with a ton of cream and dark, thick, curly hair. For more than fifty-one years, I checked the "other" box on any forms asking about my racial identity, writing on the lines allotted for explanation: "Father is Panamanian. Mother is white."

But the white police officer never asked me about my race.

"I'm taking you to jail because I don't like you," he told me as he escorted me to his squad car. I would end up living in the county jail, in a eight-foot-by-ten-foot cell, for the next six months.

It was September 2, 2016, and the officer, a plump, balding man, had been standing on the outskirts of Salt Lake City, waiting to arrest me, a homeless woman at the time, for bathing in a public river.

"African American/Black," my arrest record states.

Four years later, as I was combing through my records for my memoir, I found the officer's assumption about my racial identification. How, in the most vulnerable time of my life, had I lost my ability to define myself?

Through a quick succession of tragedies, I had lost my financial and emotional ability to stay rooted in my middle-class life. Suddenly, I plunged into a two-year-long nightmare in which I—a college-educated woman who had held good-paying jobs and owned homes—became homeless, grew severely traumatized, lost connection with myself, and got thrown in jail and locked up in psych wards.

In that state of quiet submission, in those terrifying places, I learned how those with the authority to do so could snatch me off the streets and lock me into tiny, fluorescent-lit rooms and cells, away from the fresh air, sun, and sky. I learned that I had lost control over how other people would classify me or treat me. And I learned first-hand the quintessential story of how this country can so callously de-value, even extinguish, a Black life.

Black women in the United States are almost twice as likely as white women to be incarcerated. The overall rate of Black imprison-ment for men and women at the end of 2018 was more than five times the rate among whites.

When it comes to mental health treatment, Black people are more likely to be considered mentally ill than white people. Clinicians tend "to overemphasize the relevance of psychotic symptoms and overlook symptoms of major depression in African Americans compared with other racial or ethnic groups," a 2019 Rutgers study found.

I didn't begin to put the pieces of the puzzle together until 2018, a full year after I was safely ensconced in a home, was working again, and could think about something other than staying alive on the streets. That's when I reentered the field of journalism by writing an in-depth article for the *Washington Post* about my plunge into and emergence from homelessness.

I revisited that first year, when I was repeatedly stalked, beaten, and sexually assaulted by a man who was working at the homeless out-reach center where I went to get my hygiene kits. And I remembered the best I could the start of the second year, when I began lying in desperation and nakedness on the streets of Salt Lake City.

On the occasions when the police took me to psych wards, no one bothered to ask any possible reasons behind my behavior before they injected me with court-ordered antipsychotics. If I showed any hesitation—such as backing away from the nurse administering the drugs—at least two more nurses would suddenly appear as a deter-rent to my hesitation. And so I acquiesced.

Sorting through the piles of paperwork to research my own story, I found that the diagnoses from various doctors ran the gamut from "possible civil disobedience" to "schizophrenic." But there was one consistent finding that followed me, whether I was put in a jail cell or a sterile white room: "African American/Black."

"YOU HAVE TO CHOOSE"

I wasn't raised to correlate the treatment that I received in the world with the color of my skin. Instead, I was brought up to believe that who I was had nothing to do with society's insistence, expectation, or definition.

My father had skin the color of deeply stained mahogany. My mother's skin was so white that without regular sunning, it appeared translucent.

My father had grown up in Panama, the son of a Baptist minister who encouraged his nine children to further their educations. So in his early twenties, my father left the row of humble but well-kept apartment homes where he was raised in Panama for Texas in the 1940s to attend Bishop College, a historically Black institution.

Jim Crow laws were in effect and my father was denied housing and jobs because of the color of his skin. Once, while he was sitting on a bench, a policeman physically kicked him off it. Not because my father had done anything wrong. But simply because that officer had the power to act in a hateful way and get away with it.

Vernon Yearwood-Drayton went on, through tenacity and grit, to become a microbiologist at NASA Ames Research Center, where he eventually worked on space shuttle experiments. That was the image I tried to emulate in my own life, and the one he insisted others relate to—not that of the formerly oppressed or downtrodden. Only rarely did he speak about the trauma associated with race in this country, because to do so would have made him delve into his own vulnerability. I also think that vulnerability is the reason he distanced himself from Black Americans who tried to befriend him.

It was only after my father's death, when I was researching my own memoir, that I learned my father's father had emigrated to Panama from the British-owned colony of Grenada. He was most likely the direct descendant of enslaved men and women kidnapped and shipped across the ocean from Nigeria or Ghana like livestock.

But his wife was white, as were her sons he'd adopted shortly after their marriage. So when I was born, at a Denver hospital in 1965, he insisted to the staff there that we were a white family. It was not until I began working on my book that I looked at my birth certificate and discovered I'd been officially defined as "white."

My parents didn't inform me about the racial identity they'd claimed for me. They didn't talk about race, and neither did I. Nor did I think about it much, in my early childhood, covered by my dad's cloak of protection and dreamlike naïveté. I simply had tan skin.

But it's not possible to stay naive about race in this country. My innocence was shattered in the seventh grade.

White kids from my middle school, mainly from the tony towns of the Bay Area, made fun of my voluminous hair—or simply ignored me by refusing to invite me onto their teams or to their parties. At the same time, many of the Black kids, who were being bused in from the then-almost-exclusively Black and working-class city of East Palo Alto, had taken to calling me "Oreo."

On a late fall afternoon, a bus about to cross the concrete wall and freeway that divided the affluent town of Palo Alto from East Palo Alto dropped me off. Just as I was walking beneath the bus's windows, one of the Black students spat on me.

My parents called the principal, and the next morning, a Black counselor at the school brought me to her office.

"What race are you?" she asked.

I thought about how my mother told me she had Cherokee blood in her and how her ancestors were from what was then Czechoslovakia. Like my father, she never talked about exactly how my ancestors came to this country. Perhaps she didn't know. Nevertheless, for me, the result was the same. I had been growing up with no ethnic or cultural identity in which to ground myself.

I stood in the guidance counselor's office, unsure what to say.

"I'm not any race," I finally told her. "I'm Black and white."

"You're going to have to choose," she said, shaking her head.

I didn't, though.

THE SIDELINES

As I got older, I continued to live a life on the sidelines of any racial identity. In some ways this worked for me. I majored in journalism in college and went on to land a reporting position at the *Miami Herald*, where I wrote about people from the city's wide array of racial and ethnic backgrounds—African Americans, Haitians, Cubans, and other Latinos, to name a few.

No one in the communities I covered asked me what race I was. The people I interviewed did not see me as an outsider, and yet I was, as I did not identify with any single race or culture in particular. This gave me a distinct asset in my field—a mix of outside acceptance and inner distance. I flourished in my work.

Making Black friends in the newsroom was a different story. I always felt apart from my Black colleagues, feeling as if there was always a wall between me and them.

I wasn't sure why. Sometimes I thought it was simply the competition that is part of the atmosphere of every newsroom. Other times, I wondered if my tendency to carry my past with me—and feel hurt at the slightest hint of rejection—was the problem.

Only decades later, when an old colleague from the *Herald*, who identifies as Black, contacted me on Facebook and gave some feedback about the situation, did I understand my loneliness. "There was some question amongst the Black reporters about whether you were authentically Black," he told me.

I didn't say much, but the idea of that reality made me feel angry and defensive. How could I have been any more authentically me than I already was, I thought. The truth is that back then, I never actually saw myself as Black. Nor did I see myself as white. I found my first reporting job at the Syracuse Newspapers in New York through the National Association of Black Journalists. I did feel uncomfortable identifying as Black when I didn't feel exclusively Black inside, but I had felt much more supported by my Black college professors at San Francisco State than I did by most of my white professors.

Besides, going to an NABJ conference felt more appropriate than attending the National Association of Hispanic Journalists, as my father didn't speak Spanish around me when I was a child. He and my mother didn't know how easily children can learn languages. Like a lot of parents back then, they thought it would only confuse me.

That was how, for fifty-some odd years, I navigated my way along the edges of the mainstream, learning how to live, sometimes even thrive, as an outsider in a world obsessed with race.

DIVIDE AND CONQUER

And then I was right in the middle of it, standing on a mound of grass by the river when I had bathed and then quickly dressed, with my hands locked behind my back while other people jogged and walked their dogs nearby. I could not know, of course, what that Salt Lake City policeman was really thinking when he arrested me. Is it possible that my race had nothing to do with my arrest?

But to believe that would be to cling to an incredible denial—a denial that the concept of race was created, and is still being upheld, by white people in this country to claim and maintain power for themselves. From the inception of this nation, white people have granted themselves privileges while denying those same privileges to Black people. When the barrier to Black people's right to vote was knocked down by the Reconstruction amendments, white people set it back up again for nearly another century, until the Voting Rights Act gave the federal government the power to enforce what had been in the Constitution for ninety-seven years.

That enforcement, prohibiting states from using literacy tests and other methods of excluding Black people from voting, went into effect in 1965, the year I was born. In October of 2020, *USA Today* reported that a poll worker in Memphis, Tennessee, had turned voters away who were wearing masks and T-shirts that read "Black Lives Matter." And in Cumming, Georgia, a man recorded a video of a poll worker telling him he would have to take off his Black Lives Matter shirt to vote.

Who falls into the "Black" or "white" category has always been socially determined. When I talked to Ronald E. Hall, a professor of social work at Michigan State University, about my experience with the police officer, Hall told me about the sociological concept called the master status—the aspect of a person's identity that other people take as definitive, above their other features.

He succinctly explained how it works: "I'm a professor. But a white policeman looks at me and he sees a drug dealer or a gang banger."

Hall is of mixed-race himself—his ancestry includes Cherokee, British, and African forebears—and he is the author of the book *Racism in the 21st Century* and a coauthor of *The Color Complex: The Politics of Skin Color in a New Millennium.*

"Regardless of what you do or what you say, your Blackness is the most specific aspect of your identity," he said. "Anything you do as a Black person, Black precedes it."

In 2000, the US Census Bureau began allowing people to choose more than one racial category to describe themselves. In 2013, approximately nine million Americans chose two or more racial categories when asked about their race. According to a survey by the Pew Research Center in 2015, 55 percent of the multiracial adults surveyed said they have been subjected to racial slurs or jokes.

A SHARED EXPERIENCE

At the same time I was feeling the powerlessness and shame of having my identity dictated by others, another act of identification was happening around me. Emerging from my collapse, to my surprise and comfort, I found a nearly unconditional acceptance primarily among Black people.

"Let me tell you how I can relate," so many people told me.

And when I least expected it: "I was homeless, too."

And: "Sister, I was arrested, too—and I had no idea what I had done wrong."

Again and again we would nod our heads in instant and mutual understanding.

One Black man, who founded a nonprofit in 2019 to help the indigent and incarcerated in Salt Lake City, had been homeless, spent time in prison, and lost all his friends. A Black woman who has become my closest friend in Salt Lake also lost almost everything. She went on to become a clinical social worker. And my former colleague from the *Miami Herald*?

He saw a Facebook post I had written about my collapse and wrote: "I can relate. We should talk."

We did, and he ended up referring me to the Economic Hardship Reporting Project, a news outlet that has since contracted with me to write many stories about the disenfranchised.

Don't get me wrong. I also have wonderful, steadfast friends who are white. But even in their kindness, I can't help but notice their continual shock at how the system betrayed me.

"Really?" they say. "I had no idea things were that bad."

In that surprise and denial of how broken the systems in this country truly are, I find myself too tired to bridge the distance by way of explanation. When will we stop being shocked by the police brutality so horrifyingly brought to our attention by the deaths of individuals like George Floyd and Breonna Taylor? When will we acknowledge that this country has a big problem and needs to deal with it?

I will never forget the day that I was released from jail, when I stood in front of a white judge, shackled and handcuffed, waiting for her to decide my fate.

"You have spent enough time in jail," she told me.

That charge against me was later dismissed, as my actions were proved to be a result of trauma—not a willful disobedience of the law. My mental health records have also been changed—the director of a psychological service agency that specializes in treating the homeless and formerly homeless, and who also helped me process the trauma I had experienced, went into my hospital files and erased every previous diagnosis, entering the words: "posttraumatic stress syndrome" instead.

Still, the past can never be fully erased. And that's why, today, nearly four years after my emergence, I choose to check the "Black" box.

When I check the "Black" box, I add my individual voice to the chorus of millions of others who need to be counted. On a census survey. On a hospital intake form. On an insurance form. On a housing application. In whatever way they can.

Even when I fear that I will be judged as lesser than and given unequal treatment—I sometimes still work through posttraumatic stress symptoms when I visit white doctors—I check the "Black" box.

I haven't stopped embracing the different ethnicities that make me who I am. But I was so clearly discounted for the color of my skin. And now I want that part of me to be counted as many times as possible.

Lori Teresa Yearwood is a national housing crisis reporter for the Economic Hardship Reporting Project. Her work has appeared in the *New York Times*, the *Washington Post*, the *Guardian*, *Mother Jones*, *Slate*, and many other publications. Lori is currently working on her memoir.

MY LIFE AS A RETAIL WORKER

Nasty, Brutish, and Poor

Joseph Williams

The Atlantic, March 11, 2014

> After the veteran reporter Joseph Williams lost his job, he found
> employment in a sporting-goods store. In a personal essay, he
> recalls his struggles with challenges millions of Americans return
> to day after day.

My plunge into poverty happened in an instant. I never saw it coming.

Then again, there was no reason to feel particularly vulnerable. Two years ago, I was a political reporter at *Politico*, and I spent my days covering the back-and-forth of presidential politics. I had access to the White House because of my reporting beat, and I was a regular commentator on MSNBC. My career had been on an upward trajectory for thirty years, and at age fifty I still anticipated a long career.

On June 21, 2012, I was invited to discuss race, Republican candidate Mitt Romney, and the 2012 presidential election on MSNBC. I said this: "Romney is very, very comfortable, it seems, with people who are like him. That's one of the reasons why he seems so stiff and awkward in town hall settings. . . . But when he comes on *Fox and Friends*, they're like him. They're white folks who are very much relaxed in their own company." The political internet exploded. Because I'm an African American, enraged conservative bloggers branded me an antiwhite racist. Others on the right, like Andrew Breitbart's *Big Media*, mined my personal Twitter account and unearthed a crude Romney joke I'd carelessly retweeted a month before. The Romney campaign cried foul. In less than two weeks I was out of a job.

Five months earlier my ex-wife and I had a fight. I pleaded guilty to charges of second-degree assault, and signed a court order to stay away from her and her residence. Upon completion of six months of probation, the incident would be wiped from my record. But in the wake of the *Politico* scandal, *Fishbowl DC* obtained the court documents and published a piece, "Ex-Politico WH Correspondent Joe Williams Pleaded Guilty to Assaulting Ex-Wife." Finding a new job went from hard to impossible: Some news outlets that had initially wanted my résumé told me they'd changed their plans. Others simply dropped me without saying anything.

That's how I found myself working a retail job at a sporting-goods store—the only steady job I could find after six months of unemployment in a down economy and a news industry in upheaval. In a matter of months, I was broke, depressed, and living on food stamps. I had lost my apartment, and ended up living out of a suitcase in a guest bedroom of an extraordinarily generous family I barely knew. My cash flow consisted of coins from my piggybank and modest sums earned from odd jobs: freelance copyediting, public relations, coordinating funerals, mowing lawns. So when "Stretch," the laconic, thirty-four-year-old manager of a chain store I'll call Sporting Goods Inc. called to tell me I was hired, it was the best news I'd had in a long time. (I have chosen not to name the store or its employees here, because the story is intended as an illustration of what it is like to work in a low-paid retail environment, and not as an exposé of a particular store or team.)

Of course, I had no idea what a modern retail job demanded. I didn't realize the stamina that would be necessary, the extra, unpaid duties that would be tacked on, or the required disregard for one's own self-esteem. I had landed in an alien environment obsessed with theft, where sitting down is all but forbidden, and loyalty is a one-sided proposition. For a paycheck that barely covered my expenses, I'd relinquish my privacy, making myself subject to constant searches.

"If you go outside or leave the store on your break, me or another manager have to look in your backpack and see the bottom," Stretch explained. "And winter's coming—if you're wearing a hoodie or a big jacket, we'll just have to pat you down. It's pretty simple."

When he outlined that particular requirement, my civil rights brain—the one that was outraged at New York Mayor Michael

Bloomberg's stop-and-frisk policy and wounded from being stopped by police because of my skin color—was furious.

Walk out immediately, it demanded. No job is worth it. Your forefathers died for these rights, and you're selling them for ten dollars an hour.

But Abraham Lincoln, in the form of the lone five dollar bill in my wallet, had the last word: "You, sir, are unemployed and homeless. You cannot pay for food, goods, or services with your privacy."

I'm not sure why—perhaps out of middle-class disbelief or maybe a reporter's curiosity—I pressed the issue. Seriously: I have to get searched? Even if I'm just going across the street for a soda, with no more than lint in my pockets? Even if you don't think I stole anything?

Stretch shrugged, unconcerned. Clearly he'd been living with this one for a while.

"Yeah, it's pretty simple. Just get me or one of the other managers to pat you down before you leave."

I hadn't had a job in retail since the 1980s. Perhaps youthful nonchalance and the luxury of squandering my paycheck on clothes or beer had helped camouflage the indignities of minimum-wage retail jobs, though I don't ever recall being frisked at the door. Yet over the decades, employee bag checks have become standard operating procedure in the retail environment, although some workers have pushed back.[1]

At that moment, however, I wasn't one of them. I needed something—anything—that resembled a steady job. I had to get back on the ladder. That meant sucking it up and starting at the bottom rung. So I chose two new store logo T-shirts, size 2XL. "Better make 'em roomy," Stretch suggested. "They tend to shrink in the wash."

Obtaining work in retail had changed a lot since the 1980s. What used to require a paper application and a schmooze with the manager has turned into an antiseptic online process where human interaction—and the potential for an employment-discrimination complaint—is kept to a minimum.

That put me at a distinct disadvantage.

In person, thanks to good genes, people often assume I'm younger than I am. On paper, however, I'm just another overeducated, middle-aged, middle-class refugee whose last retail experience dates to the Reagan administration.

Not to mention retail employers these days have their pick of applicants: the Great Recession added countless numbers of desperate workers like me to the annual labor-market influx of college students and high schoolers. According to an Economic Policy Institute report, "In 1968, 48 percent of low-wage workers had a high school degree, compared to 79 percent in 2012."[2] Likewise, the percentage of people in these jobs who have spent some time in college has skyrocketed, jumping from under 17 percent to more than 45 percent in the same time. All of us are in a race to the bottom of the wage pool.

Although older job candidates bring experience and skills to the table, their job applications typically blink like red warning lights to retail managers: *overqualified, overpaid, and probably harder to manage than some high school or college kid.* In a word: trouble.

"Think about it, Joey—that's why there are online applications," my sister, a veteran human-resources professional, told me. "If you apply online, and you never hear back, they don't have to tell you why they rejected you and face a discrimination lawsuit."

I soon realized the only way I'd have a shot in retail is if I dumbed down my job application, met directly with the person in charge before applying, and used my journalism storytelling skills to sell myself, stretching the truth past the breaking point.

It worked: I ambled into Sporting Goods Inc. on an inspiration one day, asked for an application, and then asked to see the manager. Luckily, Stretch bit on my fictional backstory—journalist-turned-community-college student, studying physical therapy in a midcareer change—and my real-life background as a lifelong athlete.

It was a perfect fit—at least in theory.

The first thing I noticed on my first day on the job is that in retail no one sits.

Ever.

It didn't matter if it was at the beginning of my shift, if the store was empty, or if my knees, back, and feet ached from hours of standing. Park your behind while on the clock, went the unspoken rule, and you might find it on a park bench scanning the want ads for a new job.

Another quick observation: Working in retail takes more skill than just selling stuff. Besides the mindless tasks one expects—fold-

ing, stacking, sorting, fetching things for customers—I frequently
had to tackle a series of housekeeping chores that Stretch never mentioned in our welcome-aboard chat. Performed during the late shift,
those chores usually meant I'd have to stay well past the scheduled
9:00 p.m. quitting time.

Mop the floors in the bathroom, replace the toilet paper, and
scrub the toilets if necessary. Vacuum. Empty the garbage. Wipe
down the glass front doors, every night, even if they don't really need
it. It was all part of the job, done after your shift has ended but without
overtime pay.

One afternoon, upon hearing that Sporting Goods Inc.'s top
managers were set to fly in from out of town for their annual review
of their retail troops, Stretch went on a cleaning binge, clearing junk
from the sales floor and the stockroom. When he finished, and I saw
the amount of garbage waiting for me to haul to the loading dock, I felt
like Hercules at the Augean stables.

There were five or so twenty-gallon bags stuffed with refuse along
with several piles of empty containers, cardboard boxes, and shipping
wrap. Two cases of expired energy drinks. Several unwieldy stacks of
outdated, five-foot-long cardboard displays.

The garbage run came *after* I'd already pulled my six-hour shift
on the sales floor, and done some of my usual closing-shift chores. At
the same time, since the other employee on duty was a petite young
woman, taking out the garbage was a solo operation. Forty-five minutes later, I'd finished, sweaty and slightly winded. Stretch turned off
the lights, I grabbed my things, and we headed to the door. Before
checking my backpack to see if I'd stolen anything, he said, "Thanks
for the hustle," and tossed me my bonus.

A pair of socks.

Granted, they were nice socks—high-tech, twenty-five-dollar wool
athletic socks, something I might have purchased on impulse in better
times. To the manager, it was a meaningful gesture; he seemed to sin-
cerely want to reward me for going above and beyond my usual duties.

But overtime pay, or some kind of financial reward, apparently
was out of the question. So he gave me socks.

There's an ongoing debate over whether Congress should hike the federal minimum wage from roughly seven dollars an hour, where it's been since 2008, to at least ten dollars an hour.

Proponents argue that three extra dollars an hour can lift hundreds of thousands of workers out of poverty. Opponents say a raise for hourly wage workers would keep some businesses from hiring and force others to make layoffs to stay in the black.

As a worker who earned ten dollars an hour, I say: Neither argument is entirely true.

Sporting Goods Inc., I came to realize, was fine with paying me a few dollars more than the minimum wage—officially $7.25 an hour in Maryland—because it had other ways to compensate itself, including disqualifying me from overtime or paid sick days. Requiring me to play Cinderella on the closing shift also saved management the money it would have had to pay a cleaning company to maintain the store. Yet even ten dollars an hour—about four hundred dollars a week before taxes—can barely keep a single adult afloat in a city like Washington.

A modest studio apartment in a safe neighborhood would easily consume an entire month's pay. Meanwhile, depending on circumstance, an annual salary of roughly $20,000 might not automatically qualify a retail worker for government assistance. One of my coworkers, a young single mother I called Flygirl, lived with her mom and commuted forty minutes, one-way, from a far-flung suburb to make ends meet. Most of my coworkers, in their early twenties or thirties, had roommates, spouses, or second jobs. None of them seemed to be making it on their retail salaries alone.

Even though I was living rent-free in a guest bedroom, my every-other-Thursday paycheck couldn't help me climb out of my hole, particularly after the state took half my pretax three-hundred-dollar weekly salary for child support payments. Grateful just to have a job, I didn't think twice when I noticed Stretch sometimes cut me from the daily crew and kept my hours under thirty per week—until Mike, a longtime friend and a former union shop steward, explained.

"You're part-time," he told me. "If you work forty hours or more, they'll have to give you benefits."

Because I live across town, meanwhile, I had an hour-long commute that cost as much as ten dollars a day round-trip on public transportation.

"Dude," my best friend Jamie said. "After taxes, you're making just enough to get to and from work each day."

Sporting Goods Inc.'s employee handbook has several entries about stealing from the company and its consequences: immediate termination, prosecution, imprisonment, and possible deportation. The threats were serious: I noticed about a half-dozen ceiling-mounted surveillance cameras spread across the store.

The cameras fed into a bank of monitors in the managers' office. The video feed was usually observed by a "loss-prevention officer," formerly known as a store detective. In our case it was usually a young, tattooed brother I'll call "Flex," who was built like an NFL linebacker and dressed in hip-hop style: baggy jeans, flat-brimmed baseball cap, T-shirt.

When things were slow, which was often, Flex would stroll around the sales floor, browsing the merchandise, chatting up the sales crew. I often mused that his presence in our workplace perhaps had a secondary purpose: subtly reminding Sporting Goods Inc.'s employees that the loss-prevention officer could probably chase you down and pulverize you if necessary.

But loss prevention, I soon learned, was a one-way street.

In my old salaried, white-collar life, I had the luxury of setting my own schedule, taking extra personal time if I needed it. The "flexible forty" worked because, generally speaking, my employers usually got it back when I worked through a deadline, for example, or came in on weekends to finish a project. By contrast, in the retail world, employees usually have to swipe a time card just to have lunch.

One evening, I got a stern reprimand from "Fratboy," the twenty-seven-year-old duty manager when I came back ten minutes late from my thirty-minute break. It seemed I'd lapsed into flexible-forty mode and inadvertently abandoned him on the shoe floor during an unexpected evening rush.

"I know it's not a big deal," he said. "Personally, I don't care. But what kind of manager would I be if I didn't mention it to you?"

So noted, I told him, won't happen again. Case closed.

The next day, however, when I clocked in a few minutes after the start of my 3:00 p.m. shift, Stretch sidled up to me near the outerwear rack, arms folded.

"Do you wear a watch?" he asked.

I thought it was a joke. Of course, I answered, waiting for the punch line.

"Well, Fratboy told me you came back late from your break last night. We can't have that."

Irritated by my tardiness, Stretch lectured me on time management, including an Orwellian principle found in retail: If you arrive on time for work, you're already ten minutes late. Showing up early is necessary, he said, so you can "get ready to hit the floor."

In that instant, I thought of my college football days, in full gear, psyching myself up for a game by blasting rap music into my headphones. Somehow, the metaphor didn't translate to selling Nikes and yoga pants to suburbanites.

I later realized Stretch was invoking the principle of "wage theft"— retailers expect employees to be in position ahead of time, making their life easier, even if the employees aren't getting paid for coming in early. There's even a website devoted to fighting the practice.[3]

Another loss-prevention irony: trash duty.

Under Sporting Goods Inc.'s protocol, two employees, preferably male, had to take the trash to the dumpster at closing time. One handled the trash; the other stood guard at the open loading-dock door. The refuse was tossed into a dumpster protected by both a built-in deadbolt with electronic keypad and a combination padlock.

Although the dumpster was in an access-only area with security patrols and cameras on every corner, the trash team was expected to stand watch—for thieves, it was implied, or armed intruders, or perhaps crossbow-wielding Visigoths on horseback. But as one of us carried and tossed the garbage, the other had no weapon more powerful than a shoe box.

I imagine the unstated objective was to send another subtle message about employee theft: someone is always watching, even when you take out the trash.

Perhaps the most vivid example of Sporting Goods Inc.'s obsession with internal theft was the fate of a friendly twenty-something who'd worked at the store for two years. Even the managers agreed the coworker I'll call Ike was knowledgeable, loyal, and dependable, the sort of employee who'd check out the competition on his own time and report on what he saw. As such, he was in line to become assistant manager, a promotion that would add a few dollars to his paycheck and more responsibility to his life.

One afternoon, Ike didn't show up for his shift. At the same time, the managers held a series of closed-door meetings away from the staff. Word spread like a virus: Ike had been fired for an unknown offense. The store managers refused to discuss it.

Rumor became fact about a month later when Ike came to retrieve some of his things. He told me that, before he got keys to the store, the personnel office at the company's headquarters did the requisite background check and—bad news—found an old larceny charge from when he was a teenager.

"They checked and said I didn't report it on my application. That means I lied to them," he explained, chuckling sadly at the irony. "So basically, I got fired because I got a promotion."

I knew I had to leave Sporting Goods Inc. when I realized I was turning into the sort of overeager employee who is way too emotionally invested in a crappy menial job that does its best to devalue him.

Having once supervised an eighty-member news division of a major metropolitan newspaper, the first weeks on my new job triggered a self-esteem meltdown. Flygirl, a supervisor half my age with a high school diploma, critiqued my shirt folding. I fruitlessly searched the shoe stockroom for the right size and style for an impatient customer. I silently prayed no one who knew me would come in during my shift.

As the learning curve flattened, however, my past life faded over the horizon and I gave up looking for an on-ramp back to journalism. Starved for approval after so much rejection, I started to take a weird, internal pride in my crappy menial job, almost against my will.

I felt a thrill when Stretch gave me a high-five for taking an online order from a customer without screwing it up. I quietly exulted when I correctly diagnosed that a customer needed stability running shoes and not the neutral ones he wanted. I congratulated myself on my work ethic when, instead of taking an unpaid sick day, I pushed through a Saturday shift despite a wicked, can't-breathe bronchial infection.

More than once, I fantasized that if I quit—*if I quit?*—Stretch would dangle before me the promotion that had been destined for Ike, begging me to stay.

Reality struck one afternoon, however, when a customer I'll call Jan came in for running shoes. Silver-haired, intelligent, and charming, Jan told me she'd recently retired from the US Treasury, where she'd helped oversee the 2008 financial bailout.

As I fitted her for shoes and checked her stride, we struck up a conversation about politics, finance, and the fact that not a single Wall Street banker had ended up in jail. Then, Jan hit me with a question I hadn't considered in the months since I hustled my way into a job I didn't want, had to have, and had come to accept.

"So, Joe," she asked, "What is it that you really do?"

I paused, slightly taken aback. "I sell shoes," I told her. That's my job.

"Yes, I understand," she persisted. "But what do you *really* do?"

By that point, it was clear what she meant: *Why are you here?*

Three months earlier, I would have anticipated the question, and had some vague answer handy. At that moment, though—unable to return to my chosen profession, unwilling to start thinking of an alternative—I mumbled something about being a writer, and let the subject drop.

I wish I could say that was the moment things turned around.

In a perfect world, after talking with Jan, I would have ripped off my employee T-shirt, thrown it in Stretch's face, and strode out of the store. In reality, it took another month or so before I got the opportunity to leave Sporting Goods Inc. for a temporary job as a communications director for a Capitol Hill nonprofit, a gig that paid twice as much per week as I'd earn in a month at the store. That salary still didn't come close to my *Politico* paycheck, though it was a step in the right direction.

When I called Stretch to quit, he wasn't happy, but he didn't try and convince me to stay, either, as I'd hoped. He did, however, manage to deliver a dig that all but summed up my time as a retail employee.

"So, your new job," he said, his irritation coming through the phone as he realized he needed to fill my shift for the week ahead. "They're hiring you away from here. I guess [you] don't care about hard work or loyalty."

Hard work, yes; I certainly did my share working for a store that didn't seem to value it all that much. I learned, however, that loyalty is a malleable concept—and incredibly difficult to find these days, even at ten dollars an hour.

CODA

It took a few detours, but in 2015 I found that on-ramp back to journalism when *US News & World Report* hired me as a reporter/editor. And in 2022 I took a job as a senior editor with Color of Change, an online civil rights and social justice nonprofit organization.

It's been nearly a decade since I worked at Sporting Goods Inc., but I still feel a kinship with people in thankless jobs like the one I had. That's why I was so excited to see union drives at places like Starbucks and Amazon. I loved seeing retail and hourly-wage employees using their power to stop wage theft, demand health care, and insist on their fair share of the wealth they generate for people like Howard Schultz and Jeff Bezos.

And after filing for bankruptcy protection in 2017, Sporting Goods Inc. closed the store where I worked with Stretch, Fratboy, and the rest of the crew. After a few attempts at restructuring, the company went out of business for good in 2022.

I still have both my T-shirts.

Joseph Williams is a writer in the Washington, DC, metro area.

WHAT IT'S LIKE RIDING ALONG WITH A VALET DRIVER AT A SAN FRANCISCO STRIP CLUB

Text and photos by Rian Dundon

The Washington Post, May 4, 2019

I used to park cars at a strip club in the city. It was a good gig—quick cash and free cardio running back and forth to the garage all night. And I got to photograph a little, with a view from inside my clients' cars and the urban spectacle as framed through their windows. At the time, this stretch of downtown was punctuated by a new LinkedIn skyscraper and the SFMOMA extension going up nearby. All of these things held weight to me as symbols and symptoms of the changing city. I quit the job after a year, just as a new ride-sharing app allowing users to summon a parking attendant with their phone was hitting the market. Anyone could be a valet now.

My job was fast-paced, but I had some time to make pictures on my rapid drives to and from the parking garage. I never photographed inside the club (only went in to use the restroom or drop money in the safe) but I saw meaning in the fleeting details of life outside, where half-finished construction projects were vying for room with a nightly flow of vehicles and humans. And I found a hidden thrill in studying the inside of strangers' cars for what they revealed about their owners.

Seeing the way money was spent at the club got me thinking about the influence of the tech business and all the people who make a living performing provisional labor on its fringes. These pictures are hastily made. Shot with a pocket camera, many are unsanctioned glimpses of people's personal space—a view from the driver's seat. But I'm also interested in what these spaces say about systems of labor and exploitation during a period of economic stratification in San Francisco. To the extent that they relay details from a specific nocturnal milieu, these photos are also evidence of survival.

253

"Doorman," San Francisco, 2013–2014.

"Valet Tips," San Francisco, 2013–2014.

"Self-Portrait as a Valet II," San Francisco, 2013–2014.

Rian Dundon is a documentary photographer from Portland, Oregon. He is the author, most recently, of the book *Protest City*.

YOU TALK REAL GOOD

Alison Stine

Longreads, October 21, 2019

Alison Stine confronts the ways in which being hard of hearing has made her job search more difficult.

Disability status?

It's a question I am confronted with almost daily when I fill out job applications. Sometimes I skip the question or I say I am not disabled. Sometimes I answer it truthfully, writing that I am hard of hearing (HOH), born partially deaf.

I was laid off eight months ago from my full-time editing job, and in the arduous process of searching and applying for positions, I often face this voluntary disclosure form asking what I am and what my body does and does not do. Disability isn't always included as one of the options on disclosure forms; it doesn't always count as part of diversity.

But my status has bearing on my job search. Less than 40 percent of people with a hearing loss have full-time employment, according to a study cited by NPR, in an article which profiles a woman very much like me, with hearing loss and multiple graduate degrees, who's applied to over one thousand jobs with no offers.

I've only applied to over sixty, as of this writing. But I haven't got any job offers yet.

Some who are d/Deaf would not consider me disabled, but instead, champion the identity as part of a distinct minority group. But perhaps because I was born into a family that was entirely hearing, I was raised to believe my difference was something to hide, not celebrate, a legacy of shame I am still unlearning. Deaf with a big *D* stands for the Deaf community, deaf with the little *d* stands for the physical condition of being deaf—I was so distant from Deaf culture, I didn't know this distinction until I was in my thirties.

I didn't meet another hearing-impaired person, or at least one who disclosed to me, until I was in high school. The reality is, I don't know what I am. Hard of hearing is perhaps a medically correct term, but for many people, it incorrectly conjures up the image of someone who is old and infirm. Am I disabled or not? Do I count or am I counted out?

According to the National Institute on Deafness and Other Communication Disorders (NIDCD), around two to three out of every one thousand children in the United States are born with some hearing loss. Over 90 percent of us are born to hearing parents, as I was. It's often an invisible difference, unnoticed by the larger, abled world.

I was born with less than 50 percent hearing due to a congenital issue. "A fluke," my mother told me her doctor said. I suspect, like most people as they age, I am losing more hearing, but have not been tested in years. I'm afraid to be. The last time I saw an ear, nose, and throat specialist, he wanted to "play a trick" on his medical student, to see how long it would take her to discover my hearing loss and what her reaction would be. He thought it was great fun, and was surprised when I didn't laugh. Pro tip: you can't be in on the joke if the joke is about your own body.

His joke, of course, was that most people assume everyone they meet is abled. Impairment, even to a med student, apparently, is a rude surprise.

I pass as hearing. I don't wear hearing aids, but even if I did, they would be hidden by my hair. I'm a younger, "healthy-looking" person— not the image that is conjured up when most people think of the hard of hearing. But after someone speaks, depending on how close they are to me, how loud or low or clear their voice, I have to quickly arrange the words in my head to figure out which ones logically are missing. I read lips. I'm able to make sense of a lot. But the rest is up to me. I'm a code breaker for daily living, a task I do constantly and with no support.

Because I pass, I am part of no group, without a clear identity or sense of belonging.

It doesn't always serve me to disclose. According to the National Deaf Center, a significant gap exists between employment among deaf and hearing people: only 48 percent of deaf people were employed in 2014, while 72 percent of hearing people were. The National Deaf Center makes clear, however, that this number may be so high in part because some deaf people may have given up looking for work. The Communication Service for the Deaf reports 9.6 percent of people specifically with a hearing loss are actively searching for employment but not finding it, like me.

Generally, people with disabilities are less likely to obtain higher degrees, and more likely to work part-time, according to the Bureau of Labor Statistics. Their salaries are much, much lower, too, as little as the shockingly low twenty-two cents an hour. Is it any wonder that almost 27 percent of people with disabilities live below the poverty line, according to the US Census Bureau?

"You can't tell at all," is the thing I am told most often when I do mention my hearing loss, followed by, "But you're a writer! You're gifted with language," revealing a lack of understanding that d/Deaf and hard of hearing people juggle and interact with, fight, and tame language more than any hearing person ever will. "You're so smart," is another popular, incredibly ignorant response, as if the physical process of hearing is connected to intelligence (it is not).

And my personal favorite comment about my hearing loss, which came, of course, from a hearing person: "But you talk real good!"

When I do disclose my difference, I try to make it casual. I start with "It's not a big deal . . ." Still I watch abled people's faces fall, time and again. A disabled or different person has entered their space—interrupted their life of not paying attention, not considering, or maybe not even caring—and suddenly everything has been upended. They feel bad for me; they feel bad about themselves, that they have it so easy, that they haven't had to think with each spoken interaction.

And weirdly, they feel bad that they don't know, somehow. Is it guilt, or a sense of alarm that they hadn't found me out?

I wonder if part of the aggression behind these remarks springs from abled people feeling betrayed by my identity—that they hadn't been able to guess about me, that I snuck in. If I, a person who is hard of hearing, publishes as a writer, has advanced degrees, and interacts with the hearing world so seemingly easily, who else in their space might be disabled, unbeknownst to them?

The answer, of course, is many people. According to the Centers for Disease Control and Prevention (CDC), sixty-one million Americans have a disability.

More women have disabilities than men. The unemployment rate for women with a disability was 11 percent in 2016, higher than the unemployment rate for men with a disability, and higher than the unemployment rate overall, as reported by the Bureau of Labor Statistics. Unemployment is even worse for women of color with disabilities.

Advocates have been trying to draw attention to the high rates of unemployment among people with disabilities on Equal Pay Day, the day of the year (it varies year to year) when the pay of white women (and only white women—women of color make still less) allegedly "catches up" with men's pay. But even a video on the disability pay gap from the Equality and Human Rights Commission, which lists statistics for "types of impairments"—including learning disabilities, impairments of legs or hands, and seeing difficulties—and their corresponding pay gaps, doesn't mention deafness or hearing impairments at all. Am I that invisible?

I know that, to many people, I am lacking: "You miss so much," a hearing man, a music major, said to me in college.

I know that when people find out about my hearing loss, they respond with several emotions, like that man did: disbelief, sorrow, guilt. They feel bad for me. So do some people in the Deaf community. "You're not a part of any world," a sign language interpreter once told me.

And that remark does feel true. I hear some spoken language, but not all. I know some American Sign Language (ASL), but not enough to be fluent; I've never had anyone in my life to sign to.

Hearing people also tend to feel bad that they didn't know about my difference. But how could they know? I pass, both by accident and on purpose.

Growing up, it was easier to just pretend I got everything—and for the most part, I did. I nodded at boys. I said yeah a lot. How was this different from any number of (hearing) girls, how we were all expected to be: silent, supportive, watching on the sidelines, our fingers curled around chain link fences while the boys played sports, our hips glued to the arms of couches while the boys played video games?

I blended in by falling back. My hearing loss was misinterpreted as just being shy, just being young. Just another girl who hid her body in sweatshirts and long hair; who hid her deafness in smiles.

No one worried about my job prospects because I was so "bright" and driven. No one told me that it might not matter how hard I worked. No one warned me about the unemployment rates among people with disabilities and impairments, maybe because I had no one d/Deaf in my life to tell me about their lived experiences.

When it came to daily interactions with hearing, orally speaking people, I wasn't given a key; I had to invent it. And I wasn't given a prize for figuring it out in record time, for responding appropriately, and for not letting on that I was different. Since I was a child, I've had a headache almost every day. It took another ASL interpreter to help me make sense of that. "It's from listening so hard," she said. I was concentrating so intently on interactions with hearing people, I caused myself physical pain. I'm not the only hearing-impaired person to report daily headaches.

It took insightful friends and lovers to realize: You didn't hear what I said, did you? To speak up even when I couldn't or didn't know to. Having a hearing loss has forced me to be loud, to speak up for what I need and am legally supposed to have, to speak up again when I am not believed or taken seriously the first time. Or the second time, which happens often.

It's really not a lot I need: to sit with my more profoundly deaf side against the wall so that I can hear those in the room better; to not teach or give a lecture, as I have been forced to do multiple times, right next to a loud fan or bleating air conditioner.

But the very nature of my difference is quiet.

I am so used to being dismissed, it never occurred me until recently, as I apply for job after job and receive no offers, that my hearing loss might be part of it.

Maybe there is something off about me, impacting my job prospects. You can't put your finger on it, but it's enough to mark me as other.

Dr. Brenda Jo Brueggemann, a deaf and disability studies scholar, once wrote that people thought her "accent," from her hearing loss, was German. One of my ASL teachers said there was a slight distinction to my voice, but it was minor; you had to be trained in hearing issues to understand what it might mean. She said she wouldn't have assumed about my hearing loss, even as a specialist, if I hadn't disclosed it.

It's a funny mantle to wear: difference, but difference no one really knows about unless you tell them. And then they may not trust you about your lived experience, anyway.

It's why I spent hours working up my courage to ask a friend how I could join the disability caucus of an organization for writers we both belong to. Because if people can't see inside my head, if they can't hear what I hear or know what I miss, how I fear rejection even among those with whom I am supposed to share an affinity, how will they know I'm different? How will they believe me?

I don't have it that bad, I always tell others—and myself. I was born like this. I've never known more sound. I've never missed it. And I think I'm doing okay. But I know it might be holding me back professionally—and financially.

We need to have more discussions about disability and deafness, what limits us and what doesn't limit us. I can do absolutely everything that a hearing professor, a hearing writer, a hearing editor, a hearing person can do, except hear you clearly if you whisper on my side, or if we're in a loud bar at a crowded table—and frankly, that's not in the job descriptions for those professions. Most hearing people have a hard time in those situations too.

Still, there are things people make jokes about in public spaces without shame. Deafness is one. It's also, despite being mocked, something that everyone makes claim to. "I'm a little deaf, haha," joked a woman at a conference recently where I was speaking. When it was my time to lecture, I disclosed that I am partially deaf and asked if anyone needed the handout I had printed of my remarks for accessibility reasons.

Weirdly, no one was a "little deaf" then.

Everyone is a little deaf until I speak up that I need accommodation, as required by law, and suddenly, nobody is. And nobody knows what to do about me either.

The answer is nothing. You really have to do nothing. And as my hearing boyfriend said to me recently, "It's not your job to make sure you hear me. It's my job to make sure I speak clearly. And I should be doing that work all the time, for everyone."

As I'm applying for jobs, I pause on the disclosure form. I want to tell future colleagues and employers that they should just give me a chance. You don't have to treat me differently, I want to say. You don't have to guess. You don't have to dismiss me outright. The only thing you have to do is listen to me tell you what I need. You simply have to listen: the very thing you've been expecting me—and many people like me—to do my whole life.

Alison Stine's debut novel, *The Grower*, was published by Mira in fall 2020. She lives in the foothills of Appalachia.

THE SECRET LIVES OF ADJUNCT PROFESSORS

Gila K. Berryman

Elle, December 15, 2021

On the first day of class in September 2014, my undergraduate students stared at me, surprised. They were expecting an instructor who looked more conventional, more white, more male. Yet there I was, a butch-of-center Black woman, with a boyish haircut and a men's button-down shirt, teaching their first English class at New York City College of Technology (City Tech).

To my working-class Black and brown students, I looked like I could be their neighbor. Very quickly, they grew to trust that I meant it when I said, "We can talk about anything in this class, as long as we do so respectfully." The literature we read became a springboard to discuss issues they wrestled with daily: economic survival, racism, sex, adulthood. They shared traumas and fears in their essays and lingered after class, divulging their personal struggles. I advised them on practical life skills such as navigating school bureaucracy, registering to vote, and managing emotional conflicts. In their eyes I had it together.

About halfway into the semester, I stopped by the supermarket to pick up dinner. I placed a roll and sandwich meat on the checkout counter and pulled out my EBT (food stamp) card to pay. Then I heard the cashier say, "Hi, Professor Berryman." I froze for a moment. My face heated up despite the cold. I took a breath and offered a quick, "Oh, hey, good to see you." But I couldn't meet her eyes; I was staring down at my EBT card—wishing I was anywhere else.

I was part of what the American Federation of Teachers (AFT) calls "an army of temps." I have a master of fine arts degree in creative writing from New York University, a novel-in-progress, an EBT card, and Medicaid. According to the AFT labor union's 2020 report, a quarter of adjunct faculty members surveyed depend on public assistance, 40 percent struggle to pay for basic household expenses, and one-third earned less than $25,000, putting them below the federal poverty line for a family of four. As colleges and universities increasingly rely on adjuncts—with nearly two-thirds of faculty members off the tenure track, according to a 2018 analysis by the *Chronicle of Higher Education*—the vast majority of higher education instructors face alarming economic insecurity.

I wasn't ashamed of using food stamps to afford groceries. But that day I felt like a fraud. What kind of role model was I? I was a Black woman teaching working-class Black and brown students the importance of learning to write clearly so they could get a good job, yet I couldn't support myself on my own salary.

Aside from that grocery store incident, my students had no understanding of my reality. They assumed I made good money. A few guessed my annual salary came close to $65,000. The truth: Over the decade I spent as an adjunct instructor, from 2010 to 2020, I averaged about $10,000 per year on a part-time course load and $16,000 per year on a full course load. The most I ever made in a year was $23,000; that year I took on summer classes plus twelve hours of tutoring per week. This in addition to a full academic year course load which required grading roughly six hundred papers per semester. I suffered a severe case of burnout.

Once, I was grading seventy-five assignments in my government-subsidized one-bedroom apartment in Crown Heights. Piles of student papers covered nearly every surface, teetering on the desk, the chair, the rolling file cabinet, my grandmother's walnut coffee table, and the couch. After three days of grading, my brain verged on shutting down. I closed my eyes wishing it would all disappear, but quickly forced myself to open them again. "Come on, Berryman," I said out loud, "you can do this." I took a gulp of tepid coffee and set the mug down; it was smack on top of a student's paper, but I was too tired to care.

When I returned the paper, I apologized to the student for the coffee stain. She looked bewildered, and asked why the stain was there. We stared at each other awkwardly. I didn't understand her question. "I'm sorry," I repeated. Later I realized that the student must have imagined me sitting at a tidy desk in my office, grading papers. I did have an office, but I shared the cramped space and five desks with seventy-four adjuncts in the English department. Even if there was a place to sit, it was rarely quiet enough to concentrate on grading.

Most adjuncts must hustle to survive. I met an adjunct who worked the night shift at Trader Joe's in Manhattan, because they provide part-time employees with health insurance. In the morning, when his shift ended, he commuted more than an hour to get to campus. My particular hustle involved house-sitting during the summer so I didn't have to pay for rent and utilities.

I housesat for a couple—two tenured math professors—while they vacationed in Spain with their school-aged children. They lived in a pre–Civil War era house in Western Maryland; it was surrounded by flower gardens that twisted with the contours of the landscape, and a pasture that gave way to rolling hills. The architecture was fascinating and quirky, and the setting was idyllic, but what I loved most were the living room walls lined with books. I'd run my fingers along their spines and whisper their titles to myself. *Cavedweller, Their Eyes Were Watching God, Song of Solomon.* I'd move along the bookshelf this way, reading first paragraphs and author bios, until I found a book that I couldn't put down. Then I'd plop on the couch and lose myself for half a day. I coveted this kind of space for myself, where I could be surrounded by books in a room that wasn't a living room, dining room, and office all in one— somewhere without piles of papers about to topple to the floor.

Back at home, I woke up one morning, spit something into my hand, and stared at it. I was looking at half of my back molar. I was mortified. I couldn't remember the last time I'd seen a dentist, and I could hear my grandmother's voice in my head, "You have to take care of your teeth." I stared at the bizarre-looking chunk of tooth that was supposed to be anchored into my jaw, and called my grandmother who agreed to pay for my six-hundred-dollar dental work.

When a friend and fellow adjunct had tooth pain, she had to choose between paying to see a dentist or putting gas in her car so she could get to work. She couldn't afford to have her tooth fixed. Instead, she used tea bags to draw out the infection until she could save enough money to have the tooth extracted.

In time, I got tired of not making a living wage. I wanted to stop worrying about my teeth falling out. I wanted to say yes to my friends' invitations to writing conferences in far-flung destinations. I wanted to work, but I also wanted to live. So, last summer, I stepped away from the classroom and supported myself with a combination of pandemic unemployment and freelance writing and editing jobs. I also moved from Brooklyn to Durham, North Carolina, where the cost of living is more affordable.

Adjuncts teach over half of all college classes, yet institutions treat them as if they're expendable. According to College Factual, at City Tech, a 49 percent minority faculty serves an almost 90 percent minority student body. Research conducted on the subject as well as other studies show an increase in minority students' performance, and retention rates when they see themselves reflected in the body of the faculty. Students need instructors they can relate to, and who can relate to them—people of color, working-class people, and openly LGBTQ people—so they don't feel alienated within a strange and vast institutional system. But if the policies that created the deplorable treatment of adjuncts persists, minority instructors like me will continue to leave academia.

Toward the end of the last semester I taught in New York, a young Black man lingered in front of my desk after class. He was the kind of student who sat sideways in his chair during class, feigning inattention, but offered a thoughtful analysis when I called on him. As soon as the other students were gone, he blurted out, "Do you think I should join the Marines or become a mechanic?"

I was used to students confiding in me; I often walked them to the counseling center if they needed more than just a sympathetic ear. This was different. Signing up for the military is a serious commitment; it's the kind of decision to discuss with family. I was humbled by his trust in me. But as much as I wanted to, I wasn't going to tell my student what to do with his life.

I looked up from where I sat, behind my desk, at the bright young man towering over me waiting for an answer. You can do this, I thought. And I could. I could ask the right questions—guide him through parsing fact from perception, I could help him distinguish his own values from societal expectations, so he could reach his own conclusion. It was how I conducted my classes.

I took a deep breath.

"Come," I said, "Pull up a chair."

CODA

According to the AFT, the pandemic threatened the already shaky job security of adjuncts and increased their need for government aid. Some are fighting back. On November 14, 2022, 48,000 University of California teaching assistants, graduate student researchers, post-doctoral scholars, tutors, and fellows staged a walkout, demanding a livable wage and benefits. On the other side of the country, in New York—due to a law that was implemented over half a century ago—state employees, including City University of New York's (CUNY) adjunct instructors, are prohibited from striking. The 1967 Taylor Law granted New York State's public workers the right to organize, and required employers to negotiate with them; this same law however, prohibited public employees from striking. Nevertheless, the Professional Staff Congress (PSC), the union representing CUNY's adjunct instructors, continues to make incremental progress on behalf of the workers. The 2017–2023 PSC-CUNY agreement secured up to forty-five paid office hours per semester as well as a 2 percent wage increase which went into effect on November 1, 2022.[1]

Gila K. Berryman received her MFA from New York University. Her work has appeared in *Entropy, Lilith Magazine, Mobius: The Journal of Social Change, Stitch, Transition Magazine,* and *Elle.*

THE POETRY OF LABOR

On Rodrigo Toscano and the Art of Work

Rodrigo Toscano, with an introduction by Alissa Quart
and a photograph by David Bacon

Literary Hub, March 4, 2022

The OSHA outreach trainer arrives in Walla Walla, Washington, or in Pendleton, Oregon. If he flies to Tulsa or Tucson, he then drives up to two hundred miles to wherever the union locals are. He is there to support immigrant worker centers as well as linemen and telecommunications workers, traveling so much that he can lose track of where exactly he is, teaching them how to protect themselves from being injured on the job. He will teach a thirty-hour class sometimes, with anywhere from twelve to forty students. He may ask them how many have suffered a heat-related illness on the job, and all their hands go up. They tell him about people who have died or been maimed at work and recount their own near misses. Training here is not lip service. It also is an ongoing effort to undo the lie that safety is employees' responsibility, a truism overturned more than fifty years ago with the Occupational Safety and Health (OSH) Act of 1970.

What sets the trainer in these scenes apart is that he is also an acclaimed poet, Rodrigo Toscano, author of ten books of poetry, all quite different of one another. While his day job is as the national director of the nonprofit Labor Institute, for more than twenty-five years Rodrigo has also been known in the poetry scene for his highly accomplished, vigilant, even didactic poetry. It's what tends to be called "experimental," mostly because it's both cerebral and relentlessly class-aware and political in a way that can make gatekeepers uncomfortable.

The fifty-seven-year-old's verse, like the courses that empower workers that he sets up around the country, is poetry that engages with the world of work, including its impasses and oppressions. He

269

tracks the places where refined—or literary and academic—language meets everyday speech.

The typical poetry reader may have recognized, post-Trump, that there are *bubbles* of American life, without always seeing that even their own bubble is sustained in part by political violence. That's partly due to the limits within mainstream literary culture, as Rodrigo tells me, where the range of social class identities, work and educational experience, and even ideological affinities are entirely constrained.

Rodrigo is a rarity in today's literary scene, partially because for much of the last fifty years, the labor of literary production has been siloed from other kinds of labor. There are reasons for this—reasons of norms and habits, as well as ideology. As Mark McGurl observes in his 2009 book, *The Program Era: Postwar Fiction and the Rise of Creative Writing*, American creative writing became synonymous with the university writing workshop. That narrowed not only the style and subject matter creative writers used but also narrowed who became "professional" writers in the first place, as the degree programs cost so damn much. (It's hard to underestimate the effects of these programs, multiplying more than ten-fold to 854 creative writing degree programs from seventy-nine in 1975.)

Rodrigo is very much *not* a product of this MFA regime. He was born in San Diego to a Chicano father and a Mexican national mother. His father was a tool salesman, and Rodrigo and his brothers spent some of their childhoods bundling tools for their father. His father didn't make much money, selling along the border, as the Mexican peso was devalued at the time.

As a teenager from an economically stressed family, Rodrigo didn't do particularly well in high school, although he was already a self-described autodidact, reading advanced political philosophy on his own. He was not college-tracked, so when he graduated from high school, he launched into a job where he manufactured circuit boards in a factory. At the same time, he was "taking care of my own education," as he puts it, informally (the use of the care economy to describe self-education seems apropos.) Rodrigo was, in this sense, already "swapping out," as he writes in one poem, an earlier way of thinking for a more useful new framework:

Working folks don't trade up, let alone, down
They simply—swap out, shit, folks, ideas.

After many years in Brooklyn, he now lives in New Orleans, that rare example of a city where a poet and a labor worker might afford to own a house. When I talked to him the other week on the phone, Rodrigo was still coining words, making up the word "monosectoral" to meet the needs of our conversation—to describe how little economic, class, labor, and ideological diversity there is in our literary society and how little that sphere is concerned with issues that people in other industries have to face, including injury. (This "monosectoralism" can be said to be true of journalists also.) I now will use this word myself.

Perhaps what we need to triumph over literary society's *monosectoral* vision is to do what Rodrigo writes about in his poem "Swapping Out," which like so many of his poems is achieved, demotic and immaculate, and as art sometimes electrifying. Rodrigo writes here that when "something's not working" we should take the givens—of how labor is treated, and the norms of our creative writing sphere—and "Swap that shit out," as Rodrigo writes, "let's get moving."

—**Alissa Quart**

FOUR POEMS BY RODRIGO TOSCANO
Linemen

Thirty thousand linemen in bucket trucks
Streaming into your distressed environs
Hitting sixteen-hour shifts, repairing
Lines that keep your identities well lit
The lines that give your powered distinctions
The punch they need to remain—aesthetic.
That is, when the lines are down, days on end
Your projects oblivious to these men
And the striving families they're part of
Start losing power, hour by hour.

By around the fifth day, you're like the rest
Overheated, exhausted, half crazy
And perhaps becoming dimly aware
Linemen have zero power in the arts.

Burlingame, CA. Juan Chavez, a maintenance electrician at the San Mateo County
Hospital. Public workers here are represented by the American Federation of State,
County and Municipal Employees.

Resurrection

God (yes, god) an uprooted fence, *that* one
Went on a ride during the hurricane
It was wild, it was also destructive
But only to people who love fences
And want them in place, dug in dutifully
Not flying around, god (yes, god) hurling
Smashing into shit, conjuring spirits
Muscular movements managing messes
The holes re-dug, the posts re-positioned
God (yes, god) hadn't dreamt of Hondurans
Before the wild flying, the flopping down

How battalions of migrants stand sturdy
Steadily regirding the wrecked city
Alongside good neighbors, resurrected

The Cut Point

The trashmen do come
and that's a miracle
on top of the marvel of
home water heaters
and central air cooling

Your whole life
is brained up
by designs of others
alongside others
executing plans

This density
of intentions
is the world
you navigate
even in sleep

There's a Grand Rebellion
against this world
taking many forms
one such one is
lyric poetry

These failed rebellions
deepen the myths
we tell ourselves
about ourselves
in kooky ways

Why's everything become
rejoinders
rejoinder on rejoinder
this ceaseless
chatty inflation

The trashmen know
the cut point
AC repair crews know
the cut point
some poets maybe

The density is we
the needle to cloth
is we and surely
the rivet to plate
is Zoon Politikon

The 'likes' and 'follows'
do come
dressed as miracles
vaguely intentional
fizzling fast

Behold (is an old word
meant to—behold
what's beholden
to something
say, this tub faucet)

The density
of intention here
calls up legions of
poetic actors
pushing limits

The water that flows
is a cut point
the pipes that held it
are cut points
the dam, the dials

But what about clouds
have we rebelled
against wily whisperings
are clouds merely
constructivisms

No matter, the trashmen
have arrived
on top of the marvel of
a no. 2 pencil
tracking the point

Swap Out

There's no phrase in the entire English tongue
That gives me the *tingles* more than "swap out."
Working folks don't trade up, let alone, down
They simply—swap out, shit, folks, ideas.
Something's not working? Have you tried and tried?
OK! Swap that shit out—let's get moving.
But the problem is, where get the parts, and how?
Let alone, at the time when you need them.
But even this tune of have-nots and haves
Is something folks swap out, if the tale's stale.
Working folks, you've noticed, prefer new things
Things they've thingified to—*thingaramas.*
There's another phrase that's kin to "swap out"
And that is "crap out," most folks just—crap out.

Rodrigo Toscano is a poet and essayist based in New Orleans. He is the author of ten books of poetry. His latest books are *The Cut Path* (Counterpath, 2023) and *The Charm & The Dread* (Fence Books, 2022). His previous books include *In Range, Explosion Rocks Springfield, Deck of Deeds, Collapsible Poetics Theater* (a National Poetry Series selection), *To Leveling Swerve, Platform, Partisans,* and *The Disparities.* His poetry has appeared in over twenty anthologies, including *Best American Poetry* and *Best American Experimental Poetry (BAX).*

Alissa Quart is the author of *Bootstrapped: Liberating Ourselves from the American Dream* and executive director of the Economic Hardship Reporting Project. She has written for many publications, including the *New York Times,* the *Washington Post,* and *Time.* Her honors include an Emmy Award, the SPJ Award, and a Nieman Fellowship. She is the author of four previous books of nonfiction, including *Squeezed: Why Our Families Can't Afford America* and *Branded: The Buying and Selling of Teenagers,* and two books of poetry, most recently *Thoughts and Prayers.* She lives with her family in Brooklyn.

David Bacon is a writer and photographer, former factory worker, and union organizer. He documents workers, migration, and the struggle for human rights.

ZEN AND THE ART OF UBER DRIVING

John Koopman

Fast Company, July 14, 2016

> John Koopman used to write for a newspaper; then he became an
> Uber driver: "Thanks to Uber, I am not poor. I am just . . . nobody."
> First comes rage. The rage of impotence.

It's not easy being nobody, especially when you used to be somebody. But times are tough; jobs are scarce. When you're falling straight down the financial cliff face, you reach out to grab hold of anything available to stop your descent, and there, just before you land in a homeless shelter or move in with your sister, is Uber.

It's a little after ten o'clock on a Friday night. I get called to a home in Pacific Heights. Two women are at the curb, swaying. A young woman gets in, and her friend tells me to take the woman to Corte Madera in Marin. Yeah, sure, good trip. Surge pricing.

You know when a burp is not a burp? When it's followed by vomit. The woman in the back burped. I said a little prayer, "Please don't let it be throw up." We stopped at her house and she got out. I looked in the back to make sure she hadn't left a phone or purse. I saw a puddle of something on the seat. No. No! I got out and grabbed some napkins I kept in the glove box. And there I was—master's degree, twenty-five years as a journalist, Pulitzer nominee—wiping vomit off the car seat. The napkins were small and the liquid soaked through to my hands.

That's the kind of moment that makes you question your life decisions.

I spent twenty-five years as a newspaper reporter and editor, most recently at the *San Francisco Chronicle.* I loved that job because there was never a dull moment. I loved writing on deadline. I loved covering fires and murders and wars. The greater the risk, the greater the thrill. I went to Iraq three times, embedding with Marines and Army units, and saw a lot of combat. Winston Churchill once said, "Nothing in life is so exhilarating as getting shot at without result." Yes, exactly.

It came as quite a blow when the *Chronicle* laid me off. I should have seen it coming. The economy was in the toilet and newspapers were yesterday's news. Probably, I could have made the switch to on-line news, or public relations, or some kind of writing or editing gig. But that wasn't the point: Those jobs wouldn't give me the thrill. They would not scratch the itch.

So I floundered. One day I spotted an ad on Craigslist seeking managers for several strip clubs in San Francisco. Now that was my kind of job.

What I didn't know was that I was in a downward spiral. A lot of undiagnosed depression and anxiety burned at my insides. A fire started deep in my soul and turned into rage as it burst from my head. For most people, strip clubs are bad places. Not because women are naked. Because they snort coke when they strip. Because the place is filled with sociopaths and psychopaths. Guys get drunk and try to mess with the girls, or refuse to pay their bills, or spit on the floor. Every night is fight night and I loved it. For a while, it fed my addiction. Sometimes I provoked a fight just to see what would happen.

But my fuse got shorter and shorter. My rage built like a volcano about to erupt. I had to get out. I started driving Uber, where I had to get my rage under control or lose my job and possibly die.

What I did not know—and could not foresee—was that Uber would bring me to a Zen-like state. It would soothe my soul like a river stone and bring me peace.

I'm driving along San Francisco's Embarcadero, trying to pick up a passenger at the Ferry Building. There's a bike path to my right and I move into it while looking for the fare. Two bicyclists behind me start screaming at me for blocking their way. One slams his hand on the hood of my car.

I slam on the brakes and honk my horn. I get out and snarl, "Touch my car again and I'll kill you."

I see a meter maid coming toward me and I realize I'm about to lose my job and maybe go to jail. I beat it out of there and go park. Breathe, I tell myself. Breathe. It don't mean nothing.

It's midnight on a Saturday and I pick up two tech bros. One apparently is the boss of the other, but they laugh and joke like buddies. I don't pay much attention until I smell something horrible. One of them has just let loose a fart that would gag a maggot. They're laughing; I'm not. But I bear it. We're only a couple of blocks from their destination, the Fairmont Hotel. I figure I will let it pass and get on with the night.

We pull up. One guy gets out. The other does not. It's the farter.

"Open the door for me," he says.

I'm incredulous. "You want me to get out and open your door for you?" I ask.

"Yes. This is Uber Black and the rules say you have to open my door for me," he says.

Did you ever have one of those moments where you see a whole world in your brain, an enormous and lengthy narrative of things in your life that you did, or wanted to do, or just how you see yourself? I saw myself in Iraq, dodging rocket-propelled grenades in Al Kut, and watching the statue of Saddam Hussein coming down in Firdos Square. I saw myself speaking to a rapt audience at the Commonwealth Club about the political situation in Iraq. Then I saw myself at the strip club, inviting an angry pro football player to take a punch, hoping he would. What went wrong?

I thought about getting out of the car and slamming the bro's head against the hood. It would feel so good. It would also get me fired. If I did as much as threaten this kid, I knew he could complain to Uber and they would not understand how insulting this job can be for someone who used to be somebody. Even as time stood still, the options swirled in my brain. Okay, tough guy, now what?

I got out of the car, opened the door to the back seat and let him out. Somehow he had the good sense to remain silent and not make eye contact.

I told that story to a friend. He was unsympathetic.

"You got your feelings hurt by some rich asshole?" he asked. "Now you know how the rest of the world feels."

I do not consider myself poor. Last year, I made $43,000 before taxes, working about thirty to fifty hours a week as a driver. And I could have made more. Not a lot more. But more. That's not a bad wage unless you live in the most expensive city in America. Which I do.

I like Uber. They pay on time and there's no nonsense. A lot of people hate the service, and want a lot of changes. Yeah, whatever. You know what I know? I know that if I drive a certain number of hours at certain times of the day, I will make money.

I drive for UberX, which means the company keeps 20 percent of all my fares. I pay for gas and maintenance and insurance. When it's all said and done, it's not a lot. But it's enough to get by, just barely in San Francisco if you are lucky enough to have a rent-controlled apartment like I do.

I have heard some drivers who drive limos, or own black SUVs, like Navigators and Escalades, work the airport and make $80,000, $90,000 a year. I find that a little hard to believe, but there are always ways to improve your income. You have to be smart; you have to know the best times and places to be. You have an app on your phone, and when a passenger wants a ride, the system finds the nearest drivers and sends an alert. You take it or you don't. Some of this is pure luck, but you can help yourself by knowing where those good fares will come from.

The majority of the drivers at the airport on a Sunday morning are young Middle Eastern men. Uber is these recent immigrants' ticket to the American dream. The rest are older white men like me, along with a few white women, working a second job or in the second or third acts of their work lives. For many of them, the American dream isn't working out so well. A driver I know owns a home in a swanky San Francisco neighborhood, but she has no income. She could sell the home, but doesn't want to. So she rents out a room through Airbnb and drives Uber part-time. That gives her enough cash to go on, but I always wonder, for how long?

More and more, passengers ask me about driving for Uber. Figures released last year showed Uber has more than 160,000 drivers in the United States. There were more than 20,000 in Los Angeles, and more than 15,000 in San Francisco alone. Uber doesn't care who you are and what you did in life, as long as you weren't a criminal. If you can drive and keep up your rating, you can work.

I think of Uber as a modern-day version of the Works Progress Administration during the Depression. Thanks to Uber, I am not poor. I am just . . . nobody.

When I first started driving, I talked to every passenger. I engaged in conversation about the city, life, and politics. I told them about my work as a reporter, and as a strip club manager. I felt the need to say, "I'm not really an Uber driver. I am someone too. Just like you!"

Nobody cared.

I found that I could become visible or invisible at will. It's about the voice. Say "please" and "thank you" and shut up and drive. Don't make eye contact. People come in with their antennae up and on alert. Once they see you are no threat, they turn you off.

This crushes the ego. As it turns out in my case, that's a good thing. Next comes acceptance. I am a driver. I drive. I work and go home and then work again. I speak less and listen more. People drone on about their work and lives and I nod as if to agree even as I think, mostly, "What a wanker."

Only when they initiate conversation do I join in. It just doesn't matter. Nothing matters.

And that's when the healing starts. It is "Zen and the Art of Uber Driving."

Trip after trip, the miles beat you down. Where I once seethed at downtown traffic, I am now calm. I am now cool. Nothing bothers me. When some idiot is trying to cut in front of me, I care not a bit. I breathe slowly, my mouth open slightly. Sucking in oxygen, feeling the air move across my lips and into my lungs. Breathe. Focus. Feel. This is a moment. See it and be it and experience it.

The mind-numbing traffic. The destruction of ego. The loss of identity. These things teach you that you have no power. You have no control. Whatever power you thought you had was an illusion. That epiphany scares the hell out of you at first. And then it feels liberating.

You can let go.

I don't want to fight anyone anymore. I don't yell, I don't scream. I smile and wave when cabbies honk and flip me off. I let other drivers cut into my lane and think, "Go on, man, run to your meeting."

I don't care. I'm free.

It's late Saturday night. I'm out by San Francisco State University on the far edge of the city. I get called to take a couple to the hills of

Daly City. When we get to their destination, the guy decides he wants go to the Mission District instead. But now—big surprise—the Uber app isn't working. I have no cell reception and neither does he. It's dark, it's late, it's isolated in those rolling hills. The guy says he'll give me twenty dollars cash if I just drive them where they want to go. I'm not supposed to do that, but I don't have much of a choice. I agree.

It's about a twenty-minute drive to the Mission and the fare would normally be about twelve to fifteen dollars. I pull up to a bar and they get out.

One thing you learn in the strip club world is: always get the cash up front. The guy pulls out a five dollar bill and hands it to me. "I don't think that ride was worth twenty," he says.

I look at the bill and a thousand thoughts go through my mind.

I laugh and take the bill. Because you know what? It just doesn't matter.

CODA

In late 2016, I quit driving for Uber and moved from San Francisco to Omaha, Nebraska. Both my mom and my dad (long divorced) were elderly and not in good health. After twenty-five years away, it was time to go home and help them in their final years.

So I took a job tending bar for my best friend from high school. It was a dive bar on the South Side, with a rough group of regulars, cheap booze, and fist fights. My kind of place. Mom died fifteen months later, but at least I had my time with her. I was at her side when she took her last breath. Dad died exactly five years later, December 17, and my voice was the last thing he heard. Never would have happened if I had remained in the newspaper business.

I wish I were a poet warrior, but instead I am a philosopher drunk. But I'm happy. Low stress and easygoing. In the end, that's all you can ask for in life.

John Koopman is a former reporter for the *San Francisco Chronicle* and the author of *McCoy's Marines: Darkside to Baghdad.*

SECTION 5
Class

INTRODUCTION

Astra Taylor

When I was young everyone was "middle class." The United States, we were told until the aughts, was a big undifferentiated mass. Some poor people at the bottom, sure, and a few rich people at the top, but the myth was that most people lived in between. It was an idea so fanciful that, as the comedian George Carlin said of the American dream, you had to be asleep to believe it.

The 2008 financial crisis woke the country up to the fact that the economy's rewards were not, in fact, distributed on a curve. Or, more accurately, it alerted elites to this fact (no doubt lots of people knew full well they were poor). Overnight, inequality became a matter of urgent national concern. As millions of people faced foreclosure and lost their jobs, it was clear the middle—or what was left of it—was shrinking and being squeezed. Occupy Wall Street, through its rhetoric of the 99 percent and the 1 percent, popularized a class framework that shifted the terms of the political debate, even if the terms the movement offered were still a bit fuzzy. The 99 percent, after all, includes a whole lot of people, uniting them only by the fact of they are not the megarich.

The notion of class, though more commonly discussed in earlier eras, has long been awash in confusion. Class and its assorted categories can be tools of clarification or of obfuscation, depending on who is using them and why. Class is not only about how much money you have in the bank. It relates to the role you play in society, specifically where you fit into the economy's systems of finance and production. The stories gathered here reflect some of the complexities and nuances of class in the United States today. Together they offer a prismatic view of class stratification and its personal consequences.

In their piece, the writer Erynn Brook and the illustrator Emily Flake distinguish between being poor (a lasting condition) and being

284

broke (a temporary lack of funds). Other pieces in this section look at how class inequalities are compounded by age, by having been incarcerated, or the urban-rural divide. You'll see how class is not only an economic phenomenon but also a cultural one—more money means more cultural capital in the form of access to education and other status signifiers, which in turn beget more access to opportunities to earn wealth.

At the same time, the assembled essays make clear that class divides are always reinforced by moral judgments. In other words, they challenge the common portrayal of poverty being the result of poor people's poor choices. The choices? They smoke and drink too much, take on too much debt, don't study hard enough, are lazy, and so on. In her piece, June Thunderstorm writes of the smoking bans in place to protect "self-destructive" workers that are, in fact, about social control. But such lifestyle directives cloud the truth. Economic insecurity is the inevitable product of an economy structured to let one class of people exploit another.

As these pieces help us understand, the solution to capitalism's incessant shaming and stigmatization of poor people is not to be nicer to them or create conditions of inclusion (even if being nice and inclusive are better than the alternatives). This is how class differs from other forms of identity, like race, gender, sexuality, or disability, even as class intersects with these categories in important ways. As Stuart Hall rightly observed, "Race is the modality in which class is lived."

The difference, however, is that unlike racism or sexism, the problem of class is not a problem of classism—of discrimination against or exclusion of people based on their wealth or income. Rather, the problem is class exploitation and the fact that these divisions exist at all. Thus, the solution is not to change society's attitudes about the poor, but instead to create a society in which poor people no longer exist because everyone is adequately and equally provided for.

Abolishing class requires building the power to challenge and transform capitalism, a process that requires class consciousness—an awareness among masses of people of the fact of class exploitation and a desire to challenge it. This revolutionary awareness is precisely what the myth of the middle class helped suppress. But even as that myth has lost some of its power, new mystifications have emerged to take its place. In the hands of the rich, racist reactionaries who increasingly position themselves as opponents of a shadowy liberal "elite," class becomes kitsch. When invoked by the right, the phrase "working class"—always imagined as white, male, and cisgender—becomes yet another tool of ruling-class domination.

That's why the essays like the ones compiled here are particularly important today. They are stories of both class oppression and class consciousness. Thus, they are stories that can build class solidarity, rather than lulling us into passivity. Instead, they help awaken us to the possibility of our collective power.

Astra Taylor is a documentary filmmaker, writer, and political organizer. She is the director, most recently, of *What Is Democracy?* and the author of *Democracy May Not Exist, but We'll Miss It When It's Gone.* Her previous work includes *The People's Platform: Taking Back Power and Culture in the Digital Age,* winner of a 2015 American Book Award. She is cofounder of the Debt Collective.

THE DIFFERENCE BETWEEN BEING BROKE AND BEING POOR

Erynn Brook, with illustrations by Emily Flake

Longreads, June 2018

It's a recognition that comes in the aisle of a grocery store.

Everyone I've ever talked to who has been poor and isn't anymore has the same story of the moment they realized they were no longer poor: grocery shopping.

Mine came when I was loading my groceries
onto the cashier belt and realized I hadn't done the math.

When I was poor, grocery shopping required complex
math—holding numbers in my head, constantly remembering
the pre- and post-tax prices of the things in my basket

There was also
survival math:
"If I go to bed
before the hunger
hits, then half a
bagel is enough
for dinner."

When you only have ten dollars a week for groceries—which was my budget thirteen years ago—a nickel can be the difference between "accepted" and "declined" on the card reader.

For years I didn't know how to cook meat because I couldn't afford it. I was a vegetarian from my mid-teens to my early twenties, because meat would've cost me my budget for an entire week's worth of food.

But there's a difference between being broke and being poor.

When you're poor there's no flow. There's no wiggle. There's no credit. There's no extensions. There's nothing. It's all survival. It's your manager at your café job brining tears of relief to your eyes when at the end of a long day they ask you if you want to take home the extra muffins.

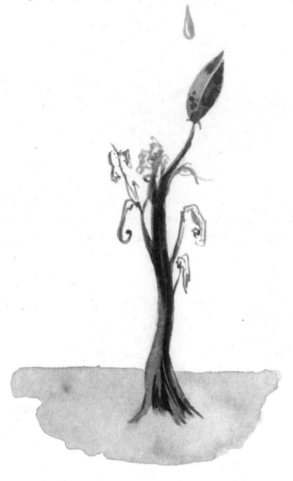

When you're broke you have flow. You have credit. You know you just need to get by for a few days or a week, and you'll budget better next paycheck.

(Or maybe you won't. You're still learning.)

When you're broke, you worry about how you would pay for an emergency expense. You get scared. You decide to plan better. You hide a $20 bill in your winter coat pocket because it'll be a nice surprise next year when it gets cold and you do't have mittens.

When you're poor every day feels like an emergency and you're drowning in it. The difference between being broke and being poor isn't a number. It's a bright light at the end of the tunnel. It's a direction. It's flow and movement and space to think.

I think about the grocery store a lot. About the time when I didn't have to do the math anymore. All the stories people have told me about their moment of realizing they weren't poor anymore and how it all had to do with grocery shopping.

Survival. Food. Rushing through the grocery store trying not to look at the things you can't afford. Seeing pasta on sale and welling up because it meant you had an extra $2 to work with that week. Being afraid of messing up the math and not having a dime "just in case."

I think about how little I survived on and how much it hurt, how it consumed me every day. Trying to calculate mealtimes so that I would be able to fall asleep before the hunger became too painful to ignore. And I think it's a fucking shame we let anyone live this way.

And it was so natural. I didn't even realize it until I was at the checkout. It just happened. I wasn't shopping in poverty. I was broke, but not poor—and it changed my world.

I don't trust a damn study, expert, article, or opinion about poor people if it can't differentiate between being poor and being broke. If you've never cried in a grocery store because it's too hard to live, you don't know what the problem is.

Erynn Brook is a feminist and freelance writer who studies media, people, communication, and culture.

Emily Flake is an illustrator for the *New Yorker*, the *Nib, MAD Magazine*, and *New Statesman*, among other places.

THAT SINKING FEELING

Ray Suarez

The Washington Post, April 30, 2020

I clung to the middle class as I aged. The pandemic pulled me under.

We were on a busy DC street, waiting for the light to change, when my teenage daughter asked, out of nowhere, "Dad, what are you afraid of?" That might have been a cue for a heartwarming father-daughter conversation about overcoming life's challenges. Nope. From my lizard brain, or from the primordial soup in my guts, came an answer I didn't even consider, out of my mouth before I had a conscious thought of it.

"Being poor. That's what I'm afraid of." Then we crossed the street.

I keep returning to that exchange over the past few weeks, as my inbox fills with coronavirus-driven bad news. A paid speaking engagement in Texas? Canceled. Several days of work at an international conference? The organizers decided not to take the risk. A gig moderating a climate change conference in Chicago? Postponed, maybe until October. When I traveled as a reporter to health crises in Africa and Latin America in recent years, exposed to malaria, tuberculosis, and pneumonia, I knew that if I got sick my health-care costs would be paid by my employer, as would any days I needed to recover. In 2010, covering the devastating Port-au-Prince earthquake in Haiti for PBS, I caught something that lingered when I got home, so I called in sick.

Now that I'm a gig worker over sixty, "sick days" are simply salary-free days off. Even if work dries up, that $2,800-a-month health insurance bill still comes due on the first of the month. The electric company won't take a podcast, a column, or a television documentary as in-kind payment for kilowatt hours.

In the first two decades of this century, wages declined for working men over fifty-five with bachelor's degrees.[1] When men over fifty who are displaced from their job finally get another one, they can ex-

295

pect their wages to fall 20 percent.[2] Such declines signal the decreasing bargaining power of older men. In a downturn, older men do hold on to their jobs more regularly than younger ones, but when they lose work it takes them considerably longer to find their next position.

Men older than fifty-five can't command higher salaries in the marketplace, but they also can't walk away and rely on their savings, which, for millions, are inadequate. Northwestern Mutual has reported that one in three baby boomers, knocking at the door of retirement, have less than $25,000 saved.[3] A study from the New School estimates that 8.5 million older workers over fifty-five would fall into poverty or near-poverty if they retired at sixty-two and began taking Social Security payments.[4] It is, the researchers found, the end point of more than twenty years of lagging behind younger men in wage increases, both among college-educated and non-degree-holding men.

An eye blink ago, I was anchoring a nightly program for the cable news network Al Jazeera America. Before that, I had long tenures with *PBS NewsHour* and NPR. When I read warnings that workers could face sudden and catastrophic losses of income in their final years of employment, I was empathetic but concluded it could never happen to me. After all, I had worked hard to build in bumpers around my life, and my career, to avoid that. I climbed the ladder in a very competitive business to jobs of greater renown, greater responsibility and higher pay. I did all the things that would have made me the hero of a financial advice column: got married and stayed married, paid off my mortgage years early, fully covered three college educations so my kids wouldn't have to borrow. Then the wheels came off. After Al Jazeera pulled the plug on its young network, I headed to Amherst College as a visiting professor while beating the bushes for jobs in radio, television, and print. I shoved down the rising panic, kept one eye on my bank balance as I started freelancing, and kept the other eye out for the next big thing. Like hundreds of thousands of men in their early sixties across the country, I had to get used to the idea that the marketplace might have already decided I was "done." Many men my age are "job bound," more convinced than their young coworkers that they couldn't find a comparable position, even in a tight labor market.

"What's this about? Corporate greed. Greed has a lot to do with it," says Nick Corcodilos, the author of the *Ask the Headhunter* blog and an employment consultant.[5] "I'll get a guy in my office who'll tell me: 'I was making $150,000. I'm scrambling to get jobs at $115 or $100. I just need a job.'" Corcodilos knows what companies say. "You'll hear explanations like, 'They cost more, their benefits cost more, they're out more often because they're sicker.' It turns out, it's all BS."

For me, the financial strain arrived quickly. As my COBRA health coverage reached its time limit, my wife and I had a long talk about how to lower our enormous monthly health-care costs. One quick fix was to drop dental coverage, so we did it. Two weeks later, I was riding my bike on DC streets when I hit an enormous, and unexpectedly deep, pothole. The shock slammed my jaw shut, but I shook it off and continued to pedal. Then the pain began—first searing, then a steady, throbbing ache radiating from my jaw to my eyes to the top of my head. It felt like my teeth were misaligned. I was having trouble chewing food. In just a few weeks I had moved from being a guy who had top-drawer health coverage to being one of the guys I read about, one of the guys I covered, who deferred health care for fear of the cost.

The pain eventually subsided, but the complications that allowed it to persist are still with me. I am years away from what I had thought of as the age when I could transition to part-time work. I have worked hard to avoid raiding my retirement savings to cover current expenses. Home repairs I would have had done without a second thought have to wait until there's money: The front steps need to be remortared and reset. A dying tree in the yard needs to be cut down and carted away.

These past few weeks indicate that I'll soon have plenty of company. Take the predicament of men my age at a time of 3.7 percent unemployment and add the army of people now filing unemployment claims—4.4 million in one recent week alone.[6] It's unclear at the moment just what federal and state government emergency programs will do for millions of self-employed and gig-economy workers, many already hustling in the best of times, who've been watching their work dry up and disappear.[7]

If my own experiences are any indication, what comes next for many of them is insecurity about self-worth, status, and place in the world. My name appears on mailing lists from my days as the old me. I'm asked to make generous contributions to organizations for which I had written big checks in the past; today, that's out of the question. I feel sheepish talking publicly about all this, because I know how many live a lot closer to the edge than I do. But I'm not whining when I say my life is different now. Even before social distancing rendered the outside world strange, I would do a walk-through at the supermarket with my wife's list in hand, to see if items close enough to what was specified were on sale. A pair of old shoes is resoled for a second time instead of being replaced. There will be no vacations for my family when this crisis ends.

And that doesn't change the fact that I have some serious decisions to make about what these years of my life, and what's left of my working years, can be. If I for once don't follow the rules, take my Social Security early and start drawing from my 401(k) accounts, I will be poorer in retirement than all my planning and saving ever assumed. I can swallow hard and realize that a chapter in my life may be over. That would mean proceeding on the theory that a cratered annual income is now the reality, rather than just an aberration. I have to scratch together the dough for my property tax, my homeowner's insurance, and my monthly premium. I'll keep an eye on the calendar and cross the line to Medicare as so many friends have begun to do.

One thing I don't ask is, "Why me?" Given my age, given the numbers, given the realities of work in America for those who are displaced, I could well ask, "Why not me?"

Ray Suarez (@RaySuarezNews) was a senior correspondent for *PBS NewsHour* and host of the public radio show *America Abroad*. He is host of EHRP's podcast *Going for Broke* and cohosts the program and podcast *WorldAffairs* for KQED-FM and the World Affairs Council.

OFF OUR BUTTS

How Smoking Bans Extinguish Solidarity

June Thunderstorm

The Baffler, December 15, 2016

The powers that be say antismoking legislation is for our own well-being. Nothing could be further from the truth. The attack on cigarette smoking does not improve the lives of those it claims to protect, be they the "self-destructive" workers who smoke or the moralizing professionals who complain about having to smell them. Antismoking legislation is, and always has been, about social control. It is about ratcheting up worker productivity and fostering class hatred, to keep us looking for the enemy in each other instead of in those who are making a killing off cigarettes and antismoking campaigns alike. It legitimates the privatization of public space, limits popular assembly, and forces the working class out of political life into private isolation via the social technology of shame. It whitewashes the violence exacted on the poor by the rich to make it all seem like the worker's own doing. It is, in short, class war by another name.

It is easy to charge hypocrisy on the part of supposedly benevolent governments concerned with "public health." Alcohol and sugar damage the consumer to an extent comparable to cigarettes, and hurt "nondrinkers" as well—ask any woman familiar with drunk men, or the cane-cutters of Latin America. But the class character of the war on smoking is so pronounced that one begins to wonder just who the "public" in "public health" is anyway. It certainly does not include Nicaraguan plantation workers, nor most Black Americans—unless we can call police murdering Eric Garner for selling single cigarettes some sort of "pro-life" operation. Of course, cops in the United States also kill Black men simply for walking around and breathing, so maybe cigarette packs should read: "Smoking Is a Leading Cause of Death Unless You Are a Black Man, in Which Case SMOKE 'EM IF YOU GOT 'EM."

Neither does the "public" protected by public health initiatives include people of the working class, no matter what color they are. If it did, initiatives would be directed first and foremost at the process of production, not consumption. And I mean production of everything. After all, anyone who works for minimum wage already expects organ damage, physical pain, a reduced quality of life, and an untimely death. And that, no doubt, is why the "If You Smoke You'll Get Sick" warnings on packs aren't working very well to inspire this particular group to quit: working shit jobs for shit pay is making the working class sicker, faster. And yet the promoter of "public health" does not concern herself with how the workers must soon enter the building to demolish rotten fiberboard all day. She is interested only in what they consume outside the door on their brief ten-minute breaks. Why should this be?

THE POLLUTING POOR

This apparent contradiction clears up once we understand that the public health campaigns of modern government have never been about protecting everyone. They are, rather, about protecting privileged citizens from the dangerously contaminating poor. "Health and safety" provided the rationale for corralling dispossessed peasants into England's workhouses and slave-trading navy, just as "health and safety" was the slogan of British imperialists working to justify colonialism and the slave ships themselves. In fact, it seems when civilized governments discuss "health and safety," what often follows is "sickness and death," so we are wise to stay on guard.

From early modern times, the emerging capitalist bourgeoisie worked to articulate its particular value in contrast to the "hedonistic" aristocrats and the "irrational" underclass, both imagined as grotesque. The masses, in particular, came to be defined by a supposed excessive enjoyment of bodily pleasures. This was in pointed contrast to the new self-denying entrepreneur, who pretended not to have any bodily functions. Orgasms, eating, sweating, and shitting were impolite, dirty things, which anxious bourgeois moralists projected onto others in a fit of collective neurosis.

Indeed, women, the poor, and "primitive" colonial subjects were all conveniently constructed as porous and leaking "mouth-breathers" driven by primal desires, while elites were rational, well-contained, and ultimately decoupled from the body and its practical functioning. The poor or racialized woman, imagined as spreading disease with her unbridled sexuality and infecting touch, was of particular concern to the new social hygienists. Hence the trope of dangerous servant women such as "Typhoid Mary," the New York cook who was quarantined for more than two decades after being apprehended in 1915 as a "symptomless carrier."

This social imaginary persists today in many guises, one of which is the dehumanization of the polluting smoker via her depiction as a series of dismembered rotting body parts (such as the nasty impaired lungs we keep seeing in antismoking propaganda), all in the interest of public health. Car emissions, soda pop, pharmaceutical medications, and nano-weaponized drones all have the potential to disturb the healthful existence of the young white bourgeois child, yet her mother supports these ventures with her taxes and consumer choices while spitting insults at the smoker waiting at a bus stop: she's just a toxic bag of body parts, after all.

I recently saw a woman brandishing the MercedesBenz of strollers walk through a sea of idling traffic toward a smoker only to say the smoker was "murdering her baby" by polluting the air. Such an act has nothing to do with protecting children, and everything to do with venting bourgeois malaise by attacking powerless people whom state authorities have constructed as abject and undeserving of respect. These same state authorities allow corporations to poison our food and water supply—so of course they don't mind if we lose our shit over some smoking neighbors instead. Indeed, the mouth-breathing neighbor with nasty black lungs is apparently more threatening than cigarette smoke itself: although the smoky wisp that has not yet been inhaled is more toxic, the great danger to nonsmokers, according to public health authorities, is secondhand smoke. Ultimately, the cigarette stands in for what bourgeois bystanders have always been most afraid of—the notion that they, too, have bodies, and that these bodies materially coexist with, and indeed create, the "vile" working class.

PUBLIC SPACE, RECLASSIFIED

I am not suggesting any sinister conspiracy of technocrats here but rather a confluence of vested interests. The push to ban smoking in the workplace in the 1980s did indeed stem from research on "Increasing Productivity Through On-Site Smoking Control"—but of course not everyone concerned about tobacco was a profit-seeking vampire, nor were foes of workplace smoking specifically targeting the poor. Smokers at the time were still considered "classy."

This is why the eighties campaign to vilify smoking was one and the same with a bid to declass it. Much as women were sold sophistication by way of Benson & Hedges, Holiday, and Parliament, with men offered similar (simulations of) power and mobility in Marlboro Country, cigarettes were to be made unappealing through new associations with foulness, odor, dirt, depravity, uncontrollable desire, and the inescapability of body parts—concepts that the bourgeoisie, in their efforts at distinction, had long projected onto the racialized working poor. In other words, cigarettes were symbolically associated with the lower classes before the poor were the majority of those (still) smoking, this being part and parcel of constructing the act of smoking as unhealthy. Smoking was consistently depicted as both unhealthy and an emerging professional-life taboo that might derail an eager yuppie's career advancement. "Cigarettes May Burn Holes in Your Career" was the alarm sounded in a 1985 magazine feature in *Career World*, with other savvy works of eighties career counseling echoing the same theme.

Now, in 2016, cigarette smoking in North America is indeed more common among people living in poverty. They smoke because they do not have the time or money to eat properly, because other, more respectable mind-altering drugs are not available to them, because it is something to enjoy. They do it because their jobs (when they still exist) are so boring and physically painful that they would rather die. Yet professionals in the wellness industry routinely describe their smoking social inferiors as "stupid" and "irrational" on the basis of their supposedly self-undermining lifestyle choices.

It's by now an iron law that whenever the poor are discussed, so are their "bad life choices." If professionals can't do something properly or fast enough, they can readily avail themselves of a diagnosis of one or another "health problem"—even something as vague and generic as "stress" or "burnout." These are conditions that are imag-ined to have stricken them randomly—as opposed to a malignant, self-inflicted malady tied to their lifestyle, upbringing, or that sketchy antidepressant they stupidly decided to take. Even though so many children of the professional class clearly have asthma due in part to the persistent bourgeois hygiene neurosis (the antibacterial hand gel all but mandated by this neurosis being a proven contributing fac-tor), they and their germophobe parents deserve empathy, time off, and specific disability rights. By contrast, working-class smokers de-serve only reproach and are asked to tiptoe around the expansive, so-cio-moral and self-induced sensitivities of the rich.

This wildly differential diagnostic treatment, which draws on age-old caricatures of the poor as case studies in lapsed self-control, parallels the entirely differential structure of empathy in the work-ing-class workplace: whenever low-income workers can't do some-thing properly or fast enough, they are simply fired, and anything that would otherwise qualify as a health problem or disability is chalked up to "personal failure." After all, this is someone who made the "bad choice" to live in poverty in the first place.

It is no coincidence that these same workers are widely perceived to deserve the exemptions of "health" as little as they deserve prop-er pay. "Public health" has always reinforced class divisions through such unequal attributions of "choice" versus "constraint." As a univer-sity student, I could not get a proper note from the Office of Students with Disabilities prescribing some time off to quit smoking because, as the nurse said, "Starting smoking is something you *chose* to do." My peer with back problems also chose to get into the car that crashed during her European holiday, yet it seems to be taken for granted that professionals simply "need" vast cosmopolitan mobility. (One can al-most hear a public health flunky confronted with this counterexample gasping at the suggestion that this health outcome was also, in some deep sense of things, an earned one: "You can't suggest that was her own doing! . . . One needs to get around somehow!")

No equivalent concept of structural "constraint" is applied to the working-class smoker, who is rather imagined to enjoy (but mishandle) infinite power and choice. This is so even though the smoker in question is brought up to smoke just as the jetsetter is to fly, and continues to do so largely because state and capital consider her undeserving of food. In fact, the smoker needs nicotine to function just as the suburban professional needs his car, and if she can't perform at work for even just two days, it will actually matter. She may lose what little food access she has. Furthermore, this smoker's daily activities, paid and otherwise, which would be curtailed by the pains of nicotine withdrawal, are generally important for the greater social good. An obvious early casualty is the caregiving labor involved in the "second shift" duties of working mothers in the domestic sphere. *Huffington Post* writer Linda Tirado says it all:

> When I am too tired to walk one more step, I can smoke and go for another hour. When I am enraged and beaten down and incapable of accomplishing one more thing, I can smoke and I feel a little better, just for a minute. It is the only relaxation I am allowed. It is not a good decision, but it is the only one that I have access to. It is the only thing I have found that keeps me from collapsing or exploding.

And so the lowest-paid workers continue to smoke, with public smoking restrictions serving only to inspire working-class shame and ruling-class belligerence. Whether because workers smoke or their friends do, the traditional places of working-class congregation are now closed to them—the pub, the diner, the park, and even the sidewalk. It is no coincidence that fifteen feet from the door stands the gutter. And how convenient for the boss that shooing smoking workers from the door downstairs makes it less likely for them to bond in conversation.

Today's student left is unfortunately complicit. Its adherents implement "scent-free spaces" prohibiting perfume, tobacco, and industrial odors in their organizing meetings, because it is apparently more important that the fraction of bourgeois professionals with allergies participates in their "anticapitalist" social movements than the majority of all people living below the poverty line. They call these maneuvers "accessibility policies."

Once, at an Occupy Wall Street assembly, standing six feet beyond the last concentric circle in the parking lot, I lit up a cigarette. In short order, I was asked to leave. I insisted on occupying. Such are the grinding wars of public accommodation in the United States—a country whose people are so poorly entitled to any public space that simply occupying a park is a big deal. In other countries around the world, workers do that sort of thing all the time. Maybe the American resistance could go and do likewise—if, that is, its leaders would welcome workers to their meetings, cigarettes and all.

SMOKERS OF THE WORLD, EXHALE!

If the lifestyle lords of the ruling class want us to quit smoking, they can provide us with the resources required to spend a quarter of our waking hours drinking kale smoothies, doing yoga, and attending trauma therapy just like them. As long as they fail to meet such elementary demands of mutual social obligation, they deserve much worse than a little secondhand smoke. Meanwhile, we members of the smoking class might consider using bourgeois paranoia to our advantage. We might start organizing "smoke-ins" fifteen feet away from high-end daycares, exhaling in their general direction until all kitchen and cleaning staff are paid five times the minimum wage plus full health and dental coverage. Persons of the educated class may suggest this is "mean" or "violent," of course, at which point we may direct them to the reputable oeuvres of Frantz Fanon and Walter Benjamin.

If the government really cared about working-class smokers' health, our political elites could easily fund our well-paid vacations, free therapy, and other support services by slashing corporate subsidies. Instead, they direct bourgeois unhappiness our way. Instead, they blame the poor for contaminating the world, while funding paramilitary offensives in defense of filthy transnational mining projects and neocolonial oil and resource wars—conflicts that will make the world much less safe for their children than a smoldering cigarette ever could. Indeed, even if government did offer smoking citizens the most tempting of golden handshakes, we might nonetheless exercise our prerogative to refuse their dirty money and blow smoke in their faces instead.

In the meantime, my last words for the smokers are simply: Never let anyone make you feel ashamed. You should be able to smoke precisely as much as you want. This is not because mass-produced cigarettes or "Big Tobacco" are beautiful things. They are not. It is, rather, because *we* are beautiful and precious. Our *lives* are beautiful and precious. Our lives, despite what the bosses say, are actually for our own enjoyment, not to make others' lives easier, cleaner, and lazier. As long as the value of professionals' lives is not measured primarily in terms of their effects on *others*, but according to their pleasure, so shall our own lives and value be measured.

Like them, we shall pursue our own desires for pleasure no matter how whimsical, and if our desire is to smoke, then offended professionals can just hold their breath for once—perhaps using this blessed interval of silence to meditate on their thieving class and its own grotesquely swollen "carbon footprint." If state and capital are going to steal our precious energies and vast hours of our lives to line their pockets with profit, leaving us with poor sleep, insufficient rent money, and a diet of 7-Eleven specials as we provide the country's most basic services, the very least we deserve is to enjoy our cigarettes in peace. So if anyone asks, it's not that smoking should be permitted because cigarettes can be proved an absolute good, which they cannot, but simply because for the time being we happen to smoke them. We might call this giving professionals a taste of their own entitlement. Heaven forbid they choke on it.

CODA

When Erica Lagalisse first appeared as June Thunderstorm, it was in David Graeber's essay "What's the Point if We Can't Have Fun?" (2013). Sitting in the grass, June makes the observation that animals play. Graeber then explores "play" as the default mode of the universe as if he came up with the rest. Lagalisse was so displeased that she briefly broke up with Graeber, at which point *The Baffler* invited Lagalisse to submit an essay of her own. Her submission, "Trickle Down

Health," was then shortened into a polemic called "Able-Bodied Until It Kills Us" (2014) that she felt she couldn't sign. "Maybe we should sign it June Thunderstorm," she proposed. "She could be *The Baffler*'s clownish caricature of class rage as well as a nameless gendered muse."

That might have been the end of June Thunderstorm, but her first fan letter arrived from Barbara Ehrenreich, who was looking for a class critique of antismokers. The original "Trickle Down Health" had attended to this matter. Plans to meet were quickly underway. Take-out meals were ordered. Ashtrays were filled. Editors' changes were rejected. June won a prize.

After years of academic and anonymous writing, Lagalisse is now known for *Occult Features of Anarchism* (2019), and is only now coming out as her heteronym June Thunderstorm. June Thunderstorm has become the unapologetic voice with which Lagalisse explores her life as a disabled working-class intellectual. For a long time, June did not receive rights or recognition for experiences of trauma or medicalized suffering as middle-class children do, because only combined with class power are one's challenges interpreted to be empathy-inducing "health" problems (a result of structure) instead of "personal failure" (a result of agency). As we join June on the healing journey of class mobility, we come to understand that while "health" is often positioned as an absolute good, health and healing are complex and opaque socially constructed categories, mobilized for political ends.

June Thunderstorm despises the professional middle class and lives to rain on their parade. She only ruins your day if your clothes are too expensive and the joy of jumping in puddles is lost on your cold, repressed, and lonely bourgeois heart.

NEVER-ENDING SENTENCES

Philip Metres

The Believer, October 27, 2020

In June 2020, I interviewed Joseph Gaston and Christana Gamble, two Black people who live in Cleveland, Ohio, about their struggles to find housing after completing prison sentences. Their experiences illuminate a mass incarceration phenomenon known as collateral sanctions—further punishments for those who have already served time. Throughout the country, formerly incarcerated people have had their rental applications routinely rejected because of past felony or misdemeanor convictions. This "Never-Ending Sentence," as the Reentry Housing Committee's 2020 report is called, demonstrates how collateral sanctions in housing is part of systemic racism. According to the "Never-Ending Sentence," 80 percent of Cleveland landlords can ban applicants with felony convictions, sometimes for life. Because of housing discrimination, many people with criminal records wind up homeless. According to Christopher Knestrick, the executive director of Northeast Ohio Coalition for the Homeless, 82 percent of the unhoused who use Cleveland's shelters are Black, and many have been housing insecure.

These collateral sanctions persist despite a 2015 US Supreme Court ruling that the Fair Housing Act makes it against the law to exclude an applicant simply because of a criminal record. Yet landlords and their management companies still routinely include questions about criminal records in their rental applications. Because Ohio incarcerates five Black people to every one white person, the consequence in housing amounts to discrimination. Though Cleveland and many other places have yet to eliminate this practice, some cities—including Seattle, San Francisco, New York, and Washington, DC—have instituted reform, eliminating criminal records as a reason for turning down a housing application.

In Cleveland, the COVID-19 pandemic has struck Gaston and Gamble particularly hard, as they and so many others struggle to find shelter and build a new life. Ms. Gamble's new reentry program, "The House of Refuge," has yet to open its doors because of the pandemic, but she's been Zooming with new clients. (Both offered key input and suggestions for revisions when I showed them the poems.)

—Philip Metres

The House of Refuge

—The Testimony of Chaplain Christana Gamble[1]

On a hot June morning during the pandemic, we Zoomed into each other's separate Cleveland rooms. Her virtual background: space, a sky of stars and a dark planet rimmed by light. Mine: an office, shelves lined with books....

I love the library

You know I'm pretty
much an open book
and I want to share my story
because it helps others

a violet flower
tucked in her
pulled-up hair

(Be with us, Lord,
as I enter
my story):

I was born in Hickman Mills, Missouri,
to a white preacher and a black mother
in the sixties

Before Cleveland, I was in the country
        riding on horses
   not living in public
      housing

When they divorced, I moved
from a white world
    to Cleveland, mom's breakdown

shock treatment

in foster care
(God blessed me quick
    but I was rebellious)

at Metzenbaum's Children's Center[2]
and public housing, I knew
    something was not right

it wasn't clean
it was wild

and I adapted to the atmosphere

My boyfriend was a dealer
    and I let him in my house
I was nineteen

The first time I went to court,
    they kept saying
                       trafficking, trafficking

and I didn't know
    what they were talking about

I was nineteen
and Judge Gaul[3] didn't ask me if I needed
    treatment, he asked me:

                what's more important
                     the drugs
                 or your child?

When I came home, I don't know
    how I ended up
in the same…

more drugs, prison
        again

    Why? You go through the programs
        and probation
           you work
      the case plan
and you still have no housing

and never knew it was illegal[4]
    until last year, you see
        the system was not made for me

the indigo
screen dances
around her
like a dreamcoat

    But God, His hand, His
                        hand

    Everything that has happened has led
    to this

(God, I cannot leave Him off my lips)

I've been in and out of County all my life

I've been in City Mission I've been in Women in Tran-
    sition
(now called Front Steps) I've been in Cats
I've been in prison I've been in foster care
I've been homeless I've lived under bridges[5]

I've been through all of that
                and so I know

Ever since I was little, my mom
        always asked why
            I brought in the strays

Don't they have a home? she'd say

    But that's how I've been

Because if you don't have a safe place to dwell
the afflictions
will descend

I looked and looked
I waited and waited
                Eden[6] Shelter Care[7]
finally
took me in   mental illness diagnosis
            unwrote my record

Northeast Ohio Coalition for the Homeless[8] has been
    my tent

and now I've made The House of Refuge

her phone rang,   (a client)
she said,
and answered it

     Chaplain Gamble
     may I help you

and all went mute
for a moment, indigo

background
dancing on her skin

her words for her
client alone

    I'm back

she said

     and so my heart

     My ministry, the House of Refuge[9]
       a peaceful restful
         place

     The House of Refuge is up and ready
       the fridge
    is full
        the microwave is ready

     because of my past I was always afraid

     I'm untaught but I'm trained by the Lord

What I want for people

is what God gave me

food, atmosphere, a people that love you

without feeling

degraded

and so my heart and I am so glad to say that I can confi-

dently

and passionately

all along I've been trained

I was walking down the street and the Lord

spoke to me

and said, open the door

And I'm not afraid of my past anymore

And the door opened

Disparate Impacts

—The Testimony of Joseph Gaston[10]

I've moved around
my whole life
    Cincinnati Columbus Nashville Cleveland

  after I got out
  of prison

     I was homeless for just
     over five years

       always in motion

                 "Judge Boyko... to take
                 senior status"
                 (Cleveland.com)[11]

nobody but nobody
would rent to me

                "I intend to maintain
                pretty much a full docket,
                but maybe a little less to
                    enable me
                to travel and sit on other
                   courts..." Boyko said.

     I went to ten different apartments
     their management companies
        all rejected me
     for felony conviction

it was discrimination

I got so fed up I asked Legal Aid
I asked the Urban League
the Ohio Civil Rights Commission
but no one would
                 represent me

everyone told me it was a useless fight
    told me the judge would rule
              against
       everyone told me to wait

    so I took three months
    filed my own case

           based on "disparate impact"

              it was a good
              lawsuit really beautiful

Plaintiff contends the Defendants engaged in discriminatory housing practices, including refusal to rent, discrimination in rental terms and refusal to make reasonable accommodations in rules, policies and practices, in violation of the Fair Housing Act. He further alleges he has a disability which substantially impairs major life functions, but he does not elaborate on what his disability is. It appears he may be suggesting his prior conviction is a disability.[12]

       every housing discrimination case
          goes to Judge Boyko

      everyone knows Judge Boyko
         Judge Boyko has performed well
            for the system

Opinion and Order: Plaintiff's Motion to Proceed In Forma Pauper-
is (Doc. No. 2) is granted, his Motion for Temporary Restraining Order
and Preliminary Injunction (Doc. No. 3) and his Motion for Appoint-
ment of Counsel (Doc. No. 4) are denied, and this action is dismissed
pursuant to 28 U.S.C. §1915(e). The Court certifies, pursuant to 28
U.S.C. § 1915(a)(3), that an appeal from this decision could not be taken
in good faith. Judge Christopher A. Boyko on 2/27/2019.(S,SR)

So I just
gave up

I wore out my eyes
I'm nearsighted now,

need

glasses to read

what I see:
the system is rigged

"It's meaningful, it's reward-
ing, frustrating at times,
just like anything else," the
judge said.

"But overall, I couldn't ask
for a better job."

Cuyahoga County is a haven
for housing
discrimination

an incestuous marriage
between the legal system

and the homeless situation

they can't let you
win

representative democracy looks like
                a good idea
but you can diminish
                the role of the populace

"Division hurts, and it's felt
everywhere, I think," the
judge said.

I was homeless for over
                five years on a waiting list at Eden[13]
                five
                years

                no one should have to wait five years for housing

some guys tried to jump me
in the shower at 2100 Lakeside
I didn't comply

they threw me out

                living in the streets, sleeping
                                in the woods

                raised enough
                                for a car, started
                                                sleeping there

                then in trains and buses

some drivers let you ride all night long

     I liked the 22nd
     downtown to the airport
     and back

          it's a long route

other drivers make you get off

          it's a hard life

     I wouldn't want anyone
     to suffer like that

          used to shower in the rec center
          kept my bag with me

          kept my hygiene up

but I never begged
     I wasn't brought up
        like that

               At the naturalization cere-
                   mony,
               Judge Boyko reads a poetic
                   statement
               by Dean Alfange:[14]

               "I do not choose to be a com-
                   mon man…
               I will not trade freedom for
                   beneficence
               Nor my dignity for a hand-
                   out

I will never cower before any
master
Nor bend to any threat.
It is my heritage to stand
erect."[15]

police spend most their time
harassing homeless people

I got a ticket for sleeping
      for sleeping!

   I looked it up
   there is no law that says
   you can't fall asleep
   in the state of Ohio

I almost died
      got shot at on West 25th
got blood clots in my legs
      from sleeping upright on buses

it's a hard life

            social justice institutions
            have become part of the system

      everyone is part
            of this system

            Federal judges often work
            hard to maintain
            their judicial indepen-

dence,
as the appointment is a
lifetime one

Judge Boyko will be rewarded well

I seek no earthly reward
        just change

I'm in Eden housing on Euclid
when I got out
of prison I wanted to leave
        the state
                they said I had to stay:

                it's called "community control"
                        to maintain parole
                they don't want the money
                        leaving the state

if I live righteously, on the day of judgment
I will not be wronged

        the change I seek in the system
        may never become reality
                but I must try

[*the line goes*
        quiet when I ask Joseph
                        his dreams]

        some day I'd like to be a cook
                or a youth advocate

        and I'd like to see the world
                look into

the Peace Corps

The judge has offer to teach
US law
... in Ukraine and Saudi
Arabia,
and having more flexibility
will allow for that.

Philip Metres is the author of ten books, including *Shrapnel Maps* (2020), *The Sound of Listening: Poetry as Refuge and Resistance* (2018), *Pictures at an Exhibition* (2016), and *Sand Opera* (2015). His work has garnered the Guggenheim Fellowship, the Lannan Fellowship, two NEAs, seven Ohio Arts Council Grants, the Hunt Prize, the Adrienne Rich Award, three Arab American Book Awards, the Lyric Poetry Prize, and the Cleveland Arts Prize. He is professor of English and director of the Peace, Justice, and Human Rights program at John Carroll University, and Core Faculty at Vermont College of Fine Arts. http://www.philipmetres.com.

THE DIGNITY OF THE THRIFT STORE

Elizabeth Gollan

Dame, November 26, 2019

> During the season of abundance, one writer reflects on the days when bargain hunting was a necessity for survival—and finds solace in the simplicity

> Through tattered clothes great vices do appear; robes and furred gowns hide all.
>
> —**Shakespeare**, *King Lear*

A few years ago, my blue dress with cornflowers started to shred. This mattered greatly, because the frock had been my last decent outfit and my family and I were broke. Our landlady, a former police officer with bobbed red hair and the kind of bangs Uma Thurman wore in the film *Pulp Fiction*, seemed to understand that this was a problem, because I was also hunting for a job. So she took me on a nine-minute walk to Warehouse Outlet—from the outside a bleak-looking box of a shop with bins and fluorescent lights—to get new threads.

"I buy all my clothes here," she said conspiratorially. "You will love it." I shuddered a little.

I was forty-six and had just moved to deep Brooklyn with my husband and our two young sons. Like so many before us, we'd moved here from another American city to chase opportunities. The problem was that our family was struggling to get by on $25,000 a year, and had almost nothing in the bank. We were not alone in our neighborhood, living on an income below the poverty line. According to local news source, Patch, approximately 27.2 percent of my neighborhood, Kensington, and adjacent Borough Park lived in poverty as we did. Before this midlife move, we'd been living off the grid, dreamy artists

323

supported by our generous families. But that was all over now, and I had a new life to create.

Our bills were piling up fast. I could barely look at the homeless shelter that went up around the corner just after we moved in, because I feared it would be our lot one day. And winter was looming.

I can attest that it's hard to build a new life when you are wearing torn pants and battered shoes.

That was why I not only went to Warehouse Outlet once to buy outfits for job interviews but also why I kept returning. While some other women who came in there were in the same monetary straits as I was, many were from vastly different backgrounds. They wore saris or burqas, and their young children clutched smartphones and plastic Spiderman figures.

We were all attracted by the same sign: "New Items Every Day. We Buy Closeouts and Liquidations." Women descended like ravens on these new shipments. (Admittedly, so did I.) They flipped through Dora the Explorer pajamas or brown (and only brown) men's medium (and only medium) down jackets or First Communion dresses. My smile didn't matter, and neither did my "excuse me's." These other shoppers have even physically knocked me down. (Never try to come between a woman and affordable clothes for her children or grandchildren.) There is a reason for this aggression. The clothes at Warehouse Outlet are often lovely: brand new, nicely designed, and good for wearing to a job interview, or the office, and keeping a baby's feet dry.

To me, the beauty of this store—as well as outlet and ninety-nine-cent stores everywhere—is that it subverts the idea that you must earn a lot of money to pass in our society; that you need one hundred dollars for a jacket to be chic or even just socially acceptable. These stores serve as an argument: there are flowers blooming in the desert. They express that true elegance comes from care and attention, not as a result of wealth or hyperconsumption.

Warehouse Outlet embodies these values. Tossed-aside pants revealed a mini bin of plastic earrings designed like wedding cakes, clusters of roses or gold filigree from India. Some were chrysanthemum-shaped—minty green or pale pink. I bought them (my choice, three dollars) and felt like an empress or an heiress. I soon had a collection of earrings. With these earrings, I could seduce someone (if I weren't married) or just enjoy the weight on my neck or feeling put together and proper. Nobody needs to wear earrings. They are by definition luxurious. I felt rich, even though my kitchen is linoleum and my apartment needs a paint job to cover the cracks in the hallway. For far less than a bag of groceries, I could go on a shopping spree.

A mega bin filled with baby clothes sits under the front window. Mothers and grandmothers sort through them, touching each outfit with great discrimination. Yes? No? Maybe? The women sort and sort, as women have done in markets for a thousand years. I do the same and find a white linen shirt. Six dollars! (My landlady was right.)

"Naisha, you got bras?" Steven, the manager, shouts from the backroom to a clerk.

"Steven, can I tell you something?" she shouts back. "From three thirty to six we were down in the basement sorting." The saleswomen work long hours and FaceTime their kids at the dinner hour.

Of course, there can be a dark side. I've witnessed a fight between two female shoppers, both seemingly down on their luck, scrapping over glossy high heels. One tried to steal the shoes. The owner chased her out, screaming that he'd call the cops.

In tony Park Slope, Cobble Hill, and Brooklyn Heights, you might not see such a skirmish in a shop. For one thing, Amazon Prime runs like water into brownstones and apartment buildings. And the stores are almost all high-end—Rag & Bone, Bird, their names like urban prayers.

But who needs them?

It's interesting how your mindset changes if, like me, you have devoted yourself wholly and out of necessity to outlet shopping, with the occasional vintage-store foray. Once I needed a swimsuit, so I popped into Victoria's Secret on Fifth Avenue, remembering it from my youth as selling midrange clothing. After three years of shopping at Warehouse Outlet, I was stunned to find that fifty dollars at Victoria's Secret bought virtually nothing. Stupefied, I rode escalators in a crazy spiraling wave. After the outlet, the store seemed like a Disneyfied Guggenheim, floor after floor of perfectly folded displays of bras and panties.

I could afford neither its padded bras nor its demeaning idea of womanhood, but the store itself filled me with longing: Where were the shrewd grandmothers, restless kids in the corners, and toddlers' Superman pajamas stuck between dish racks and men's slippers? Where were the flowered potholders? The random blue raincoats? And where was the pleasure of leaving with two new dresses and a pair of jeans, all for twenty bucks?

So what if the outlet shoppers didn't always share well. I knew they were looking for dress shirts for their husbands and their children, shirts that were cotton and that they could afford, and I understood.

I wondered if Warehouse Outlet would make it though the pandemic, since they couldn't have done business when the world was shut down. The first time I came back, afterward, even the previously unfriendly owner smiled when I said I was happy to see them open. He said he was too. Now, once again, men in vans park in front in the afternoons. In gold chains, parkas, and scowls, they unload boxes from a double-parked van. The Greek Diner down the block sells avocado toast, now, and says so proudly on a sign in the window. Warehouse Outlet seems unchanged. Currently for sale: a ceramic pie pan, its once-fluorescent orange price tag now faded to peach: $27.99, but not here. Here it is six dollars. A cake plate on the base of a ceramic monkey, sits next to the bins Spider Man pajamas and acrylic shawls with indigo leaf patterns.

I still go in regularly. It's Black Friday, and well beyond, every day, here. A shirt is six dollars, pants are two or six, depending on the rack. The lady behind the counter still eats rice from a Styrofoam container, in the back of the store. She still calls her kids, who must be older now, and tells them to do their homework and feed their sister, while the sky outside on Church Avenue turns black. She smiles at me, now, and remembers that I don't need a bag.

Prince Harry had just married Meghan Markle when I wrote this piece. I remember hearing it broadcast in the shop; struck by the contrast between the wedding's pomp and the shop's bins; and the women looking through them. The store is still there, but Prince Philip has died. Queen Elizabeth died. The queen's groom cried when her pony came out. I cried. Victoria's Secret doesn't have "angels" anymore, for a complex set of reasons. But ladies still come to the store, and although I don't *need* to, to survive anymore, I am one of them. A universe, generative, waits under those fluorescent lights. You just have to walk in.

Elizabeth Gollan is working on a book about her work as a caregiver and personal chef and the political and cultural meaning of those professions.

CLASS DISMISSED

Alison Stine

Longreads, February 2019

When she attends an elite private college on scholarship, Alison Stine discovers that education isn't quite the equalizer she expected it to be.

I had never seen so many tennis courts in my life. I had never heard of rugby or lacrosse. I mispronounced genre in class because I had only ever read the word. I didn't know girls my age owned pearls. I felt equally stunned by black dresses and those pearls at the dining hall on display Sunday nights, something many in sororities wore. I didn't own pearls, or a nice black dress. I was born in Indiana, where our neighbors grew popcorn. I was raised in rural Ohio. My public high school was small, flanked by fields. The last day of senior year, a student drove up in his family's tractor. It had taken him hours to get there, puttering along back roads. I was the first person in my family to attend an elite private college, partially on multiple scholarships, and partially, I think, on my parents' sheer will to get me out.

I wasn't the first person in my family to go to college—I was the second generation, after my parents—and on teachers' and guidance counselors' advice, I had applied to several schools, including state universities. But the private colleges were the ones that seemed to really want someone like me. They courted me. They offered me money, and I couldn't say no to that. I couldn't afford to.

I would soon learn that private colleges in this country have a social class problem. Each year, as spring break approaches, I think back on my time in school with particular sharpness, remembering other students going to warm islands or ski resorts. Unlike me, my classmates definitely knew how to ski. They parked their Land Rovers and BMWs on campus, and they landed coveted unpaid internships in the summer—something only rich kids can afford to do.

All of these trappings of wealth were new to me in 1996. But it appeared I was going to get an education in class privilege as well as liberal arts.

I was hardly alone in my experience of class bewilderment. Now, as then, there is no special orientation for students who identify as poor or rural, no workshops on the culture clash we might experience in college. Based on the price of required books, most professors had no idea of our financial reality. Students are reprimanded for not buying books on time, or not having money on a copy card, or for personal printers running out of pricy inks—but these are real and valid issues for those not raised in wealth. While our intellects can keep pace with our wealthy classmates, our wallets can't.

I sometimes think it is difficult for our former professors to reconcile the academic and intellectual successes that I and my fellow scholarship kids had in college with our difficulties after graduation. A friend who works as a stay-at-home mom, raising multiple children, admitted to me she couldn't face going to back to campus and seeing beloved teachers. Another friend, struggling to find work at the time, had a visceral, violent reaction to an annual fund request, sent on expensive, engraved paper only weeks after the Wall Street bailout in 2009. A few years after graduation, I returned to campus for a memorial service for a community member. One of my favorite professors asked me what I was doing. When I answered, "Teaching high school," he said, "That's a waste."

I know he meant I was spending all my time working a very difficult job—and not the one for which I had studied—rather than writing. But for most of us, difficult, nondream jobs are all we have, all we can hope for.

I didn't know any of these potential perils or stigma of class, of course, when I first landed at the campus on a hill, overlooking the prettiest small town I had ever seen: houses with porches and gingerbread trim, manicured lawns, and residents who walked everywhere, greeting each other by name. The college boasted a towering chapel, a healthy endowment, and an annual tuition of over $65,000 as of last year.

There, for the first time, I met kids who had gone to private high schools, kids who had gone to boarding schools. Kids very different

from me. Most of my close friends at college ended up being scholarship kids who had gone to public schools like I had, or were from
rural areas, or were poor. When wealthy students defiantly took their
frozen yogurt out of the dining halls, which we were not supposed to
do, they joked, "We're paying for it."

My high school had a good graduation and college attendance
rate, but many of my classmates there went on to The Ohio State University, in Columbus, about an hour away from where I was raised.
Some lived at home and attended community college or "the branch,"
our name for the OSU satellite campus in our hometown. Nationally,
according to 2015 data from the National Center for Education Statistics, only 14 percent of low-income students graduate from a bachelor's or higher degree-granting program within eight years; only 29
percent of middle-income students do.

Some of my high school classmates went on to private colleges, of
course—a comparable number of low- and middle-income students
enroll in private colleges as enroll as in state universities, according to
the National Association of Independent Colleges and Universities—
but no one from my graduating class went to mine. That seemed important to me at the time, important to my starting over.

But I *couldn't* start over, couldn't leave my upbringing behind. It
was there with me the whole time, informing every one of my choices
and experiences.

I felt I needed to compensate for my upbringing by working extraordinarily hard. My first year, I dressed up for class, to which I
would arrive half an hour early, waiting outside the classroom door.
I took frantic, copious notes, but professors often said words I didn't
know—and didn't explain them. Rereading my notes at night, I stayed
up until two, until four, trying to figure everything out, trying to learn
this new language for a world I still felt I was denied entrance to: a
world of learning, but also of wealth.

It didn't take long before I stopped raising my hand. My theology
professor admitted to me that he missed that fiery, eager student who
had debated so much in our first few weeks. But that student had finally heard the snickers from the back of the class.

I had never read Nietzsche, Kafka, Nabokov—or many books at

all by women, or writers of color. When I was growing up, we had one bookstore: a Walden Books in the mall. I would go straight to the classics section, a short shelf, and stand there while Muzak from the lobby washed over me. In that way, I read George Eliot and the Brontës, purely by chance, out of desperation.

I had never heard of Immanuel Kant. In high school, I had never taken or even heard of philosophy. We had no advanced placement classes there. I had registered, my parents had paid for, and I had taken several advanced placement *tests*, in the hope of exempting out of some introductory college classes, as did a group of my classmates. I think we did okay, but not great, having not studied for these tests, having never been exposed to much of the subject matter, having never been tutored or seriously prepped for them. When I asked the administration about this, the vice principal said, "All of our classes are AP classes."

But they weren't. I had some wonderful teachers, of course. Several of them encouraged me in meaningful ways that still stand out today. One of these high school teachers later told me when she had tried to deviate from the syllabus the other teachers had all agreed to use—among her changes, she wanted to include more contemporary authors—her fellow teachers had shunned her.

Other words I mispronounced: *manic, gesture, lingerie.*

Another thing I didn't know: There were exceptions to rules, that some people broke the rules and got away with it. Some had been getting away with rule-breaking their whole lives. That wasn't an option for me. Following the syllabus and course policies to the letter, I came to class ill, I came to class exhausted. I was never late. I didn't ask for a sorely needed extension on a paper, not any paper—something many students request and many professors grant—until I was a senior. It didn't even occur to me to try.

When you're poor, when you're on scholarship, when this is your first and only shot, you can't afford to break the rules. You can't get in trouble. You can't afford a single mistake. Early in my college career, when I was at a party broken up by campus security, my boyfriend and I, both scholarship students, both underage, climbed out a window.

Not coming from a world of privilege made college confusing, difficult, and at times, dangerous.

I had never done much drinking. I remember having just a couple of drinks in high school: a wine cooler and Zima, procured from somebody's older brother. That was it. Our parents didn't drink with us. We didn't have fake IDs. We didn't have the money to buy gas, let alone beer. We didn't go to parties where waiters served wine.

In college, suddenly, liquor was everywhere, glittering and expensive. Surrounded by kids with enough money to buy drugs, to buy the best alcohol, to secure it for their parties, I went to dorm rooms with full bars set up on dressers. One of my first-year roommates kept a crystal wine goblet in our room, which she brought with her to fill with wine at frat parties. It was actual crystal, a present from her parents. A professor bought my boyfriend Bombay Sapphire gin for his twenty-first birthday. It was the most expensive liquor we had ever seen.

Certainly, cheap beer flowed like a constant, sticky river. Boys lined bathtubs with garbage bags filled with "jungle juice," which was every bottle of alcohol in the dorm poured together, with a lot of malt liquor thrown in; it was always red. But many of my classmates had had the access and allowance to drink for years before I could. They were familiar with alcohol and used it to their advantage; they continued to lavish cash on partying expensive and hard.

And rarely faced consequences.

Because I feared getting in trouble, because I had no safety net and was terrified of losing my scholarships, I didn't drink much. This further outcast me. I couldn't even party like the others, bonding at frat parties. Not having had high school or family experiences with drinking also made me vulnerable. I tried to keep my drink with me at all times to stay safe, but I certainly couldn't hold my liquor.

It wasn't experience that kept me from getting hurt those years, it was dumb luck and my own terror.

Not coming from the world of privilege made navigating the real world after college challenging. I didn't have student loans, surviving on a combination of scholarships, work study, summer jobs, and what my parents had saved, but many of my college friends weren't as lucky. Our wealthiest classmates didn't have this burden of repayment; they weren't starting out already buried by debt.

On a teaching assistantship, I went to graduate school: another academic institution wound by wealth. I was surprised that many of my classmates said they were there just to learn; I was there hoping to ultimately land a good job with my degree. I *had* to have a job to live: learning was an afterthought.

My boyfriend at the time never finished the program, due to financial constraints. My longtime partner later in life had had the same experience: dropping out of a PhD program because his car broke down and he couldn't get to class. He was one of the only ones among his graduate school class with a day job.

As an undergraduate, I had first come face to face with my own inexperience, my own lack. But I also was supported by professors who buoyed my confidence, invited me over for fancy dinners with visiting writers and scholars, and supported my ideas and ideals.

But the real world wasn't like that. In the real world, it didn't matter that I worked hard, that I stayed out of trouble. Bank accounts mattered more than my brain, the result of class and connections, which could never be taught or earned, but were birthrights.

Did I expect to make a large income after college? No. Did I expect to live up to my promise? I had hoped to.

I didn't expect to see frat boys running the world, and running it just the way they went through college: like the money would never end, the alcohol would never stop, the party would never be busted, the paper would never come due, other people would never matter or know. And they would never get caught.

In that way college prepared me more for the real world than I could have ever dreamed.

Alison Stine's debut novel, *The Grower*, was published by Mira in fall 2020. She lives in the foothills of Appalachia.

FOR YEARS, I'VE TRIED TO WORK MY WAY BACK INTO THE MIDDLE CLASS

Lori Teresa Yearwood

MIT Technology Review, February 23, 2021

Early this winter, I took a long walk in the Salt Lake City park in which I had been arrested for bathing in a river when I was homeless.

About thirty minutes into that walk, I stood across from the park's granite meditation temple, thinking: "Three and a half years ago, I slept under that building's awning."

I can still feel how hard that temple's cold stone floor was; I remember how people strolled by my bed of cardboard and clothes and stared with what struck me as a combination of concern, contempt, and pity. Now I see that these are also the lenses through which I have often judged my own progress in my new, not-yet-middle-class life.

These days, I often wonder: Am I really doing as well as I should be after all this time? How did I ever allow myself to fall so far? Trying to get back the economic security I had before that collapse is so hard! Is it even possible?

I am the daughter of Vernon Yearwood-Drayton, a Black Panamanian immigrant who came to the US in the 1940s—the era of Jim Crow laws—to become a microbiologist at NASA's Ames Research Center. My father made certain I graduated from college. He ate a lot of rice and beans to ensure that he left me with an inheritance he thought would keep me safe in a world without him.

Yet I am also a woman who, after a quick succession of traumas, plunged out of the protected realms of the middle class and into two years of homelessness. My experience is surprisingly common. From June to November 2020, nearly eight million people in the US fell into poverty in the face of the pandemic and limited government relief, according to research from the University of Chicago and the University of Notre Dame.

Poverty is a complicated thing. It can be generational or situational and temporary—or anything in between. For me, climbing out of poverty has been as much about mindset as it has been about the dollars in my bank account. "I am going to do this," I tell myself over and over again. "I have inherited the strength from my father to do this."

In the spring of 2017, I finally left my last makeshift "home"—a slatted wood park bench in that same park. My first job during my recovery was as an eleven-dollar-an-hour grocery clerk at a Whole Foods store where my twenty-something bosses handed me preset timers whenever I took a bathroom break. As a former journalist who had risen through the ranks of the *Miami Herald* to write cover stories for the paper's Sunday magazine, I stood at my register, struggling to hold back tears.

Well-meaning people tried to encourage me by pointing out how far I had come. "You're working!" they said, "You're housed!" And the declaration I found most diminishing: "I'm so proud of you!"

I was fifty-two and I did not mark my progress by those measurements. Rather, I marked my progress by how far I had fallen. What did it mean that I was earning enough to rent a room in someone's house when just a few years ago, I had owned a three-acre horse ranch in Oregon?

One of the most debilitating symptoms of posttraumatic stress is that people who suffer from it avoid the things that hurt them most. For me, that meant I avoided myself.

I was full of shame and self-hatred. Hatred that I—someone who had once had hundreds of thousands of dollars in the stock market—had collapsed. Hatred that I had become one of "them."

Through tears, I told my trauma therapist how I was regularly stalked and beaten by a man who worked the front counter of the homeless outreach center where I had picked up my daily hygiene kits.

"If you don't love that part of yourself that you have so successfully distanced yourself from, you will not be able to fully heal," my therapist said.

Slowly, after many sessions, I came to feel great compassion for the desperate woman I once was. I envisioned myself sitting beside her in the streets, holding her and telling her: "I am so sorry. I will never separate myself from you again. I will take care of you."

My incremental but steady steps forward did not come from the expected governmental or community resources. They came from a series of strangers who cared about my welfare. The systems that our society has in place to lift people out of poverty are fragile and full of holes, so I learned to look elsewhere.

My first home out of homelessness, for example, was offered by the executive director of a small Salt Lake City nonprofit. Housing lists had one- to two-year waiting lists at the time, so she offered me a room in a home of formerly incarcerated women in exchange for managing the other women in the house.

That house experienced funding issues and closed six months later. But another stranger, a woman I met quite by chance at a neighborhood gathering, offered me free shelter in her Airbnb for a month and then rented me a small bedroom in her home for four hundred dollars a month, about a hundred less than market rate. My eleven-dollar-an-hour cashiering job was just enough to pay my expenses and to cover the trauma therapy I knew I needed to keep moving forward.

If there is any single piece of advice I could give anyone else in the midst of collapse, it would be this: No matter what the world tries to project onto you, stop judging yourself. Learn about trauma and its impact on your psychology and physiology.

By many measures, my life today could once again be counted as successful. My jobs have become increasingly suited to what I now see as my purpose—to help people, including me, say the things that need to be heard. I'm now a full-time freelance journalist who specializes in integrating trauma awareness into my stories. I am under contract with the Economic Hardship Reporting Project and have been published in major media outlets such as the *Washington Post, Slate,* and the *Guardian.* I love my one-bedroom apartment in Salt Lake City, where I live with my two cats, Iggy and Kanab.

But I began this piece by talking about a simple walk in a park for a reason. To an onlooker, it would have looked like a completely ordinary act. But for me to walk in that park without resenting myself for all that had occurred there was just as much of an accomplishment as any job I had landed. When I stood in front of that white stone meditation temple and thought of that past me lying on its floor, I accepted her.

That's progress.

Lori Teresa Yearwood is a national housing crisis reporter for the Economic Hardship Reporting Project. Her work has appeared in the *New York Times*, the *Washington Post*, the *Guardian*, *Mother Jones*, *Slate*, and many other publications. Lori is currently working on her memoir.

WHAT DOES IT MEAN TO BE "BAD WITH MONEY"?

Joshua Hunt

The Believer, September 1, 2020

When I was twenty-five, I fell in love with a college boy. He was frugal, despite growing up rich, while I spent money faster than I could make it, despite growing up poor. This vexed and confused him. My parents, after all, had given me a road map to misfortune, which seemed to him as good as a road map to its opposite. What else was a childhood surrounded by poverty, addiction, and crime if not a lesson in how not to live?

One day, my boyfriend came home from class with his own lesson to impart: I was bad with money, a professor had explained to him, because I'd grown up in "a culture of poverty," absorbing values and behaviors which would forever thwart my escape from the underclass. I'd been aware from a young age what kind of statistics were associated with being an Indigenous Alaskan—more likely to suffer sexual abuse or commit suicide—but I'd never before had my life experience reduced to theory. Still, I was a high school dropout and he was a college boy, and I had to admit that he had a point.

It isn't quite as simple as being bad with money. Every so often, I'm gripped by an urge to spend frivolously. Deprivation breeds irrational appetites, but there's something deeper behind these urges of mine; it sometimes feels like I'm chasing a gambler's high by ratcheting up the stakes of my own life and betting everything on the belief that I'll somehow come through all right. How I spend the money is almost beside the point.

Once, after losing a job, I spent everything I had on a ten-day trip to Iceland, unsure of how I'd pay my rent after I got home. Then there was the time I bought an iPad, used it for a week, and sold it for grocery money at a price much less than I'd paid. Occasionally I'd buy some rare, out-of-print record or book, which would mock me from a shelf while I lived off instant ramen noodles until my next paycheck. For years I put this kind of behavior down to an excess of the working-class joie de vivre captured in Les Blank's 1971 film *Spend It All*. But the subjects of Blank's documentary "work like hell to make some money, then spend it all having a good time," and sometimes I have no fun at all spending money. What I do feel, invariably, is *present*. I am, for the duration of the spree, fully engaged with the world around me.

Growing up in poverty is like growing old and dying once each month. In my house there was a smothering malaise that deepened with each passing day as the money and food stamps dwindled; by the end of the month, when the cupboards were empty of everything except one mysterious can of pumpkin pie mix, we were reduced to the role of spectators in our own lives. When paychecks and food stamps arrived on the first of the month, it's wasn't just a relief. It was like coming up for air. More than having enough food to eat, the first of the month meant a week of booze and cigarettes for mom, and Doritos and Coke for us kids. It meant two weeks of sleep without worry. It meant three weeks without hunger. It meant, for however long we could hold out, a reprieve from tears, fighting, and shame.

The residue of these experiences is difficult to explain. Once in a while, when I come into a bit of money, I find myself wanting to celebrate by buying something I otherwise would not. It's a natural enough urge, I think. But it doesn't always end there. What begins as a celebratory impulse sometimes becomes something more nihilistic—an overwhelming desire to spend relentlessly until I am free of my last dollar. While I am spending the money, I feel completely engaged with life, like a gambler watching his horse as it makes its way around the track; once I am broke, I feel briefly elated. Then I feel nothing.

When I was thirty, I earned my GED, then I became a college boy, too. I lived abroad, went to graduate school, and learned many theories, none of which clarified my relationship with money. After graduate school, I was hired to work in a newsroom in Tokyo, which I celebrated by spending twelve hundred dollars on a pair of dress shoes. Then I asked my new boss if I could borrow enough money for my flight to Japan.

Joshua Hunt is a former Tokyo correspondent for Reuters and an adjunct professor at Columbia University's Graduate School of Journalism. His writing has appeared in *Vanity Fair,* the *New York Times Magazine, GQ,* and *Harper's.*

ACKNOWLEDGMENTS

We would first like to thank this book's project editor Laura Ross, who orchestrated this collection so well. Gratitude then goes to this book's editors Katy O'Donnell and Anthony Arnove at Haymarket, who were so helpful at every juncture, as well as to the five stellar essayists who wrote the introductory pieces in this anthology.

At EHRP, we've received great assistance from our seamlessly skilled Operations Manager George Lozano, our senior editor Deborah Jian Lee, our dedicated and clever social media editor Rachel Sanoff, our elegant copyeditor John Webb, our wise counsel attorney Lynn Oberlander of Ballard Spahr, and our publicity team Kylee Siaw, Zachary Halper and Andrew Smith. Thanks also to the gifted designers Dean Pappalardo and Penny Blatt. Praise must also go to EHRP's governing board Duy Linh Tu, Bruce Morrow, Sarah Safer, Matthew Annenberg, Rimjhim Dey, Nikhil Swaminathan and Jim Ledbetter.

We are also grateful to our funders including the JPB Foundation, Ford Foundation, Omidyar Network, Open Society Foundations, the James Irvine Foundation, Melville Charitable Trust, Acton Family Foundation, the Simons Foundation, The Puffin Foundation and to many other individual donors, as well as our former fiscal sponsor, the Institute for Policy Studies.

Others who offered help along the way include agents Jill Grinberg and Denise Page, Stephanie Steiker and John Timpane.

Finally, we'd like to offer both respect and affection to EHRP's many writers, photographers, filmmakers, poets and illustrators, in particular the ones who have contributed with such honesty and dedication to this collection.

NOTES

The Body: Introduction

1. This is part of Talila A. Lewis's working definition of ableism. See "Working Definition of Ableism – January 2022 Update," Talila A. Lewis's personal website, updated January 1, 2022, https://www.talilalewis.com/blog/working-definition-of-ableism-january-2022-update.

I Did My Own Abortion Because Texas . . .

1. Esmarie's name has been changed to protect her privacy.
2. Raga Justin, "No Abortions in Texas Unless the Mother's Life Is in Danger, Texas Attorney General Says as Coronavirus Spreads," *Texas Tribune*, March 23, 2020.
3. Jennifer Gerson, "Fake Health Clinics Are Tricking College Students," *Cosmopolitan*, February 1, 2019.
4. *Dobbs v. Jackson Women's Health Organization*, 597 US (2022).
5. Oriana González and Jacob Knutson, "Where Abortion Has Been Banned Now That *Roe v. Wade* Is Overturned," Axios, updated January 6, 2023, https://www.axios.com/2022/06/25/abortion-illegal-7-states-more-bans-coming.
6. Marielle Kirstein, Joerg Dreweke, Rachel K. Jones, and Jesse Philbin, "100 Days Post-Roe: At Least 66 Clinics across 15 US States Have Stopped Offering Abortion Care," Guttmacher Institute, October 6, 2022, https://www.guttmacher.org/2022/10/100-days-post-roe-least-66-clinics-across-15-us-states-have-stopped-offering-abortion-care.
7. "Communities Need Clinics: The New Landscape of Independent Abortion Clinics in the United States," Abortion Care Network, 2022, https://abortioncarenetwork.org/cnc2022/.
8. Weiyi Cai, Taylor Johnston, Allison McCann, and Amy Schoenfeld Walker, "Half of U.S. Women Risk Losing Abortion Access Without *Roe*," *New York Times*, May 7, 2022.
9. Benjamin Rader, Ushma D. Upadhyay, Neil K. R. Sehgal, et al., "Estimated Travel Time and Spatial Access to Abortion Facilities in the US Before and After the *Dobbs v. Jackson Women's Health* Decision," *JAMA*, November 1, 2022, https://jamanetwork.com/journals/jama/article-abstract/2798215.
10. Laura Huss, Farah Diaz-Tello, and Goleen Samari "Self-Care, Criminalized: August 2022 Preliminary Findings," If/When/How, Accessed March 15, 2023, https://www.ifwhenhow.org/resources/self-care-criminalized-preliminary-findings/.
11. Renee Bracey Sherman, private communication, December 2022.
12. Rachel K. Jones, Elizabeth Nash, Lauren Cross, Jesse Philbin, and Marielle

Kirstein, "Medication Abortion Now Accounts for More Than Half of All
US Abortions," Guttmacher Institute, February 24, 2022, https://www.
guttmacher.org/article/2022/02/medication-abortion-now-accounts-more-
half-all-us-abortions.
13.   Laurie McGinley and Ariana Eunjung Cha, "Conservative Group Sues FDA
to Revoke Approval of Abortion Pill," *Washington Post*, November 18, 2022.

The Twisted Business of Donating Plasma

1.   "Baxter Continues Its Dominance of the Plasma Industry," Press release,
Companiesandmarkets.com, April 16, 2013, https://www.mynewsdesk.com/
uk/companiesandmarkets-com/pressreleases/baxter-continues-its-domi-
nance-of-the-plasma-industry-856305.
2.   Lucy Reynolds, "Selling Our Safety to the Highest Bidder: The Privatisation
of Plasma Resources UK," openDemocracy, April 24, 2013, https://www.
opendemocracy.net/en/ournhs/selling-our-safety-to-highest-bidder-privati-
sation-of-plasma-resources-uk/.
3.   Paul Gallagher, "'Is There No Limit to What This Government Will Priva-
tise?': UK Plasma Supplier Sold to US Private Equity Firm Bain Capital,"
Independent, July 18, 2013; Christopher Doig, Andreas Laupacis, Meera
Dalal-Burns, "Paying for Plasma—Canada's Double Standard?," Healthy
Debate, April 17, 2014, https://healthydebate.ca/2014/04/topic/cost-of-care/
paying-plasma/.
4.   Centers for Disease Control and Prevention, "HIV Transmission Through
Transfusion—Missouri and Colorado, 2008," Morbidity and Mortality
Weekly Report (MMWR), October 22, 2010, https://www.cdc.gov/mmwr/
preview/mmwrhtml/mm5941a3.htm.
5.   Jeffrey L. Winters, "Complications of Donor Apheresis," *Journal of Clinical
Aphresis* 21, no. 2 (2006): 132–41.
6.   S. Vansteelandt, E. Goetghebeur, I. Thomas, E. Mathys, and F. Van Loock,
"On the Viral Safety of Plasma Pools and Plasma Derivatives," *Journal of the
Royal Statistical Society (Series A)* 68, no. 2 (2005): 345–63.

To Help the Homeless, Offer Shelter That Allows Deep Sleep

1.   "2011 Health Sleep Study," House the Homeless, February 18, 2011, https://
housethehomeless.org/2011-health-sleep-study/.

Inequity in Maternal Health Care . . .

1.   Harita Raja, "Postpartum PTSD: Beyond Postpartum Depression in
Maternal Mental Health," Psychiatry Advisor, May 12, 2017, https://www.
psychiatryadvisor.com/home/topics/anxiety/postpartum-ptsd-beyond-post-
partum-depression-in-maternal-mental-health/; Zainab Shaban, Mahrokh
Dolatian, Jamal Shams, Hamid Alavi-Majd, Zohreh Mahmoodi, and Homeira
Sajjadi, "Post-Traumatic Stress Disorder (PTSD) Following Childbirth: Prevalence and Contributing Factors," *Iranian Red Crescent Medical Journal* 15, no.
3 (2015): 177–82.
2.   Dylan Scott, "Medicaid Is a Hassle for Doctors. That's Hurting Patients,"

Vox, June 7, 2021, https://www.vox.com/2021/6/7/22522479/medic-aid-health-insurance-doctors-billing-research.

3. "Maternal Vulnerability in the US—a Shameful Problem For One of the World's Wealthiest Countries," Surgo Ventures, accessed March 15, 2023, https://mvi.surgoventures.org/.

4. Maggie Clark, "Maternal Depression Costs Society Billions Each Year, New Model Finds," Georgetown University Health Policy Institute, May 31, 2019, https://ccf.georgetown.edu/2019/05/31/maternal-depression-costs-soci-ety-billions-each-year-new-model-finds/.

5. Centers for Disease Control and Prevention, "Racial and Ethnic Disparities Continue in Pregnancy-Related Deaths," press release, page last reviewed September 6, 2019, https://www.cdc.gov/media/releases/2019/p0905-ra-cial-ethnic-disparities-pregnancy-deaths.html.

6. Saraswathi Vedam, Kathrin Stoll, Tanya Khemet Taiwo, Nicholas Rubashkin, Melissa Cheyney, Nan Strauss, Monica McLemore, Micaela Cadena, Eliza-beth Nethery, Eleanor Rushton, Laura Schummers, Eugene Declercq, and the GVtM-US Steering Council, "The Giving Voice to Mothers Study: Inequity and Mistreatment during Pregnancy and Childbirth in the United States," *Reproductive Health* 16 (2019).

7. Katherine J. Igoe, "Parents with PTSD Are More Likely to Struggle with Breastfeeding," *Parents*, April 27, 2021.

8. Lauren Wellbank, "Do Postpartum Depression Symptoms Look Different in a Pandemic?," *Parents*, December 30, 2020.

9. "American Birth Story: The Changing Face of Birth in America," *Parents*, April 10, 2020.

10. "New Study Uncovers the Heavy Financial Toll of Untreated Maternal Men-tal Health Conditions," Mathematica, April 29, 2019, https://www.mathe-matica.org/news/new-study-uncovers-the-heavy-financial-toll-of-untreated-maternal-mental-health-conditions.

11. "Postnatal Depression and Perinatal Mental Health," Mind, April 2020, https://www.mind.org.uk/information-support/types-of-mental-health-problems/postnatal-depression-and-perinatal-mental-health/about-mater-nal-mental-health-problems/.

12. Lyra Matin's personal website, accessed March 15, 2023, https://lyramatin.com/.

13. Beba: A Center for Family Healing website, accessed March 15, 2023, https://beba.org/.

14. Cassie Shortsleeve, "There's Now a Medical Textbook for Reproductive Men-tal Health—Here's What That Means," *Parents*, updated on May 20, 2022.

15. White House, "Vice President Kamala Harris Announces Call to Action to Reduce Maternal Mortality and Morbidity," fact sheet, December 7, 2021, https://www.whitehouse.gov/briefing-room/statements-re-leases/2021/12/07/fact-sheet-vice-president-kamala-harris-announc-es-call-to-action-to-reduce-maternal-mortality-and-morbidity/.

16. National Patient Advocate Foundation website, accessed March 15, 2023, https://www.npaf.org/.

Home: Introduction

1. National Law Center on Homelessness and Poverty, "Homelessness in America: Overview of Data and Causes," January 2015, https://homelesslaw.org/wp-content/uploads/2018/10/Homeless_Stats_Fact_Sheet.pdf.
2. "Measuring Housing Insecurity in the American Housing Survey," PD&R Edge, November 19, 2018, https://www.huduser.gov/portal/pdredge/pdredge-frm-asst-sec-111918.html.
3. "Average Rent Increase in the U.S. in 2022," Credit Karma, updated October 20, 2022, https://www.creditkarma.com/insights/i/average-rent-increase#:~:text=It's%20also%20worth%20noting%20that,increased%20from%20%241%2C093%20to%20%241%2C339.
4. Rachel Bogardus Drew, "New Census Data Show Growing Share of Americans Struggling to Pay Rent," Enterprise, September 15, 2022, https://www.enterprisecommunity.org/blog/new-census-data-show-growing-share-americans-struggling-pay-rent.

Meet Tomeka Langford

1. Quiet Title, accessed March 15, 2023, https://quiettitle.com/.
2. "Increased Foreclosure Activity in First Six Months of 2022 Approaches Pre-Covid Levels," ATTOM, July 14, 2022, https://www.attomdata.com/news/market-trends/foreclosures/attom-midyear-2022-u-s-foreclosure-market-report/.
3. "Every Tax Foreclosure in Detroit 2002–2016," Regrid, accessed March 15, 2023, https://taxforeclosure.regrid.com/m/every-tax-foreclosure-in-detroit-2002-2016#b=.
4. Patrick Cooney and Amanda Nothaft, "Stopping the Eviction Machine in Detroit," Poverty Solutions at the University of Michigan, policy brief, October 1, 2019, https://poverty.umich.edu/publications/stopping-the-eviction-machine-in-detroit/.
5. Peter Hepburn, Renee Louis, and Matthew Desmond, "Racial and Gender Disparities among Evicted Americans," Eviction Lab, December 16, 2020, https://evictionlab.org/demographics-of-eviction/.
6. Emily Moss, Kriston McIntosh, Wendy Edelberg, and Kristen Broady, "The Black-White Wealth Gap Left Black Households More Vulnerable," Brookings Institution, December 8, 2020, https://www.brookings.edu/blog/up-front/2020/12/08/the-black-white-wealth-gap-left-black-households-more-vulnerable/.
7. Christian E. Weller and Richard Figueroa, "Wealth Matters: The Black-White Wealth Gap Before and During the Pandemic," Center for American Progress, July 28, 2021, https://www.americanprogress.org/article/wealth-matters-black-white-wealth-gap-pandemic/.
8. Kai Ryssdal and Richard Cunningham, "Eviction Filings Hit Pre-Pandemic Levels a Year after the End of the Moratorium," *Marketplace*, July 29, 2022, https://www.marketplace.org/2022/07/29/eviction-filings-hit-pre-pandemic-levels-a-year-after-the-end-of-the-moratorium/; Tim Ellis, "Rental Market Tracker: Typical U.S. Asking Rent Surpassed $2,000 for First Time in May," Redfin News, June 9, 2022, https://www.redfin.com/news/redfin-rental-report-may-2022/.

Evictionland

1. Taylor Marr, "Millions of Renters Face Eviction—Why Today's Housing Market Is Partially to Blame," Redfin News, December 12, 2016, https://www.redfin.com/news/millions-of-renters-face-eviction-why-todays-housing-market-is-partially-to-blame/.

2. Chris Salviati, "Rental Insecurity: The Threat of Evictions to America's Renters," Apartment List, October 20, 2017, https://www.apartmentlist.com/research/rental-insecurity-the-threat-of-evictions-to-americas-renters.

3. Elizabeth Flock, "Eviction Companies Pay the Homeless Illegally Low Wages to Put People on the Street," *Washington City Paper*, February 23, 2017, https://washingtoncitypaper.com/article/192058/eviction-companies-pay-the-homeless-illegally-low-wages-to-put-people-on-the-street/.

4. "Express Evictions," Yelp, accessed March 15, 2023, https://www.yelp.com/biz/express-evictions-san-bernardino.

5. Tanay Warerkar, "Low-Income New Yorkers Facing Eviction Now Guaranteed Legal Representation," Curbed New York, August 11, 2017, https://ny.curbed.com/2017/8/11/16135812/low-income-new-yorkers-housing-court-legal.

6. Boatwright Memorial Library, 2016-17 OneBook | Evicted: Poverty and Profit in the American City by Matthew Desmond: Statistics & Data, updated February 23, 2023, https://libguides.richmond.edu/c.php?g=509505&p=3832530; Andrew Flowers, "How We Undercounted Evictions by Asking the Wrong Questions," *FiveThirtyEight*, September 15, 2016, https://fivethirtyeight.com/features/how-we-undercounted-evictions-by-asking-the-wrong-questions/.

7. "In a Typical Year, Landlords File 3.6 Million Eviction Cases," Eviction Lab, accessed March 15, 2023, https://covid19.census.gov/documents/weekly-eviction-data-2020/explore.

8. Martine Paris, "These Are the Most Expensive US Cities for Renters, with Some Prices Up 41%," Bloomberg, July 26, 2022, https://www.bloomberg.com/news/articles/2022-07-26/these-are-the-most-expensive-cities-for-renters-led-by-nyc-and-sf.

37,000 US Veterans Are Homeless—I Was One of Them

1. "Veterans," National Alliance to End Homelessness, updated April 2021, https://endhomelessness.org/homelessness-in-america/who-experiences-homelessness/veterans/#:~:text=On%20a%20single%20night%20in,as%20part%20of%20a%20family.

2. "Pharmacy Benefits Management Services," US Department of Veterans Affairs, updated August 21, 2020, https://www.pbm.va.gov/pbm/cmop/va_mail_order_pharmacy.asp.

3. Lisa Nagorny and Dan Pick, "5 Reasons Why Employers Are Not Hiring Vets," Military.com, accessed March 15, 2023, https://www.military.com/hiring-veterans/resources/5-reasons-why-employers-are-not-hiring-vets.html.

4. Alex Miller, "In Need, in New York," *New York Times*, June 21, 2012.

5. Veteran Suicide Prevention Act, H.R.1123, 117th Cong. (2021–22).

6. Richard A. Oppel Jr. and Michael D. Shear, "Severe Report Finds V.A. Hid Waiting Lists at Hospitals," *New York Times,* May 28, 2014.

7. Joe Davidson, "Whistleblower Says There's a Secret VA Wait List for Care. The Department Says That's Not True," *Washington Post,* June 3, 2019.

8. Joe Davidson, "Whistleblower Says VA Ordered Fake Appointments to Cut Waiting List," *Washington Post,* June 27, 2019.

9. Call of Duty Endowment, accessed March 15, 2023, https://www.callofdu tyendowment.org/; The National Coalition for Homeless Veterans, accessed March 15, 2023, https://nchv.org/; Stack Up, accessed March 15, 2023, https://www.stackup.org/.

A Fierce Desire to Stay

1. West Virginia Department of Health and Human Resources, "West Virginia Drug Overdose Deaths: Historical Overview, 2001–2015," August 17, 2017, https://oeps.wv.gov/outbreaks/documents/data/special/wv-drug-overdos-es-2001_2015.pdf.

2. Evan Comen, "The Fastest Growing (and Shrinking) States: A Closer Look," *USA Today,* accessed March 15, 2023, https://eu.usatoday.com/story/money/economy/2018/01/15/fastest-growing-and-shrinking-states-closer-look/1019429001/.

My Marriage Was Broken—the Coronavirus Lockdown Saved It

1. "Coronavirus: Spain Closes Borders," EU Observer, March 17, 2020, https://euobserver.com/tickers/147766.

My Sister Is a Recovering Heroin Addict . . .

1. Rosalind Adams, "Sobering Conditions at Narco Freedom's Three-Quarter Houses," *Al Jazeera America,* October 27, 2014, http://america.aljazeera.com/articles/2014/10/27/narco-freedom-soberhomesalanjasonbrand.html.

2. Lisa Riordan Seville and Graham Kates, "Drug Treatment Moguls Lived in Luxury on Medicaid Cash, Say Prosecutors," NBC News, January 5, 2015, https://www.nbcnews.com/news/investigations/drug-treatment-mo-guls-lived-luxury-medicaid-cash-say-prosecutors-n276386.

The Underground Economy of Unpaid Care

1. "Family Caregiver Services by State," Family Caregiver Alliance, accessed March 15, 2023, https://www.caregiver.org/connecting-caregivers/ser-vices-by-state/?state=national.

My Pandemic Year behind the Checkout Counter

1. Tara Parker-Pope, "How Do I Make Thanksgiving Shopping Safer?," *New York Times,* November 23, 2020.

2. Julia Belluz, "Still Going to the Grocery Store? With New Virus Variants Spreading, It's Probably Time to Stop," *Vox,* updated January 15, 2021, https://www.vox.com/22220301/covid-spread-new-strain-variants-safe-gro-cery-store-n95-masks-vaccine.

3.   "High Rate of Symptomless COVID-19 Infection among Grocery Store Workers," *Science Daily*, October 30, 2020, https://www.sciencedaily.com/releases/2020/10/201029191116.htm.

4.   Michael Corkery, David Yaffe-Bellany, and Rachel Wharton, "When Stocking Grocery Shelves Turns Dangerous," *New York Times*, March 21, 2020.

5.   Abha Bhattarai and Hannah Denham, "Stealing to Survive: More Americans Are Shoplifting Food as Aid Runs Out during the Pandemic," *Washington Post*, December 10, 2020.

6.   "Week 18 Household Pulse Survey: October 28–November 9," United States Census Bureau, November 18, 2020, https://www.census.gov/data/tables/2020/demo/hhp/hhp18.html.

My Life as a Retail Worker

1.   Dara Kerr, "Apple Slapped with Lawsuit over Mandatory Employee Bag Checks," CNET, July 29, 2013, https://www.cnet.com/tech/tech-industry/apple-slapped-with-lawsuit-over-mandatory-employee-bag-checks/; Alice Hines, "Forever 21 Class Action Lawsuit Filed By Employees," *Huffington Post*, January 18, 2012, https://www.huffpost.com/entry/forever-21-lawsuit-class-action_n_1214359.

2.   Lawrence Mishel, "Low-Wage Workers Have Far More Education than They Did in 1968, yet They Make Far Less," Economic Policy Institute, January 23, 2014, https://www.epi.org/publication/wage-workers-education-1968/.

3.   Wage Theft, accessed March 15, 2023, http://wagetheft.org/wordpress/.

The Secret Lives of Adjunct Professors

1.   The City University of New York Agreement between the City of New York and the Professional Staff Congress/ CUNY, December 1, 2017–February 28, 2023, accessed March 15, 2023, https://www.cuny.edu/wp-content/uploads/sites/4/page-assets/about/administration/offices/labor-relations/28283961_cuny-psc_2017-2023_agreement.pdf.

That Sinking Feeling

1.   Grace Ferguson, "Studies: Older Workers' Wages are Declining," Multi Briefs, March 17, 2020, https://exclusive.multibriefs.com/content/studies-older-workers-wages-are-declining/association-management.

2.   Richard W. Johnson and Corina Mommaerts, "Age Differences in Job Displacement, Job Search, and Reemployment," Center for Retirement Research at Boston College, January 2011, https://crr.bc.edu/working-papers/age-differences-in-job-displacement-job-search-and-reemployment/.

3.   "1 in 3 Americans Have Less Than $5,000 In Retirement Savings," Northwestern Mutual, May 8, 2018, https://news.northwesternmutual.com/2018-05-08-1-In-3-Americans-Have-Less-Than-5-000-In-Retirement-Savings.

4.   "20+ Years of Older Workers' Declining Bargaining Power," Schwartz Center for Economic Policy Analysis at The New School, Older Workers Report, August 7, 2019, https://www.economicpolicyresearch.org/jobs-report/2019-q2-older-workers-report.

5. Ask the Headhunter, accessed March 15, 2023, https://www.askthehead-hunter.com/.
6. Rachel Siegel and Andrew Van Dam, "4.4 Million Americans Sought Jobless Benefits Last Week, as Economic Pain Continued across the United States," *Washington Post*, April 23, 2020.
7. Shelly Steward, "Five Myths about the Gig Economy," *Washington Post*, April 24, 2020.

Never-Ending Sentences

1. Special thanks to Chaplain Christana Gamble for her conversation, warmth, and testimony. Christana wanted to thank Sister Linda Catanzaro for her mentorship in the Ignatian Spirituality Project while Christana was in County Jail, and director Sherri Horton-Brandon for her program Women in Transition (Front Steps), which provided shelter and training for Christana as she transitioned from homelessness.
2. Metzenbaum Center is a temporary shelter for housing juveniles in the justice system. For more on the history of child services in Cleveland see https://case.edu/ech/articles/c/child-care.
3. For more on the controversial judicial practices of Judge Daniel Gaul see https://serialpodcast.org/season-three/2/transcript.
4. For more information about routine housing discrimination for those with criminal records, please read: http://www.thehousingcenter.org/wp-con-tent/uploads/2019/12/A-Never-Ending-Sentence-2020.pdf and https://www.cleveland.com/business/2020/01/a-criminal-record-is-a-never-end-ing-sentence-for-cuyahoga-county-housing-applicants-report-says.html. In 2015, the US Supreme Court ruled that the Fair Housing Act included disparate impact claims, which now makes it against the law to exclude an applicant simply on the basis of having a criminal record. Special thanks to attorney Maria Smith (Legal Aid Society of Cleveland) for her insights into what is known as collateral sanctions—ongoing punishment for those who have served their time.
5. For more information about City Mission see https://www.thecitymission.org/; for more information about Women in Transition (now called Front Steps) see https://www.frontstepsservices.org/our-history.
6. Eden, Inc., short for Emerald Development and Economic Network, Inc. (EDEN) is a 501 (c)(3) agency of the Alcohol Drug Addiction and Mental Health Services Board of Cuyahoga County, dedicated to "providing housing solutions to people facing housing insecurities and homelessness." See https://www.edeninc.org/about/.
7. Shelter Care Plus is one of the programs offered by Eden, Inc. See https://www.edeninc.org/program-shelter-plus-care-2/. It provided a workaround to provide Christana with housing, despite her record.
8. For more information about the Northeast Ohio Coalition for the Homeless, check out https://www.neoch.org/. Special thanks to Chris Knestrick for connecting me with Christana Gamble.
9. To contact the House of Refuge emergency hotline for services call 216-713-

8364. To contribute to the House of Refuge, you can send a check to House of Refuge Inc., P. O. Box 17327, Cleveland, OH 44117. www.houseofrefugeinc.org.

10.   Special thanks to Joseph Gaston for sharing his story. Thanks as well to Maria Smith of the Legal Aid Society of Cleveland for connecting us.

11.   On Judge Daniel C. Boyko's taking senior status see https://www.cleveland.com/court-justice/2019/05/federal-judge-in-cleveland-to-take-senior-status-next-year.html. Quotes from this article appear throughout this poem.

12.   For more information about the case, please read https://www.govinfo.gov/app/details/USCOURTS-ohnd-1_18-cv-02440. For more information about routine housing discrimination for those with criminal records, please read http://www.thehousingcenter.org/wp-content/uploads/2019/12/A-Never-Ending-Sentence-2020.pdf and https://www.cleveland.com/business/2020/01/a-criminal-record-is-a-never-ending-sentence-for-cuyahoga-county-housing-applicants-report-says.html.

13.   Eden, Inc., short for Emerald Development and Economic Network, Inc. (EDEN) is a 501 (c)(3) agency of the Alcohol Drug Addiction and Mental Health Services Board of Cuyahoga County, dedicated to "providing housing solutions to people facing housing insecurities and homelessness." https://www.edeninc.org/about/.

14.   On Judge Boyko's naturalization ceremony see https://apnews.com/e8faf64a-fa8a42f7895b8ed42c24ddbb.

15.   For the full text of Dean Alfange's "My Creed" go to https://www.goodreads.com/quotes/82410-my-creed-i-do-not-choose-to-be-a-common.

INDEX

ABOUT HAYMARKET BOOKS

Haymarket Books is a radical, independent, nonprofit book publisher based in Chicago. Our mission is to publish books that contribute to struggles for social and economic justice. We strive to make our books a vibrant and organic part of social movements and the education and development of a critical, engaged, and internationalist Left.

We take inspiration and courage from our namesakes, the Haymarket Martyrs, who gave their lives fighting for a better world. Their 1886 struggle for the eight-hour day—which gave us May Day, the international workers' holiday—reminds workers around the world that ordinary people can organize and struggle for their own liberation. These struggles—against oppression, exploitation, environmental devastation, and war—continue today across the globe.

Since our founding in 2001, Haymarket has published more than nine hundred titles. Radically independent, we seek to drive a wedge into the risk-averse world of corporate book publishing. Our authors include Angela Y. Davis, Arundhati Roy, Keeanga-Yamahtta Taylor, Eve L. Ewing, Aja Monet, Mariame Kaba, Naomi Klein, Rebecca Solnit, Olúfẹ́mi O. Táíwò, Mohammed El-Kurd, José Olivarez, Noam Chomsky, Winona LaDuke, Robyn Maynard, Leanne Betasamosake Simpson, Howard Zinn, Mike Davis, Marc Lamont Hill, Dave Zirin, Astra Taylor, and Amy Goodman, among many other leading writers of our time. We are also the trade publishers of the acclaimed Historical Materialism Book Series.

Haymarket also manages a vibrant community organizing and event space in Chicago, Haymarket House, the popular Haymarket Books Live event series and podcast, and the annual Socialism Conference.

ALSO AVAILABLE FROM HAYMARKET BOOKS

*After Life: A Collective History of Loss
and Redemption in Pandemic America*
Edited by Rhae Lynn Barnes, Keri Leigh Merritt, and Yohuru Williams

Build Yourself a Boat
Camonghne Felix

Can't Pay, Won't Pay
The Case for Economic Disobedience and Debt Abolition
Debt Collective, foreword by Astra Taylor

From #BlackLivesMatter to Black Liberation (Expanded Second Edition)
Keeanga-Yamahtta Taylor, foreword by Angela Y. Davis

Not Too Late: Changing the Climate Story from Despair to Possibility
Edited by Rebecca Solnit and Thelma Young Lutunatabua

Remake the World: Essays, Reflections, Rebellions
Astra Taylor

The Sentences That Create Us: Crafting A Writer's Life in Prison
PEN America, Edited by Caits Meissner

Socialism . . . Seriously: A Brief Guide to Surviving the 21st Century
(Revised & Updated Edition)
Danny Katch

*So We Can Know: Writers of Color
on Pregnancy, Loss, Abortion, and Birth*
Edited by Aracelis Girmay

Speaking Out of Place: Getting Our Political Voices Back
by David Palumbo-Liu